HOW TO SURVIVE THE ORGANIZATIONAL
REVOLUTION

BIS Publishers
Building Het Sieraad
Postjesweg 1
1057 DT Amsterdam
The Netherlands
T +31 (0)20 515 02 30
bis@bispublishers.com
www.bispublishers.com

ISBN 978 90 6369 521 7

Text: A.P. de Man, P. Koene and M. Ars
Editor: Mike Corder
Design and illustrations: Buro BRAND

HOW TO SURVIVE THE ORGANIZATIONAL
REVOLUTION

Ard-Pieter de Man, Pieter Koene & Martijn Ars

BISPUBLISHERS

CONTENT OF THE BOOK

FOREWORD

Over the past few years numerous new organizational forms have emerged. We noticed that many practitioners remain unfamiliar with these forms or, if they are familiar with them, find it difficult to determine whether they are the right solution for their own organization. This book aims to help leaders and professionals in organizations answer that crucial question. We believe new organizational forms can be beneficial for many organizations. At the same time we are concerned that hypes and rigid application of organizational models may do more harm than good. This book acts as a first guide to recent developments in the world of organizing and will help professionals make the right decisions if they are considering restructuring their organization.

Many people and influences shaped this book. We would like to recognize the following people and organizations. This book started during Ard-Pieter's time as Dean of Sioo, the leading Dutch training institute in the areas of consulting, organization design and change. For Sioo's Consulting Program & Community (CP&C) he developed a workshop on new organizational forms. Special thanks to the participants in CP&C who contributed many insights and relevant literature that found their way into this book. A substantial part of this book was written at the Royal Melbourne Institute of Technology (RMIT), where Ard-Pieter spent a short sabbatical in 2018 as an honorary visiting professor. Thanks to professors Gerda Gemser and Mark Leenders and RMIT's Graduate School of Business and Law for their hospitality and for creating an environment that enabled Ard-Pieter to concentrate on writing.

Pieter and Martijn contributed to this book based on their experience leading PwC's global community on enterprise agility and new contemporary organizational models. We thank all PwC colleagues across the globe for their ideas, support and sponsorship for this project and for sharing their thought leadership in this area with us.

We are very grateful to the organizations who made their time available for us to interview them. We specifically would like to thank the following interviewees for giving access to their cases: Nick Jue (ING), Harm Jans (bol.com), Sally Wang (International SOS) and Natalie Peters (Telstra). Thank you all!
A final group of people deserving our gratitude are those involved in the production of the book. We are indebted to the creativity of Buro BRAND for designing the book and the wonderful illustrations.

We are very happy with the look and feel
Nikki Langkemper, Samily Metselaar, Hester
Naaktgeboren, and Simone Prick of Buro
BRAND created. BIS Publishers and in particular Bionda Dias and Sara van de Ven were
very helpful throughout the process of getting
this book to market. Mike Corder was a
flexible editor who corrected our English and
ensured consistency in our use of language.

Ard-Pieter de Man
Pieter Koene
Martijn Ars

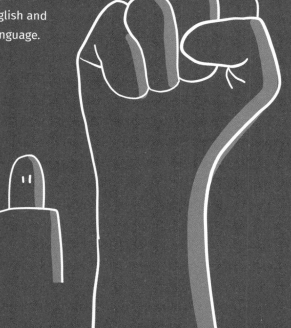

INTRODUCTION

In this book we present an overview of new organizational forms and their pros and cons. Our aim is to help managers understand the different organizational design options they have, so they can make an informed decision about whether or not to adopt a new organizational form. We focus on this topic because in our consulting practices we found there was a need among managers for a clear overview of non-traditional organizational forms. Managers asked us for a guide to help them navigate through the variety of new organizational forms that have emerged over the past few years. Many traditional assumptions about organizing are being challenged, leading to a revolution in our thinking about organizations. But when does this organizational revolution become relevant for your organization?

WHAT DO WE MEAN BY 'ORGANIZATIONAL REVOLUTION'?

The organizational revolution refers to the process of development of new organizational forms that coincides with the transition from an industrial to an informational society. Our increased ability to gather, process and share information affects the business environment organizations face. Few businesses for example have no online competitor. Luckily, this new ability to work with information also gives us the tools to develop new organizational forms to meet the demands of that new environment. For example, better information sharing with new information technology makes it possible to rely more on self-organization and agile ways of working. Technology, however, does not enforce a single organizational form upon firms. Instead, various new organizational forms come into being and practice will establish what works and what doesn't. The organizational revolution is a long term process in which organizations search for new organizational models that fit new business requirements. It is not a sudden, brief period of change, but a prolonged period of development and experimentation that has been going on for some time. The organizational revolution will probably not make all traditional organizational models obsolete either. In the midst of change, there always is continuity too.

Even though we believe that information and information technology are core drivers of the organizational revolution, we are not technological determinists who believe that all organizations will inevitably become a blockchain. We also do not believe in the growing spiritual branch of management, which believes that 'human consciousness' has now evolved in such a way that it makes self-organization possible. We also don't believe in lean and agile fundamentalists, who claim that only lean or agile can lead to successful organizations. We need to look deeper and find out how the new benefits and costs of gathering, processing and sharing information help us to formulate new answers to age old organizational questions.

Information may be a dominant factor in the new organizational solutions that have developed over the past decades, but it is not prescriptive in the sense that it forces every organization into the same model. And it is certainly not the only force shaping organizations. Therefore there are many possible solutions to organizational questions. In addition, each organization is unique which makes it even more unlikely that one size will fit all. It is best to take a pragmatic approach to organizing: the most important thing is that an organizational form works for your organization. It is less relevant whether you follow all the detailed prescriptions that an agile or holacracy guru may provide.

WHAT THIS BOOK DOES AND DOES NOT DO

The core of this book consists of chapters that describe six new organizational forms.

We do not advocate one new organizational form over another. We don't even advocate that new organizational models are better than traditional organizational forms. That all depends on the situation and it is very likely that the functional organization, the business unit or the matrix are still appropriate for a number of organizations. During the writing of this book we also found that they can be combined with newer forms. What we do aim for is to analyze the new forms that have emerged in practice. We do so by describing these forms in a structured way based on work by Puranam, Alexy and Reitzig[1]. They describe new organizational forms along four dimensions:

How are tasks divided?
This refers to the question of how the different tasks that need to be done are split up and who determines which tasks have to be done. This requires translating the organizational goals into activities and determining the priority among those activities. Priorities can be set through budgets, rules, consensus and the like.

How are tasks allocated to individuals?
Tasks need to be assigned to people and groups of people that carry them out. Managers can do this, but people can divide work among themselves as well. In some cases an IT system allocates the work (think Uber and Lyft).

How are rewards provided to motivate people?
Rewards need to be provided to stimulate people to do the work assigned to them. The term rewards however is broad and does not only include financial incentives. People are also motivated by their colleagues, challenging assignments or an appealing vision.

How is information provided so people can make the right decisions?
In order for people to do their work they need to have the right information. This includes information about when they need to coordinate with others. IT systems can provide information, but reports, meetings and chats at the coffee machine provide information as well.

We describe new organizational forms in terms of these four elements. Next we provide information leaflets for each organizational form. This is inspired by the information leaflets you get from your pharmacist when you pick up your medication. We believe such information leaflets should be mandatory for management concepts as well. They should state how it works, why it works, when it does not work and what the side effects are of using any management concept. All too often, management literature is overconfident with the prescriptions it gives. A mandatory information leaflet could tame the guru ambitions of many a management thinker.

HOW TO READ THIS BOOK?

The book consists of three elements (see figure 1). *First* there are chapters that provide the backbone of the book. Chapters 2 to 7 describe the new organizational forms. They are the multidimensional organization, the Spotify model, holacracy, the platform organization with an ecosystem, value proposition based ecosystems and open source organizations. Chapter 1 describes the big trends in organizing and why they occur. Chapter 8 provides an antidote to success stories and highlights some of the drawbacks of new organizational forms. Chapter 9 gathers information about new mechanisms for internal governance that have been developed in practice, many of which can be applied across the six organizational forms we describe. The final chapter 10 provides guidelines to help managers choose the appropriate form for their organization and shows how forms can be mixed in hybrid solutions.

The second element of the book is cases. The cases illustrate the new organizational forms, but they also show that in practice organizations adapt them to meet their own unique needs. The common denominator is that they tweak organizational models to make them fit.

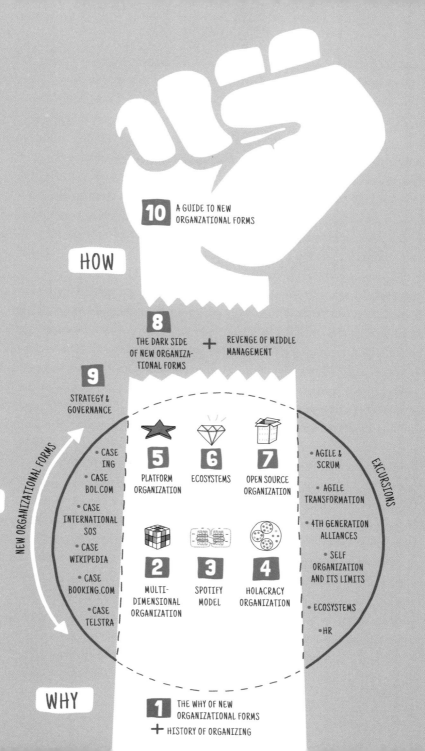

The third element of the book is excursions that dive deeper into some themes that we find relevant or provide background knowledge to help you better understand the six organizational forms discussed in chapters 2 to 7. Depending on your existing knowledge or your curiosity, you can choose to take a deeper dive.

Each chapter and excursion starts with an 'Idea in brief' section. This summarizes it and helps you to determine whether you want to know more about it or move on to the next topic. It is possible to read the book from cover to cover. Obviously, we believe that that is the most valuable experience. Otherwise we would not have taken the trouble to put the chapters, excursions and cases in this order. But being aware of the modern manager's impatience, the book also makes it possible for you to jump right to topics you are the most interested in.

WHAT IF YOU WANT TO KNOW MORE?

Our book gathers existing information, structures it, analyzes it and presents it in a coherent form. The book provides an overview and not a detailed discussion of all the ins and outs of new organizational forms. It is an introductory text, not a full-blown analysis.

We have added further references for those who are interested in delving further into a certain topic. We selected references that do justice to those who put forth the ideas we summarize here, but that also are helpful for managers who want to know more.

References also show classic texts that are still worth reading today because they explain fundamental insights. If you want to dig deeper into the background of a certain idea, the older and more academic references are the ones you may turn to. If you are more interested in how you can apply those ideas today, the more recent articles, white papers and websites are the place to look. If you are a teacher, the references can be useful to give your students assignments to probe beyond what we write here.

---

[1] *Puranam, P., Alexy, O., & Reitzig, M. (2014). What's "new" about new forms of organizing?. Academy of Management Review, 39(2), 162-180.*

THE WHY OF NEW ORGANIZATIONAL FORMS

A CHANGING ENVIRONMENT

We live in a time of widespread experimentation with new organizational forms. For many decades organizations used varieties of only a few basic organizational forms like the functional form, the business unit and the matrix. These organizational forms were very successful in meeting the demands of the 20th century industrial economy[1]. Once adapted to the specific circumstances of a company, and despite continuous bickering about the disadvantages of hierarchy and bureaucratic policies, these organizational forms actually enabled managers to run companies of unprecedented size. The economies of scale and scope they generated laid the foundation for the economic successes of the previous century[2].

Then came the information society. In the information society the processing of non-tangibles like data and images is of more significance than the transformation of physical materials[3]. The costs of gathering, manipulating and sharing information have declined immensely. The impact of this trend on management is substantial. After all, one of the core questions of organizing is how to ensure that any individual in an organization has the right information to make the right decision at the right time. For example, the role of the middle manager in the business unit organization was to interpret information gathered by staff units, make decisions based on that information and to communicate these decisions to his subordinates. At the time of the invention of the business unit in 1923 this was an optimal use of information. In 1923 information could not be interpreted automatically and sharing information was expensive. Currently, artificial intelligence and algorithms interpret information and cheap online tools are available for information sharing that can reach millions of people in a

The idea in brief
- **The information society requires other organizational forms than the industrial society**
- **They are less hierarchical, more dynamic and information based**
- **Be careful following the latest fads: traditional ideas still have their uses**
- **Each organization is unique, therefore there is no one best way to organize**

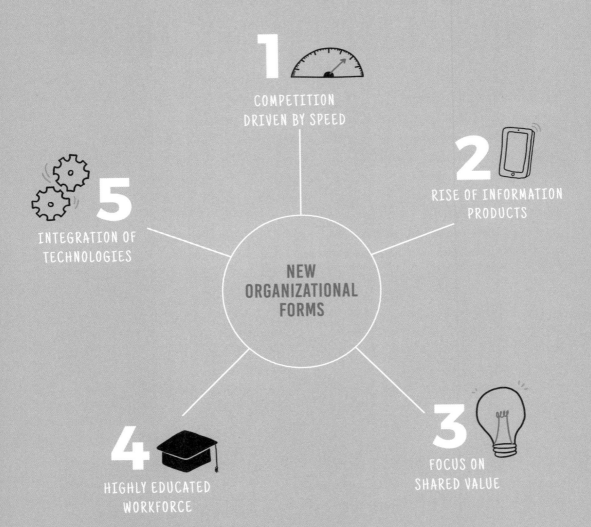

1 COMPETITION DRIVEN BY SPEED

2 RISE OF INFORMATION PRODUCTS

5 INTEGRATION OF TECHNOLOGIES

NEW ORGANIZATIONAL FORMS

4 HIGHLY EDUCATED WORKFORCE

3 FOCUS ON SHARED VALUE

second. Therefore the traditional role of the middle manager in interpreting and sharing information becomes less and less relevant[4]. Somewhat counterbalancing this trend, information technology leads to an increase in the number of top managers (an increase from five top managers per organization to ten between the mid 1980s to the mid 2000s)[5]. The reason is that information technology enables the centralization of administrative functions, each of which is led by a C-level executive. Many organizations now have chief legal officers or chief human resource officers. Yet the net effect is that many managers lose their information monopolies and thus their hierarchical status. The current trend away from hierarchy and towards more self-organization would have been impossible without cheap information sharing. The declining cost of information enables the rise of new organizational forms.

Even though the cost of information is a dominant factor in the emergence of new organizational forms, it is not the only one. There are a number of other trends that affect the way we think about organization. To mention just a few:

Competition is driven more by innovation and speed than by economies of scale and scope. In the industrial society, production costs were an important factor in the competitive battle as they determined the sales price. Of course costs of production remain important, but innovation and speed have become more relevant in today's affluent markets. The implication of this for organizational forms is that fast decision making, increasing creativity and combining diverse capabilities become more important than predictability, stability and refining capabilities.

Information products replace physical products. The development and production processes of information products are different. Production processes for information products can be organized quite differently than those for tangible products. Their cost structure also differs. In industrial societies fixed costs and variable costs of production are high. In the informational society the initial costs of creating an information based product may be very high, but the variable costs are zero[6]. Information products like movies or software are expensive to produce, but cheap to copy. Different cost structures imply other business models can be developed to recoup investments. In turn, new business models may require new ways of organizing.

With so many basic needs met in the rich countries and with the financial crisis behind us, many people feel that the exclusive focus on creating shareholder value is too narrow. Apart from economic side effects of this focus, many people are looking for new ways of sensemaking in their work. Hence we see a move from a focus on shareholder value to shared value[7], aimed at creating shareholder value while solving societal problems. Such a shift in strategy has far-reaching implications for organizations. The internal governance no longer can be focused on one sided financial measures but now needs to include broader measures of success and other policies that support the focus on social goals[8].

High levels of education also affect organizational forms. Decision that once were left at the manager's discretion because of her analytical skills can now be made by a highly educated workforce lower in the hierarchy - even more so when employees have online tools available that support them in their decision-making. Again, this opens up opportunities for selforganization rather than hierarchical coordination of activities.

Integration of technologies is another interesting trend. Dubbed the Fourth Industrial Revolution, the integration of technologies that were previously separate requires organizations to foster new ways of collaborating internally and externally[9]. When brains are tied to bionic arms and cars increasingly become information platforms, domains that were separated have to be integrated. This has led to the emergence of new forms of collaboration, often between organizations. Modularization of technology enables this trend. The more final products are created from individual modules that are connected with other modules via common standards, the more companies can focus on delivering modules and integrating them with those of other organizations.

CHANGING ORGANIZATIONS

All these trends put strain on existing forms of organization. Because these trends will affect different organizations differently, each organization will have to adapt to them at their own pace. For some that may imply that smaller changes suffice. For many however the tensions caused by traditional ways of organizing in a changing context, can only be fundamentally resolved by implementing radically new organizational forms.

Table 1 shows some trends around organizational forms. The drawback of tables like this is that they put the extremes next to each other, whereas in reality there are many shades of gray. So below we discuss these trends, but also emphasize their limits.

Departments are out; processes are in

One of the complaints about traditional organizational forms was that optimization occurred in silos to the detriment of collaboration. New organizational forms break through this by focusing on how processes flow through the organization. Information supports this trend because nowadays information is available on a process level, instead of only at a departmental level. Underperforming processes are spotted more easily and the lessons derived from that can be translated into process improvements. But: Organizations still need to be divided up into subgroups. Even though the these subgroups may work quite differently than in the past and may have exotic names like tribe, council or circle, they are in essence still departments.

Out	In
Departments	**Processes**
Hierarchy	**Self-organization**
Internal	**External**
Planning & control	**Experiment & iterate**
Mechanistic	**Organic**
Orders	**Information**
Hard controls	**Soft controls**

Table 1: Trends in organizational forms

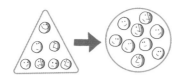

Hierarchy is out; self-organization is in

Hierarchical coordination is replaced by self-coordination in teams. The extent to which this occurs differs widely. Sometimes it is limited to cutting the number of management layers. Sometimes teams are given a task and resources and decide themselves how they organize their activities. Occasionally teams are allowed to set their own goals*. The increase in self-organization does not imply all management tasks disappear. Instead, many of these tasks like planning and HR are executed in the teams. The term 'self' is a bit misleading as well. The boss may be gone, but the systems and procedures in place to make self-organization work are usually elaborate. Nevertheless, there is an unmistakable trend away from 'being managed' towards 'selfmanagement'. But: Hierarchy is never far away. Sometimes it is informal. Often there are still formal hierarchical layers in organizations. Hierarchy tends to remain valuable when decisions need to be made quickly, key knowledge is concentrated at the top and

several decisions need to be coordinated. Also top managers tend to set the rules and processes that guide self-organization.[10]

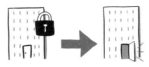

Internal is out; external is in

The internal and the external organization were strictly separated in the industrial society. In fact the large scale vertically integrated enterprises aimed at keeping the outside world outside as much as possible. The less dependent a company was on outside partners, the more it could realize the goal of uninterrupted, smooth and efficient production. In the course of the 1990s the boundaries of the firm started to fade with an increase in the number of alliances, particularly in IT, pharma/biotech and airlines. Pressured by competition, companies started to realize that specializing in a few core competences had its benefits and that complementary competences needed to be delivered by partners. Gradually this trend spread to other industries, to the extent that internal and external have now become blurred. Improved

---

Despite this variety we have opted to use the term self-organization because it is so commonly used. Note however that many different definitions of the term exist. When somebody uses the term it therefore makes sense to ask what they mean by it. Operationally it can just mean employees organizing their own daily work (self-management). Tactically it can mean employees making changes to the structure and internal governance. Strategically it can mean employees setting the organizational goals. The first one is most common.

information systems have made it possible to monitor the often far-reaching extent of external collaboration. But: This trend does not imply everything can be contracted out to partners. On the contrary: To be an effective partner is demanding. A company has to be interesting to work with. Without top notch capabilities, an interesting service and a strong business model few partners will want to work with you.

increasingly use forms of soft control. They pay great attention to the role of culture and norms and values to govern the organization. Rather than a strategy tied to bureaucratic control mechanisms, an overarching vision or purpose binds the people and guides them in the decisions they make[11]. But: This does not imply that anything goes. The new instruments and process are as elaborate as the traditional ones.

Planning & control is out; experiment & iterate is in

The traditional methods of governing organizations like hierarchical decision-making, planning & control processes and top down accountability are less prominent in new organizational forms. The business environment requires more experimentation and iteration. Traditional planning cycles are annual. That is too long to adapt to changes that occur throughout the year. Abolishing planning & control altogether creates a potential risk for organizations: How do you know employees make the right decisions for the whole? How do you avoid costly mistakes that may bring down an organization? To fill the control gap, new instruments are invented with new meeting structures. In addition, organizations

Mechanistic is out; organic is in

In a continuously changing business environment the ideal to achieve is organic adjustment of the organization to changing conditions. New organizational forms therefore try to embed continuous change in the organization design. This is in contrast to the more mechanistic approach of traditional organizational forms. Their ideal was to ensure as much stability as possible, so as not to disrupt the efficiency and optimization of production processes. But: not everything is fluid. People also need things to give them direction and stability when they have to make decisions. Therefore organizations implement processes to ensure this.

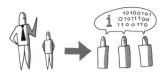

Orders are out; information is in

This trend is derived from the trend away from hierarchy towards self-organization. The traditional chain of command was top down, with higher management giving marching orders to lower management who would next instruct the operational level. In new organizational forms, relevant information about the opportunities and threats is shared across the organization, independent from the hierarchical or unit structure. This enables anyone in the organization to decide which action to take to profit from the opportunity or limit the threat. But: many decisions affect others and that is why new meeting structures are put in place to solve conflicts of interest. That may be the disappointing takeaway from this book: Meetings are here to stay (although they can be made more fun and productive).

NO ONE BEST WAY OF ORGANIZING

The broad outlines of how changes in the business environment lead to changes in organizational forms are easily sketched and may not be very surprising. It is clear that the search is on for new organizational forms that fit that environment. Even though undoubtedly some elements are overhyped, the long-term developments in the economy and society point to the need for other ways of thinking about organizing. The precise outcome however is not easy to predict. At the same time, some caveats are in order. They all revolve around one idea: There is no one best way of organizing.

First, the search for the new always masks the continuity that is also present. New organizational forms never are completely new, but usually emerge from existing forms. At the same time, if history is any guide, then we may conclude that not all organizations will move away from the old towards the new. Older organizational forms may still have their use in certain circumstances. It is not hard to spot the remnants of the medieval guilds even in modern societies.

Second, new organizational forms need to meet institutional demands. A striking observation in that regard is that even though organizations are looking for flexibility, society and politicians demand more accountability and control from organizations. These developments are at odds with each other and yet they occur simultaneously. This suggests that somewhere a balance needs to be struck and that the rise of new organizational forms will have its limits.

Finally, each organization has its own history and faces its own unique environment. For that reason alone organizations will never adopt the exact same organizational form, but need to adopt forms to fit their own specific situation. Differences may also be sectoral. For reasons of safety and security some organizations, for example pharmaceutical companies, may not be willing or able to delegate too much decision authority to the individual. And importantly, cultural demands play a role as well. Non-hierarchical forms of organizing may not be effective at all in countries and cultures that traditionally are accustomed to hierarchy. In addition, many new ways of working fit better with information products than with physical products. That is why many new organizational forms are developed in the software and service industry. When ideas spill over to other organizations, they have to be adapted.

So we need to look beyond the hype to see what makes sense in the long-term and what does not. The next challenge for managers is to determine what those trends mean for their organization. The most important guideline is not to mindlessly adopt a form that works elsewhere. The second most important guideline is not to listen to people who claim that a certain organizational form is clearly the best. One size does not fit all. There is no one best way of organizing. You need to tweak and search when developing a new organizational form.

[1] Kogut, B. M. (Ed.). (1993). Country competitiveness: Technology and the organizing of work. Oxford University Press; Teece, D. J. (1980). The diffusion of an administrative innovation. Management science, 26(5), 464-470.
[2] Chandler, A.D. (1990). Scale and scope, the dynamics of industrial capitalism. The Belknap press.
[3] https://en.wikipedia.org/wiki/Information_society, retrieved March 5th, 2019.
[4] Zammuto, R. F., Griffith, T. L., Majchrzak, A., Dougherty, D. J., & Faraj, S. (2007). Information technology and the changing fabric of organization. Organization science, 18(5), 749-762.
[5] Guadalupe, M., Li, H., & Wulf, J. (2013). Who lives in the C-suite? Organizational structure and the division of labor in top management. Management Science, 60(4), 824-844.
[6] Shapiro, C., & Varian, H. R. (1998). Information rules: a strategic guide to the network economy. Harvard Business Press.
[7] Porter, M.E., & Kramer, M. R. (2011). Creating Shared Value. Harvard Business Review. 89(1/2), 62-77.
[8] Birkinshaw, J., Foss, N. J., & Lindenberg, S. (2014). Combining purpose with profits. MIT Sloan Management Review, 55(3), 49-56.
[9] Schwab, K. (2017). The fourth industrial revolution. Crown Business.
[10] Foss, N. J., & Klein, P. G. (2014). Why managers still matter. MIT Sloan Management Review, 56(1), 73-80; Sanner, B., & Bunderson, J. S. (2018). The Truth About Hierarchy. MIT Sloan Management Review, 59(2), 49-52.
[11] Ghoshal, S., Bartlett, C. A., & Moran, P. (1999). A new manifesto for management. MIT Sloan Management Review, 40(3), 9-20.

A BRIEF HISTORY OF ORGANIZING

Over time humanity continued to invent organizational forms of increasing complexity. The earliest form of organization is the specialization of individuals in those activities and crafts in which they excelled. The emergence of medieval guilds, ecclesiastical forms of organization and armies all influenced human thinking about how to organize work. It wasn't until the 1840s however that the first people emerged who were paid for dedicating all of their time towards the management of enterprises. The American railroad companies invented the functional form of organization and with it the person who was indispensable for its success: the full time, salaried manager[1].

The next great breakthrough took place in 1923 at General Motors with the invention of the divisional or business unit organization. GM recognized that different market segments existed that could each be served by a separate business unit that included all the resources necessary to serve that segment. A Board would oversee the various divisions, allocate investments across them, start new divisions or wind down existing ones and set targets for each business unit manager. This system unleashed entrepreneurship at the business unit level, while also enabling a company to bring a variety of products to the market. The latter was difficult to do within the functional organization.

It is somewhat arbitrary to start a historical timeline of organizational forms with the business unit, but for the purpose of this book it serves well, because most organizational forms that developed over the past hundred years are either refinements of the business unit or attempts to break away from it. More importantly the business unit still shapes many people's mental model of how to organize (more about this later). New organizational forms try to break through this mental model and therefore are often met with skepticism and disbelief.

The idea in brief
- **Organizational forms develop out of each other over time**
- **For historical reasons, the mental model of the business unit dominates much thinking about organizing**
- **New organizational forms depart from this mental model**
- **We are in a period of widespread experimentation with new organizational models**

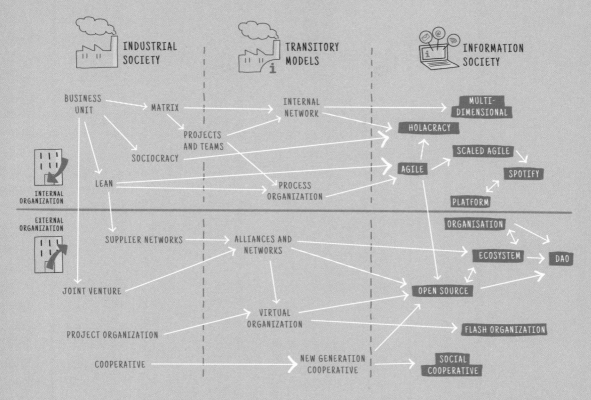

INDUSTRIAL SOCIETY

TRANSITORY MODELS

INFORMATION SOCIETY

BUSINESS UNIT → MATRIX → INTERNAL NETWORK → MULTI-DIMENSIONAL

PROJECTS AND TEAMS

SOCIOCRACY

HOLACRACY

AGILE

SCALED AGILE

SPOTIFY

LEAN

PROCESS ORGANIZATION

PLATFORM

INTERNAL ORGANIZATION

EXTERNAL ORGANIZATION

ORGANISATION

SUPPLIER NETWORKS → ALLIANCES AND NETWORKS

ECOSYSTEM

DAO

OPEN SOURCE

JOINT VENTURE

VIRTUAL ORGANIZATION

PROJECT ORGANIZATION

FLASH ORGANIZATION

COOPERATIVE → NEW GENERATION COOPERATIVE → SOCIAL COOPERATIVE

Figure 2: A brief history of organizing

Figure 2 presents an overview of organizational forms. The business unit is the main starting point, but project organizations, cooperatives and lean thinking provide inspiration for new ways of organizing as well. We will return to these later and start with developments from the business unit onwards.

The top line of the figure shows different organizational forms derived from the business unit, but each of them trying to remedy its limitations. A major drawback of the business unit structure is that the independence of each business unit prevents learning across units. There is no incentive for business unit managers to collaborate. As a consequence, all kinds of synergies that are possible in theory, are not realized in practice. For General Motors it was a conscious decision in *1923* to organize like this. The entrepreneurship of the business unit manager and his complete focus on optimizing his own unit, delivered the main benefits. Any further collaboration would probably only distract the manager from his most important task. Yet over time the disadvantage of limited cross-unit collaboration started to become more painful. Once the major benefits of optimization of units have been reaped, further benefits can only be gained by collaboration across units. The matrix organization proposed a solution for this, as it tries to combine the best of both worlds. For example, a consultancy firm with three business units focusing on retail, automotive and banking, might have people with functional expertise in strategy, marketing and HR in each of its units. In order to ensure that the functional expertise is also maintained, consultants can have two bosses: one ensuring the consultant contributes to the retail market and another focusing on the consultant's contribution to the strategy branch. The difficulty of having two bosses proves too much for many people and hence we see many watered down versions of the matrix in which there is no formal boss for the strategy branch, but somebody with a less formal status who tries to bring strategy consultants together to exchange knowledge and build expertise. In many cases this worked satisfactorily.

Another way of dealing with the challenges of the business unit is to define projects and assemble teams, usually on a temporary basis, to solve issues emerging from lack of interunit collaboration. In many cases this works.

A further step away from the business unit was the internal network organization, as pioneered by ABB[2]. ABB took a radical step by changing the structure of the organization in such a way that individual units, called competence centers, would not have all resources available to serve a particular market segment. It did the opposite: it made units too small to serve a market segment, thereby forcing them to collaborate because no competence center could go to the market alone. The idea behind this is that for the particular business-to-business market that ABB serves, each project is unique. Having fixed units is less useful as competences for each project need to be brought together from across the organization. It is much more important to have top-notch knowledge that can be combined to deliver big engineering projects. Because each competence center has its own profit responsibility, an incentive is built in to be entrepreneurial as well. To avoid disintegration, processes exist about how to engage with customers, a centralized information system keeps watch on all competence centers and top management continuously travels the world to emphasize its vision and manage conflicts.

Whereas the internal network organization changed the structure of the business unit, the multidimensional organization leaves the structure in place, but changes the governance. The main difficulty that was recognized but not solved by the preceding organizational forms was that organizations want to do multiple things at the same time: serve a market segment, sell a product, focus on a certain geographical area. The information requirements to do all this are very high: sales and costs need to be made transparent across all these different dimensions. Until recently the cost of the information infrastructure needed to do so was prohibitive, requiring organizations to choose one dimension (e.g. market segment) as the axis of optimization and maybe manage one other axis (e.g. product) on the side. With the declining cost of information however, sales and cost figures can be sliced and diced endlessly at limited additional cost, provided that a good information infrastructure is in place. This enables the multidimensional organization. A small branch of the business unit family

tree that has been gaining traction lately, is the sociocracy and holacracy movement. A main problem of the business unit is its top down, hierarchical character. Even though the original idea behind the business unit is not that communication should be predominantly top down, in practice bottom up communication often was limited. This meant that middle and senior managers had to make decisions about issues about which they were not particularly well informed. It also led to complacency on the work floor: knowledge available on an operational level remained unused. Sociocracy, invented in 1970, tried to change this by structurally ensuring bottom up communication through a system of double links[3].

In this system any lower ranking unit (called 'circle' in sociocratic lingo) elects somebody

"Organizing is what you do before you do something, so that when you do it, it is not all mixed up."

> Alan Alexander Milne

to represent them at the next higher hierarchical level and vice versa: the higher level elects somebody to represent them in the lower circle. In addition, each circle has a high degree of autonomy in deciding how they do their work. This system keeps hierarchy and the structure in place, but takes off many of the sharp edges. Holacracy is the 20th century reincarnation of sociocratic principles.

A third branch emerging out of business unit thinking is the branch that eventually leads to agile thinking. This branch focused much more on the organization of work at an operational level, rather than on overall organization designs. It also was an accident of history. Toyota developed a different manufacturing philosophy because after the Second World War it did not have the capital to buy cutting edge American technology[4]. Inspired by American supermarkets, it developed a system of production that did not build to stock, but builds to order. This required detailed attention to the production process, requiring the input of workers on

the assembly line and therefore giving them substantial authority, including the right to halt production. The first experiments with this system called 'lean thinking' were done in 1947. Important in the bigger picture of organizational forms, is the fact that it put business processes center stage. Using employees' knowledge, any part of a business process that does not deliver value for customers is eliminated as waste. The focus on processes has since been present in much thinking about organizations, as can be seen in process organizations but also in the emphasis agile organizations place on simplification of processes for customers.

Around the year 2000, ideas emerged among software developers who found that the traditional process of writing software had too many drawbacks and therefore proposed a more flexible and customer driven process, with more autonomy for software developers. Under the name of agile this has taken the world by storm, since this term was coined in 2001. It worked well on a project basis and therefore the question arose whether it

American railroads appoint middlemanagers		Functional form	GM organizes in business units		Toyota extends Lean to suppliers	Sociocracy and system of double linking	
		1860	1923		1961	1970	1988
1841	1844						
	First cooperative structures			1947 Toyota implements Lean organization		Increasing use of matrix structure	ABB implements internal network organization

would be possible to apply agile at the level of whole departments or even organizations. Scaled agile (*2006*) and the Spotify model (from *2012*) are attempts to come up with ways of making entire organizations agile, rather than only the individual projects. The development of agile organizations is especially relevant for platform organizations that have a presence online, like Google and Facebook. To rapidly and continually update their platform, fast deployment of software is critical. Agile working ensures this. Platform organizations have a further interesting feature, namely that they depend on external partners to join their platform, be it as a supplier, advertiser, app developer or user. Together these are called the ecosystem around the platform. Ecosystems form the culmination of another long-term trend in organizing: the gradual loosening of the boundaries of the firm. Toyota contributed immensely to that trend when it decided in *1961* to extend its lean thinking to its suppliers as well. This integrated the external world into the internal world of the corporation. This was a fundamental break with the business unit's focus

on optimizing the internal organization. Collaboration across boundaries had existed for a while but had mainly taken the form of joint ventures: a separate company set up by two or more parent companies and often managed quite independently of its parents.

In the *1990*s the idea that maybe not all problems could be solved internally and that collaboration with other companies was necessary to take advantage of market opportunities took further hold and translated into massive growth in alliances and networks[5]. Most networks however were the sum of bilateral relationships. In ecosystems the relationships are multilateral: everybody collaborates with everybody else.

Another organizational form with a long tradition behind it, is the project organization in which various organizations or individuals team up to jointly produce an outcome. This way of working is very common in the world of construction, where different contractors each deliver part of a building project. Movies are good examples of these temporary forms

Alliances and JV's take center stage
1990

First framework to scale Agile
2006

Spotify to organize in Tribes & Squads
2012

Decentralized autonomous organizations
2018

2001
Launch of Agile manifesto

2007
Sociocracy reincarnates through Holacracy

2017
Flash organizations

of organization as well[6]. The idea of virtual organizations is basically the same except that technology plays a greater role in connecting these organizations[7]. The very recent notion of flash organizations are an even flashier version of this. Gigster in the software business, and Artella, for animated pictures, are examples of platforms that connect freelancers to execute temporary projects. They select freelancers based on data points they gather about them from, among others, their team members. Using artificial intelligence they can then assemble the right flash team for the right job[8].

Flash organizations are temporary organizations but still have a central point, be it a person or a platform, that brings people together. Open source organizations on the other hand are not temporary and people sign up for them themselves. Yet they still take inspiration from virtual organizations in that their work force is not stable and work is done online. They also tend to follow agile management principles of software development. Some of them, like Linux, developed into platforms with their own ecosystems.

The final line in figure 2 is dedicated to co-operatives. With a history dating back to the *19th century* cooperatives have united mostly smaller organizations around specific issues. By sharing credit risks, farmers were able to provide finance to each other. Or by creating

scale, farmers could jointly purchase supplies at a lower cost. New generation cooperatives have put more emphasis on offensive moves, like stimulating innovation and joint brand creation[9]. The latest form they take are social cooperatives in which people unite to solve pressing societal issues such as global warming or inner city development. Open source organizations can be seen as a modern form of cooperative as well. The combination of open source, ecosystems and platforms spawns the rise of the decentralized autonomous organization (DAO, see box 1).

Decentralized Autonomous Organizations

The DAO, decentralized autonomous organization, is so new that even its name still needs to be agreed upon. Some call it a distributed autonomous organization others a decentralized autonomous company. Decentralized refers to the idea that the DAO is owned by peers, none of whom is able to dominate the others. Autonomous refers to the idea that the DAO operates without human intervention and works through algorithms instead.

The blockchain and Ethereum are examples. The idea is that relevant rules that guide the operations of the organization are programmed into smart contracts and that thereby the DAO avoids the problems of many human based organizations, like opportunistic behavior, the forming of dominant coalitions and opaque decision-making.

However, both the words 'decentralized' and 'autonomous' may be taken with a grain of salt. Even though DAOs are supposed to be egalitarian, in reality some of its peers may be more equal than others. A pure DAO could in theory be run autonomously (that is: without human intervention), but in practice many DAOs elect people to manage the organization. Besides, the rules always need to be programmed by humans, so the idea of an organization without human intervention seems to be elusive: technology always functions in a social setting. Even DAOs that were set up as pure DAO require human intervention. This is shown by the case of an Ethereum based DAO, simply named 'The DAO', in which a small group of people took countermeasures when the system was under attack. Many DAOs therefore operated more like platforms with ecosystems of people around them that make use of the DAO as an infrastructure.

It would be a stretch to say DAOs are an alternative to organizations at this point in time. They are only successful in executing routine tasks of low complexity. In particular, they are inflexible: organizations are better able to adapt to changing circumstances and it is difficult to see how all functions of an organization can be written into code. Nevertheless, advances in technology will undoubtedly broaden the applicability of DAOs.

Technology may help to coordinate large groups of actors like developers, bitcoin miners and token holders. For that reason the experiments with DAOs are relevant and may hold interesting implications for how to organize. Problems that still need to be solved concern the legal status of DAOs, how to write smart contracts that are watertight and how to balance the human and technology side of DAOs.

Box 1: DAO's[10]

PURE AND MIXED FORMS

Even though figure 2 does not show a simple and straightforward picture, it does show how organizational forms both build on and divert from their predecessors. It traces the red line in the developments. Reality of course is always messier. In many organizations we see combinations of these models, adaptations of them to specific circumstances or implementations that have stopped halfway. Many will consider this a violation of the principles of organizing. This is not necessarily so. We do not believe that there is one pure organizational form that works best; not for an individual organization let alone for organizations in general. Instead, organizing requires tinkering, borrowing parts of ideas from different forms and molding them into something that works for you. Maybe the end result is not pretty from a theoretical perspective, but what matters is whether it works in practice. That does not imply any mess is good: even organizations that use several forms simultaneously or in a mix must understand the principles behind these forms and, more importantly, why they diverge from them.

THE STRENGTH OF A MENTAL MODEL

In many ways the development of new organizational forms is a search process. Completely new models do not show up overnight, but emerge over time. The business unit towers over 20th century management just like networked and non-hierarchical forms will tower over the 21st century. The search process is often difficult because it requires letting go of many of the assumptions of the business unit. The mental model of the business unit is strong. Consider this:

- *One person has to be the boss*
- *There is an annual cycle of business planning and budgeting*
- *Each unit needs to have ownership of all resources needed to perform the task it has*
- *Clear market segments need to be defined*
- *Clear financial performance indicators are necessary.*

At first glance, nobody can object to this list. Yet the new organizational forms that are emerging depart from one or more of these principles. There is not one single boss in an ecosystem. Agile operations run counter to annual cycles. Many resources relevant for platforms are outside the organization that owns the platform. And they certainly don't define stable market segments but let markets emerge on their platform. Financial performance is relevant to all organizations, but is not the only thing. Open source organizations find that good software or a good encyclopedia (Wikipedia) is valuable in itself.

Thinking about organizational forms needs to grounded in the realization that many things we take for granted, in fact are only things we agreed upon to make things work in an earlier period of time. Recognizing such assumptions and understanding which are worth keeping and which should be left behind, is the first step to successful change towards new models. The information society enables new organizational models and the latest organizational forms can all be seen as experiments aimed at finding out which new models work.

[1] Chandler Jr, A. D. (1977). *The visible hand: The managerial revolution in American business.* Harvard University Press.

[2] Bartlett, C. A., & Ghoshal, S. (1993). Beyond the M-form: Toward a managerial theory of the firm. *Strategic Management Journal*, 14(2), 23-46.

[3] Romme, A. G. L. (1995). The sociocratic model of organizing. *Strategic Change*, 4(4), 209-215.

[4] Cusumano, M. A. (1988). Manufacturing innovation: Lessons from the Japanese auto industry. *MIT Sloan Management Review*, 30(1), 29-38.

[5] De Man, A. P. (2004). *The network economy.* Edward Elgar.

[6] DeFillippi, R. J., & Arthur, M. B. (1998). Paradox in project-based enterprise: The case of film making. *California Management Review*, 40(2), 125-139.

[7] Chesbrough, H. W., & Teece, D. J. (1996). When is virtual virtuous. *Harvard Business Review*, 74(1), 65-73.

[8] *The New York Times International Edition*, 2017, Employers embrace pop-up plan for staffing, July 18, p. 1 and 12; *The Economist*, 2017, The human cumulus, August 28, p. 54.

[9] De Man, A. P., & van Raaij, E. (2008). Making horticulture networks bloom, in: De Man, A.P. (ed.). *Knowledge Management and Innovation in Alliance Networks*, Edward Elgar, 122-144.

[10] This section is based on Walsh, D. (2014). DACs vs the Corporation, *Bitcoin Magazine*, 18 November; DuPont, Q. (2017). Experiments in algorithmic governance: A history and ethnography of "The DAO," a failed decentralized autonomous organization, in: Campbell-Verduyn, M. (ed.), *Bitcoin and Beyond.* Routledge, 157-177.

2 THE MULTIDIMENSIONAL ORGANIZATION

A key problem for multinationals that operate several product lines for different market segments in different countries is how to optimize profitability across all these dimensions: country, product, segment. The business unit structure focuses on one of these dimensions and the matrix tries to optimize two. Other dimensions are neglected, even though they may be important. Until recently, there was no organizational form that had the ability to optimize across more than two dimensions. Usually one or two dimensions were chosen and other dimensions were managed via temporary projects, working groups or individuals tasked with looking after dimensions that would otherwise be neglected[1]. The multidimensional organization provides a more integrated solution that would not have been possible without the use of modern information technology[2].

A multidimensional organization balances several dimensions (product, geography, market etc.) to optimize overall profitability. In a multidimensional organization, managers are accountable for the contribution their dimension makes to the overall company performance. Having managers accountable ensures two things. First, that each relevant dimension gets sufficient management attention. Someone has to spot new opportunities in market segments or for product development. In addition, managers need to assign resources to projects. Second, it ensures clients can do business with the organization in the way they want: on a product basis, a regional basis or in any other way they desire. However, all these accountabilities increase the risk of conflicts between managers about which clients to serve with which resources. To solve these conflicts, the multidimensional organization prioritizes decisions based on the profitability per client. Resources are assigned to the project that contributes most to that profitability.

The idea in brief
- **The multidimensional organization balances several dimensions rather than only one or two (e.g. geography, product, client and expertise)**
- **A manager is responsible for each dimension**
- **Conflicts are solved and priorities are set based on profitability per client**
- **Supported by one undisputed source of information and a collaborative culture**

To make that decision, the organization needs to have an undisputed source of information that enables the company to decide which action is the most profitable. In addition, information has to be available for each dimension about which revenues and costs it generates, so as to ascertain their contribution to overall company profitability.

This means that for any transaction with clients, the company needs to register all this information in one centralized database. For example, if an IT company sells hardware, software and services to an oil company in China, it needs to register all this information to be able to trace how each product category performs, how well they do in the oil sector and in China. The same revenue and cost of the transaction can next be reported across all these dimensions. That also makes it possible to compare performance within the dimensions: for example, by sharing information across different regions, managers can see in which region things are going well and in which region less so. They can next contact each other and discuss possible improvements.

This way of operating requires a number of additional mechanisms. The first is that there needs to be an overarching logic that is shared within the firm about how to serve clients and which clients to serve first. An example is IBMs logic that they prefer to sell integrated solutions to clients, rather than individual products. Developing and maintaining such a logic and next defining the relevant dimensions that need to be measured in keeping with that logic, is a top management task. Having such a logic in place also helps to resolve conflicts about resource assignment: conflicts are prevented when everybody knows the priorities.

Second, the higher levels of management are rewarded not on the profitability of their own dimension but (mainly) on the overall profitability of the firm. This creates an incentive for them to collaborate to increase profitability per client, rather than profitability of the dimension under their own management. Third, and following on from the previous

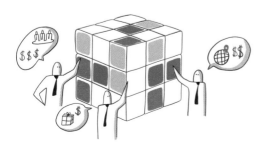

requirement, this requires managers to have a collaborative mindset. Managers that prefer to run their own shop are less suitable to work in a multidimensional organization, because in the multidimensional organization a manager is not solely responsible for the end result. The end result is a joint, not an individual, result.

As can be seen from the discussion above, the multidimensional organization focuses more on getting the information sharing and the behavior right than on creating the right departments that operate autonomously. Below the level of top managers however traditional departments can continue to exist. The higher management echelons determine the actions to take based on the information they receive and communicate these in their departments. The key organizational characteristics of the multidimensional organization are summarized in table 2.

Table 3 presents the information leaflet for the multidimensional organization. It lists the relevant ingredients of the form and the side effects. The key problem solved by the multidimensional organization is sub-optimization that occurs through focus on only one or two dimensions. The fact that the multidimensional organization can monitor several dimensions at the same time gives management a much better insight into opportunities. A second problem that is overcome by the multidimensional organization is the lack of collaboration across units in

HOW ARE TASKS DIVIDED?	· TOP MANAGEMENT DETERMINES WHICH DIMENSIONS ARE MOST IMPORTANT · CONFLICTS BETWEEN PROJECTS ARE SETTLED BASED ON DISCUSSIONS ABOUT MAXIMIZING PROFITABILITY PER CLIENT
HOW ARE TASKS ALLOCATED TO INDIVIDUALS?	· TOP MANAGEMENT DETERMINES WHO IS RESPONSIBLE FOR WHICH DIMENSION · ON AN OPERATIONAL LEVEL, MANAGERS FOR THE DIMENSIONS DECIDE WHO WILL WORK ON WHICH PROJECTS
HOW ARE REWARDS PROVIDED TO MOTIVATE PEOPLE?	· HIGHER MANAGEMENT IS MAINLY REWARDED BASED ON THE OVERALL PROFITABILITY OF THE COMPANY
HOW IS INFORMATION PROVIDED SO PEOPLE CAN TAKE THE RIGHT DECISIONS?	· ALL DATA ARE IN ONE TRUSTED SOURCE · OVERALL PROFITABILITY IS REPORTED ACROSS ALL DIMENSIONS, GIVING EVERYBODY INSIGHT IN ALL RELEVANT DATA

Table 2: Core elements of the multidimensional organization

an organization. The focus is on the overall profitability of the organization, not on the profitability of individual units. Costly turf wars over who owns which clients, resources and budgets are avoided or at least mitigated. An additional gain lies in the execution of large projects. In the business unit or matrix organization, a large project is often difficult to fit into the organization, as it gives rise to all kinds of forms of transfer pricing and discussions about which unit gets what. Because the multidimensional organization measures the contribution of each dimension to overall profitability, such discussions are much more limited.

The multidimensional organization of course also has its downsides. Because people are rewarded based on the overall profitability of the organization, there is less individual accountability for actions. This may open up opportunities for freeriding behavior. This problem cannot be mitigated by formal performance reviews, but can only be solved by behavioral mechanisms. Hence, the selection of people with a collaborative mindset is crucial for making this organizational form work. The multidimensional organization also requires continuous negotiation and discussion about opportunities in the market and how to react to them. In a traditional business unit organization it is up to the business unit manager to decide which opportunity to pursue. In the multi-dimensional organization

many opportunities require discussion and managers need to agree on which opportunities get priority. The focus on client profitability is helpful in this. It can be implemented by using client scorecards that show, per client, the financial elements and future opportunities at that client. It is not one number that presents the overall client profitability, there are various elements that need to be weighed, requiring discussion and negotiation. Finally, even though the basic idea of the multidimensional organization is elegant, it is not easy to grasp for everybody. It is a complex form of organization: with many dimensions to optimize, senior managers need to have a high cognitive ability to work in this setting.

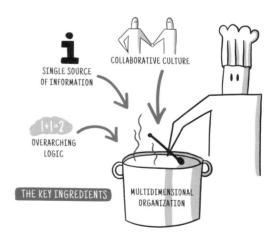

For this reason, this organizational form is not suitable for everybody. It is only relevant for multinationals operating in multiple markets with multiple products, facing complex client

PROBLEMS SOLVED	· SUBOPTIMIZATION DUE TO NEGLECTING RELEVANT DIMENSIONS · LACK OF COLLABORATION · DIFFICULTY OF EXECUTING LARGE PROJECTS
DISADVANTAGES	· LOSS OF INDIVIDUAL ACCOUNTABILITY · CONTINUOUS NEGOTIATION AND DISCUSSION · HIGH DEGREE OF COMPLEXITY
SUITABLE FOR?	· COMPLEX MULTINATIONALS OPERATING IN MULTIPLE MARKETS WITH MULTIPLE PRODUCTS · FACING COMPLEX CLIENT DEMAND · WITH GREAT PROFIT POTENTIAL IN INTEGRATED DELIVERY OF PRODUCTS AND SERVICES TO CLIENTS
NOT SUITABLE FOR	· ORGANIZATIONS THAT HAVE LITTLE TO GAIN FROM INTEGRATED PRODUCT DELIVERY
KEY INGREDIENTS	· OVERARCHING LOGIC TO SET PRIORITIES · WIDESPREAD AND TIMELY AVAILABILITY OF TRUSTED INFORMATION · COLLABORATIVE CULTURE
RISKS	· COMPLEXITY OF THE SYSTEM · ABSTRACT GOALS THAT LEAD TO LOSS OF IDENTIFICATION
LEADERSHIP	· COMMUNICATE THE OVERARCHING LOGIC · TOP NEEDS TO RESOLVE CONFLICTS BETWEEN MARKET OPPORTUNITIES AND AVAILABLE RESOURCES · DEFINING THE RELEVANT DIMENSIONS

Table 3: Information leaflet multidimensional organization

demand and having a great profit potential in integrated delivery of products and services to clients. This organizational form is not for smaller organizations and organizations offering single products that do not require integration with other products or services. For those organizations traditional forms like business units, functional or matrix organizations remain a better option.

The key ingredients that make the multidimensional organization work are easy to identify (but hard to implement). There needs to be an overarching logic to set priorities in the organization. There has to be one trusted and accepted source of information that registers all transactions according to several dimensions. This source needs to be available widely in the firm and deliver information in a timely fashion. Finally, a collaborative culture needs to be in place, at least at the higher levels of management. This list of ingredients also contains the seeds for the main risks a multidimensional organization faces. The complexity of the system may imply few people really get it, and that undermines the system's legitimacy. Similarly, the overarching logic is often an abstract idea that people may not buy into so easily.

As identification with goals is a main success factor for multidimensional organizations, there lies a task for the leadership here. It may be one of the great clichés that management has to communicate well, but that does not make it less true. Communication of the overarching logic and ensuring widespread understanding of it in the organization is a major responsibility for the most senior leadership. Second, one key problem is not resolved in this organizational form and that is the conflict between market opportunities and available resources. At any given point in time, there may be more opportunities than there are resources available to meet them. The overarching logic and focus on profitability per client may go quite some way in resolving this conflict, but inevitably some conflicts will remain. This is where management needs to step in and make the call.

Finally and obviously, top management needs to define the relevant dimensions for the organization and ensure that the information that measures these dimensions is captured. To ensure the latter is often a major IT challenge. To build one integrated IT system is costly and takes time. The good news

is that once it is in place using the latest technology, it may not be that difficult to add dimensions or stop registering a certain dimension when market circumstances change. Because the structure of information is no longer tied to the structure of the organization, changes can be made without requiring major upheavals. This is in contrast to the business unit structure: there all information centers around the business unit, often with each unit having its own information systems. A change in the structure therefore requires a change in information systems and vice versa.

IBM: THE PIONEER

The organization that did the most pioneering work in developing the multidimensional organization was IBM under Louis V. Gerstner in the 1990s[3]. The overarching logic that emerged over time was that IBM should deliver integrated solutions for the largest organizations instead of individual products for each and every one. IBM would always be outcompeted by specialists if it focused on selling individual products. By offering solutions to large companies however, IBM could profit from the broad range of products it has to offer. That logic fit well with all the different businesses IBM was in. It also clarifies where the priority lies: IBM still serves local clients, but the focus lies elsewhere. The relevant dimensions for the organization were defined as products, regions, channel and customer. Global account managers were put in a crucial role. They took the lead in integrating all IBM resources in projects for clients. The consequences of this change in strategy were immense. For example, it also required retraining of sales managers to focus on selling overall solutions rather than individual products.

Information was a key factor in operating the multidimensional enterprise. Regarding the financial systems, since the mid-1990s IBM worked on creating one general ledger. Each transaction can be registered in 1,000 columns. The first columns are the same for each transaction across IBM and that enables data to be consolidated by product, by customer, by channel and by region. The second part allows for any other information to be registered that different managers find useful for themselves. The system has the capability to consolidate weekly and to provide the relevant information across the four dimensions. The fact that this organizational form is not just about systems, but people as well,

becomes evident in the fact that almost 40 per cent of the top managers were changed in the years after the new way of working was introduced. It was important for top managers to feel like part of one team and in many places that required new people to step in.

Clear priorities are set to facilitate this process: number one is acquiring new projects, next optimizing IBM results; optimizing results of the manager's own unit only comes in third place. Collaboration between units is vital to achieve the first two priorities and is enabled by the one trusted source of information. Competence profiles for employees were updated to better support this way of working. Job rotation, bonding mechanisms and a focus on personal development further supported the new organizational form.

[1] Goold, M. & Campbell, A. (2002), Designing Effective Organizations, New York, NY: Jossey-Bass.
[2] This chapter is based on the next publications. Campbell, A., & Strikwerda, H. (2013). The power of one: towards the new integrated organisation. Journal of Business Strategy, 34(2), 4-12; Strikwerda, H. (2008). Van unitmanagement naar de multidimensionale organisatie. Uitgeverij Van Gorcum; Strikwerda, J., & Stoelhorst, J. W. (2009). The emergence and evolution of the multidimensional organization. California Management Review, 51(4), 11-31; Zammuto, R. F., Griffith, T. L., Majchrzak, A., Dougherty, D. J., & Faraj, S. (2007). Information technology and the changing fabric of organization. Organization Science, 18(5), 749-762.
[3] All information about IBM is taken from Campbell, A., & Strikwerda, H. (2013) ibid. and Strikwerda, H. (2008) ibid.

"Through modular organizing, deploying the method of multidimensional information spaces, large companies can succeed in organizing for uncertainty in a constructive, entrepreneurial way."

> Hans Strikwerda

AGILE, SCRUM AND THE SCALED AGILE FRAMEWORK (SAFE)

Undoubtedly one of the most influential streams of thinking in business is the agile movement. Technically, agile is not an organizational form as such, but rather a way of organizing projects. Agile originated in software development in 2001 and aimed to remedy problems of traditional software development projects. Traditional projects often were long running, expensive, did not deliver what the client wanted, were not able to deal with changing requirements during the project and were accompanied by endless documentation nobody ever read. In 2001 a number of software developers got together and produced the Manifesto for Agile Software development (see table 4). In a broader sense the term agile has been used to denote the organizational ability to quickly reconfigure strategy, structure, processes, people, and technology toward value-creating and value-protecting opportunities[1]. This broader use of the term agile would include the organizational forms discussed in this book. Below our focus is first on agile defined in the narrow sense and next on some approaches to scale agile to the broader organization.

The idea in brief

- Rooted in software development projects, agile focuses on delivering working software faster
- It has fixed roles (product owner, multifunctional teams) and a fixed process with meeting structures (scrum, sprints)
- SAFe is a framework that enables the application of agile on an organizational level instead of a project level
- It helps to improve time to market in organizations with a complex legacy IT architecture

AGILE AND SCRUM

The basic ideas behind agile on a project level are that individuals and interactions between them are more important than processes and tools, working software is better than comprehensive documentation, customer collaboration is preferred over contract negotiation and responding to change is better than following a fixed plan. Many applications of agile make use of a method called Scrum, developed in the 1990s. In the Agile/Scrum methodology a 'product owner' acts as the client and defines what task he wants to have done in what order.

OUR HIGHEST PRIORITY IS TO SATISFY THE CUSTOMER THROUGH EARLY AND CONTINUOUS DELIVERY OF VALUABLE SOFTWARE.

WELCOME CHANGING REQUIREMENTS, EVEN LATE IN DEVELOPMENT. AGILE PROCESSES HARNESS CHANGE FOR THE CUSTOMER'S COMPETITIVE ADVANTAGE.

DELIVER WORKING SOFTWARE FREQUENTLY, FROM A COUPLE OF WEEKS TO A COUPLE OF MONTHS, WITH A PREFERENCE TO THE SHORTER TIMESCALE.

BUSINESS PEOPLE AND DEVELOPERS MUST WORK TOGETHER DAILY THROUGHOUT THE PROJECT.

BUILD PROJECTS AROUND MOTIVATED INDIVIDUALS. GIVE THEM THE ENVIRONMENT AND SUPPORT THEY NEED, AND TRUST THEM TO GET THE JOB DONE.

THE MOST EFFICIENT AND EFFECTIVE METHOD OF CONVEYING INFORMATION TO AND WITHIN A DEVELOPMENT TEAM IS FACE-TO-FACE CONVERSATION.

WORKING SOFTWARE IS THE PRIMARY MEASURE OF PROGRESS.

AGILE PROCESSES PROMOTE SUSTAINABLE DEVELOPMENT. THE SPONSORS, DEVELOPERS, AND USERS SHOULD BE ABLE TO MAINTAIN A CONSTANT PACE INDEFINITELY.

CONTINUOUS ATTENTION TO TECHNICAL EXCELLENCE AND GOOD DESIGN ENHANCES AGILITY.

SIMPLICITY--THE ART OF MAXIMIZING THE AMOUNT OF WORK NOT DONE--IS ESSENTIAL.

THE BEST ARCHITECTURES, REQUIREMENTS, AND DESIGNS EMERGE FROM SELF-ORGANIZING TEAMS.

AT REGULAR INTERVALS, THE TEAM REFLECTS ON HOW TO BECOME MORE EFFECTIVE, THEN TUNES AND ADJUSTS ITS BEHAVIOR ACCORDINGLY.

Table 4: Principles behind the Agile Manifesto[2]

These tasks end up on a 'product backlog'. A self-managing team selects tasks from the highest ranked items on the product backlog. In a 'sprint planning', the team divides these tasks among the team members in such a way that they can execute a coherent set of work during a short 'sprint' (a fixed time period of one to four weeks in which they have to deliver the tasks). In a daily scrum meeting, team members discuss progress of the sprint and what they need to finish on time. Such a meeting lasts a maximum of 20 minutes. In a sprint review the results of a sprint are presented. At the end of a sprint, team members evaluate the process in a sprint retrospective.

A scrum master or agile coach facilitates this process, ensures the way of working is maintained and introduces new ways of working to the team, if and when necessary (figure 3). The scrum master also is the interface between team and product owner. In short: Scrum has four meetings (sprint planning, daily scrum, sprint review, sprint retrospective) and three roles (product owner, team, scrum master).

Agile thinking has a strong focus on delivering value for the client via continuous improvement and focuses on using the autonomy and knowledge of individuals, rather than

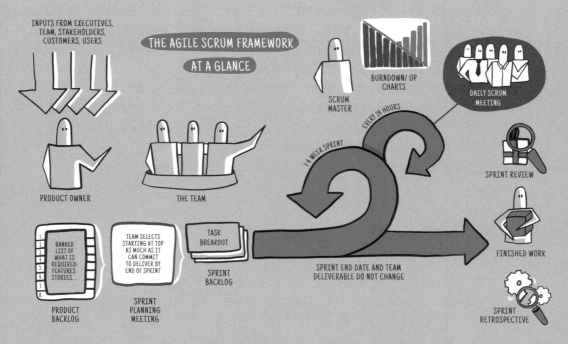

Figure 3: The Agile Scrum Framework[3]

on organizational procedures and processes. Product owners define what to do, but how to do it is left to the team. The benefit of this way of working lies in the ownership people feel of their work and the fact that they have control over it. This provides a strong motivation for them to deliver. In addition they can focus on getting the job done, rather than discuss the process in endless meetings. The focus is on delivering for the client, the product owner. Apart from the daily meeting, coordination relies highly on visible information. The product backlog is visible, there is a task board and 'burn-down charts' show the progress made towards the end of the sprint. All this also requires a scrum team to work in one single space, enhancing communication between team members.

Agile/Scrum solves a number of problems. Because sprints are short it is easier to react to changes that emerge during the project. Many projects falter because by the time they meet the initial goal, the goal has become irrelevant. By providing many opportunities to adjust to changing demand, agile project management is able to work with changing client demand during the development of software.

Agile thinking is not universally applicable. Not every individual is comfortable with the fact that the end goal of the project remains unclear. In an environment where people identify with end goals, instead of a fixed process, agile working may be counterproductive. Also the fixed process that often is adhered to rigidly may lead to a feeling of 'going through the motions' or can be experienced as a straitjacket. Finally, it may cause problems when parts of organizations have to work together, where one part works according to agile principles and the other one does not. Differences in work rhythm may lead to tensions between the teams.

Table 5 presents some further conditions for agile to work. Agile works well in swiftly evolving markets where demands change. When markets are predictable, traditional ways of working based on planning and detailed specifications may perform better. When customer requirements are clear at the outset, traditional methods work better, but when they are not clear or become clearer along the way, agile is the way forward. Customers also need to be available for regular collaboration with the teams. Complex problems with unknown solutions requiring cross-functional teams fit better with agile methods than known problems that can build on existing solutions using a functional team. Furthermore, the idea of working in sprints assumes that delivering small parts of work is also viable for a client; for example, an incremental improvement in a website or an algorithm that can easily be integrated in an existing website. If such improvements do not exist and substantial functionality needs to be in place before it is useful for a client, agile is less suitable. Finally, agile makes sense if mistakes made during the process can easily be remedied and can therefore be seen as learning experiences pointing to solutions that work and those that don't work. If mistakes during the project are fatal to the overall outcome you will want to exercise more control than is possible in an agile environment.

	FAVORABLE	UNFAVORABLE
MARKET ENVIRONMENT	CUSTOMER PREFERENCES AND SOLUTION OPTIONS CHANGE FREQUENTLY	MARKET CONDITIONS ARE STABLE AND PREDICTABLE.
CUSTOMER INVOLVEMENT	CLOSE COLLABORATION AND RAPID FEEDBACK ARE FEASIBLE. CUSTOMERS KNOW BETTER WHAT THEY WANT AS THE PROCESS PROGRESSES.	REQUIREMENTS ARE CLEAR AT THE OUTSET AND WILL REMAIN STABLE. CUSTOMERS ARE UNAVAILABLE FOR CONSTANT COLLABORATION.
INNOVATION TYPE	PROBLEMS ARE COMPLEX, SOLUTIONS ARE UNKNOWN, AND THE SCOPE ISN'T CLEARLY DEFINED. PRODUCT SPECIFICATIONS MAY CHANGE. CREATIVE BREAKTHROUGHS AND TIME TO MARKET ARE IMPORTANT. CROSS-FUNCTIONAL COLLABORATION IS VITAL.	SIMILAR WORK HAS BEEN DONE BEFORE, AND INNOVATORS BELIEVE THE SOLUTIONS ARE CLEAR. DETAILED SPECIFICATIONS AND WORK PLANS CAN BE FORECAST WITH CONFIDENCE AND SHOULD BE ADHERED TO. PROBLEMS CAN BE SOLVED SEQUENTIALLY IN FUNCTIONAL SILOS.
MODULARITY OF WORK	INCREMENTAL DEVELOPMENTS HAVE VALUE, AND CUSTOMERS CAN USE THEM. WORK CAN BE BROKEN INTO PARTS AND CONDUCTED IN RAPID, ITERATIVE CYCLES. LATE CHANGES ARE MANAGEABLE.	CUSTOMERS CANNOT START TESTING PARTS OF THE PRODUCT UNTIL EVERYTHING IS COMPLETE. LATE CHANGES ARE EXPENSIVE OR IMPOSSIBLE.
IMPACT OF INTERIM MISTAKES	THEY PROVIDE VALUABLE LEARNING.	THEY MAY BE CATASTROPHIC.

Table 5: Conditions for agile[4]

THE SCALED AGILE FRAMEWORK (SAFE)

As can be seen from table 5 many business environments nowadays fit with agile working. This explains the popularity of the concept. It also makes it attractive to think about applying such thinking not only on a project level but on an organization level as well. However, what works well for an individual project does not always work well for a complete organization. It may be possible to work with a handful of scrum teams, but the problem in many organizations is that scrum teams cannot be designed to work independently from each other. If that is the case coordination across teams needs to take place. A simple way of doing that is to install a scrum-of-scrums, that is a team to coordinate the teams. Yet experience shows a scrum-of-scrums becomes difficult once more than five teams need to be coordinated.

Organizations therefore look at a variety of other models to scale agile such as Disciplined Agile Delivery (DAD), Large Scale Scrum (LeSS), Enterprise Scrum, Scrum at Scale, ScALeD, XSCALE or Nexus[5]. Currently the Scaled Agile Framework (SAFe) is the most frequently used model to scale agile and

Why frameworks to scale Agile are necessary

scrum across organizations. SAFe provides a way of implementing agile thinking in complex organizations that cannot be easily redesigned to make the Spotify model work (see chapter 3 for the Spotify model). An important reason why the Spotify model may not work is the presence of tightly connected IT architectures. One of the preconditions for the Spotify model to work is that tribes can work independently in IT systems without impinging too much on each other's work. In most organizations however, the IT architecture is not so streamlined but instead resembles spaghetti. Changes that one team wants to make therefore will affect the work of other teams and hence coordination is necessary. When IT creates such interdependencies between teams, SAFe may provide a solution.

One of the more humorous aspects of the agile movement is their less than agile use of language. Much effort has been invested in creating terminology that is as inscrutable as possible. Here are the core concepts used in SAFe[6]. First of all, SAFe relies on value streams. *A value stream* is a sequence of steps that deliver value to the customer. A value stream includes a *trigger*: for example a client request or an idea for a new product may trigger the start of a process to deliver on that request or create that new product. A value stream ends with the delivery of value to the customer. *Value stream mapping* is the process to map the steps necessary to deliver the value. Value streams tend not to be short projects, but are long lived. For example, the process of a patient entering the hospital, being treated, leaving and paying is an example of a value stream. In practice however most value streams are not this type of *operational value streams*, but are *development value streams*. That is: they build the IT systems to support the operational process. Whereas in the Spotify model business and IT are always present in a squad, in most implementations of SAFe, business and IT are still separate and somebody in IT coordinates with stakeholders in the business (this person is called a *proxy product owner*).

Value streams are delivered by *Agile Release Trains* (ARTs). Other than the name suggests this is not a machine or a piece of wam of people of flesh and blood. An ART is a virtual team of all the people necessary to deliver a value stream. It is a long-lived combination of agile teams, which, along with other stakeholders, develops and delivers solutions incrementally, using a series of fixed-length iterations. A *release* is a piece of software that can be deployed (used). Every two to four months the teams coordinate their work in a Program Increment meeting. A *program increment* is the two to four months period that elapses between program meetings. During the program increment, teams work on their deliverables and release software when they see fit. The Program Increment meeting is not the deadline at which deliverables have to be finished. Its purpose is to coordinate work for the next period (or in SAFe speak: program increment).

The ART aligns several multidisciplinary teams to a common business and techno-logy mission. These teams are called *feature teams*. Each ART is a virtual organization (50 – 125 people) that plans, commits, and executes together. Note the word 'virtual': the team may consist of people working in different geographies, functions or business units. An ART is not a separate department in an organization; instead existing departments make people available to work in the ART. Existing organization structures do not have to be changed to work with ARTs. Ideally, an ART is as independent as possible from other ARTs and can release independently. More often a *release planning* is necessary to plan and prioritize work across sprints and teams. A single value stream may have only one ART, but varieties to this model may exist. One ART may be able to work on multiple smaller value streams. A large value stream may have multiple ARTs (this is then called a *solution train*).

There are three layers in SAFe:
1. The portfolio layer comprises the value streams in an organization. By adding or dropping value streams a company makes strategic choices about which markets it wants to be active in.
2. The program layer consists of the ARTs that needs to coordinate the teams.
3. The team layer executes the work.

If you understand the next sentence, you will pass the SAFe 101 test. The feature teams in multiple ARTs work in a solution train to de-liver program increments for a value stream. There is nothing to it, really.

New functions emerge in the SAFe framework like release train leads and value stream leads. Value stream leads need to coordi-nate priorities among each other. Each value stream lead next prioritizes the work to be done.

3 MONTHS

5-12 TEAMS

INCREMENT

RELEASE TRAIN ENGINEER

The release train lead coordinates the teams in the ART in such a way that the prioritized work gets done. Each team also has a product owner. Budgeting in the SAFe framework is done based on the initiatives on the portfolio level. Through budget allocation management ensures that people work on those value streams and projects that deliver the most value.

Table 6 summarizes the differences between SAFe and Spotify. The key issue lies in the IT architecture that creates interdependencies that need to be coordinated in SAFe. The Spotify model does not require that coordination. If the IT architecture in an organization is streamlined, coordination requirements are much lower.

That enables an organization to work with autonomous teams and restructure itself more radically, as Spotify has done. When the architecture looks like spaghetti, teams cannot be autonomous but need to coordinate extensively with other teams. A restructuring along the lines of Spotify will not improve the situation. In that case SAFe applies.

Still, it is possible to make an organization more agile by using SAFe, although the speed will always be lower than in the Spotify model. The key is that SAFe reduces hand-offs between teams and thus removes an important cause of mistakes and delay.

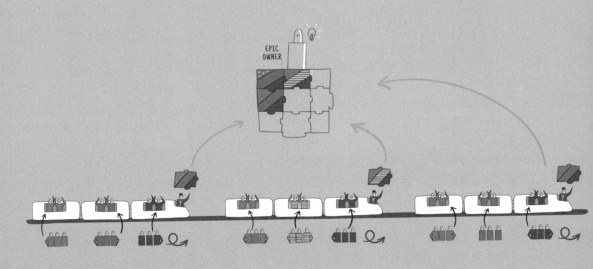

SAFe	Spotify model
IT architecture is spaghetti	IT architecture is streamlined
Therefore teams are interdependent	Therefore teams can work independently
This requires coordination in an ART and among value stream leads	There is no need for a coordination layer; the tribe lead coordinates with the product owner
While maintaining an existing organization structure	And the organization can be restructured to the tribes and squads model
Effect: higher speed than traditional organizations, but lower than in Spotify model	Effect: high speed of software deployment

Table 6: SAFe versus Spotify

"The shift to Agile is not just a matter of adopting one or two particular management tactics. A single fix is not enough: companies need systemic change."

> Steve Denning

[1] Ahlbäck, K., C. Fahrbach, M. Murarka & O. Salo. (2017) How to create an agile organization. October, https://www.mckinsey.com/business-functions/organization/our-insights/how-to-create-an-agile-organization

[2] http://agilemanifesto.org/

[3] https://agileforall.com/

[4] Rigby, D. K., Sutherland, J., & Takeuchi, H. (2016). Embracing agile. Harvard Business Review, 94(5), 40-50

[5] VersionOne (2018), 12th Annual State of Agile Report, https://explore.versionone.com/state-ofagile/versionone-12th-annual-state-of-agile-report

[6] The definitions are based on https://www.scaledagileframework.com/identify-value-streams-and-arts/, retrieved 11 October 2018.

3 THE SPOTIFY MODEL

The popularity of agile ways of working at a project level raised interest in the possibility of building entire organizations according to agile processes. In agile dialect, the question is: how to scale agile? Especially in online environments in which speed of innovation is critical, the search for organizational forms that enable fast deployment of software has been vigorously pursued. The necessity of making new or improved applications available to customers fast is very high in these industries. It is no coincidence then that one of the scaled agile models that attracts most attention emerged at Spotify, the online music streaming service. The Spotify model received much attention and is a source of inspiration for many organizations.

Figure 4 depicts the basic form of the Spotify model[1]. The model builds on five elements:

Product owner

The product owner performs the same role as in agile/scrum processes. She or he determines the deliverables that need to be made and prioritizes the work to be done, but does not specify how the work should be done. The product owner represents the client and does so based on data. In an online setting, client behavior is monitored and the product owner uses the data gathered to determine which functionality is needed.

Squad

A squad is a multifunctional team that creates those deliverables. For example, a squad can focus on payment solutions. An interesting feature of a squad is that, provided a fixed process is followed, individuals in a squad can make new functionalities available online without asking for permission of a higher hierarchical layer. This is one way of ensuring speedy deployment of new features. Another

The idea in brief
- **The Spotify model aims to speed up software deployment**
- **It scales agile by using autonomous, multifunctional teams called squads**
- **Each squad is part of a tribe: a department focusing on a certain business issue. Product owners in the tribe determine which functionality squads need to develop**
- **Each squad member is part of a chapter, together with other members of his tribe who have the same functional expertise. The chapter lead is their hierarchical boss**
- **The model is suitable for software development, non-routine activities and requires a streamlined IT architecture**

way to create speed is to organize squads so that they can function as independently from each other as possible. Each dependency is likely to slow down the process because it requires meeting and coordination. This also requires a streamlined IT architecture. The fewer the interconnections between IT systems the lower the need for coordination, allowing squads to make changes in IT systems without a need to align with other parts of the organization. Squads may consist of around nine people.

Tribe

A tribe is a collection of squads working in a related area, like back-end infrastructure or the Spotify music player. In the Dutch bank ING, tribes are product related, for example daily banking or mortgage services[2]. The tribe lead is responsible for creating the right habi- tat for people to be effective and coordinates with product owners and other tribes to set priorities. Tribe leads report to for example a COO. The number of people in a tribe varies across organizations in the range of 100 to 200. People in a tribe are co-located to enhance collaboration. The tribe lead receives a budget and allocates that to different squads.

Chapter

A chapter bundles expertise in the organization. It contains people with similar skills in the same tribe. For example, a chapter may focus on data analytics or user experience. Without chapters, there would be no learning from each other. An interesting feature here is that the chapter lead reports to the tribe lead or the CIO. The chapter lead fulfills line manager tasks like performance management, ensuring development of individuals and

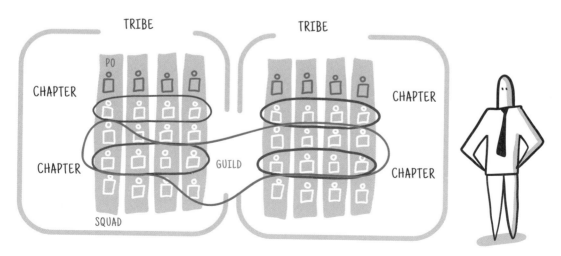

Figure 4: The Spotify model

finding and sharing best practices. If there is hierarchy in the Spotify model it lies with the chapter lead. However, the chapter lead is not a fulltime manager, but is also part of one of the squads. This way of working is interesting because the focus of the line manager is mainly on maintaining high quality knowledge in the group that reports to him.

Guild

A guild is a group that shares knowledge on a voluntary basis across the organization. Guilds tend to connect similar chapters in different tribes but they are open for everybody to join.

A final but smaller role is that of system owner. This is a role somebody may have in addition to a squad membership or chapter lead role. It exists to ensure the overall system remains coherent. With so many different squads working independently and making changes, there is a real risk that consistency can be lost. The system owner role is kept small though, so as not to impinge too much on the independence of the squads.

Budgets are allocated to the tribe lead. This is relatively straightforward because the number of people in the tribe determines the budget. The tribe lead next allocates budgets based on the number of squads and sprints that are necessary. This can be changed during the year, depending on new issues emerg-

ing. In this way short-term priority setting is decoupled from long-term funding, allowing for both budgetary clarity at the organizational level and adaptability at the operational level.

Is this a matrix organization? That depends on how you define matrix, but the model looks conspicuously like one. However there are a few notable differences with the classic, pure matrix structure. In a matrix, similar skills are grouped together in departments whereas squads contain a variety of skills. In a matrix, work is often project based meaning that team composition changes form project to project, but in the Spotify model team composition is more stable. Third, in the pure version of the matrix, each member of the organization is accountable to two line managers. In the Spotify model there is only one: the chapter lead. A squad member is told what to do by the product owner and how to do it by the chapter lead. But the chapter lead does the performance review. This safeguards the quality of the technical knowledge. Fourth, this last point also signals a departure from the matrix. A manager in a matrix is responsible for the product, process and people. In the Spotify model these responsibilities are split between the product owners, agile coaches and chapter leads[3]. A final difference lies in the governance. Mandates lie much lower in the organization than in a matrix. Many decisions can be taken by the teams without involving a higher level manager. So people and teams report to each other in the daily start-up, not to the boss.

Probably more relevant than a discussion about whether this structure is really new and different is the realization that structure is only a small part of the story. Even though it provides the skeleton for the organization, it is the behavior and culture that makes it come alive. The high level of selforganization and autonomy is what really sets it apart from the more traditional organization designs. It is hard to see how a traditional organization can be reconciled with the authority of each individual to make changes to the product. Yet that is what Spotify does. That requires a high sense of responsibility and collaborative spirit. A focus on learning, collaboration, and a sense of community is

important, as well as hiring the right talent. Office lay out stimulates collaboration. The Spotify HR blog shows how Spotify deals with all these issues[4]. For example, Spotify is very reticent with financial incentives. The main motivation must come from the opportunities for development an individual is exposed to within Spotify. Hence also the emphasis of the chapter lead on this aspect. Table 7 summarizes the core elements of the Spotify model.

The core problem solved in the Spotify model is a speed of operation that is too low to stay ahead of the competition (see table 8). With decision authority low in the organization and the organization focused on deployment, new product features are introduced on a continuous basis. Through the mechanism of the product owner the innovation also is

HOW ARE TASKS DIVIDED?	· PRODUCT OWNER AND TRIBE LEAD DETERMINE WHICH TASKS ARE TO BE DONE AND WHAT THE PRIORITY IS · TOP MANAGEMENT DETERMINES WHICH FIXED ROLES EXIST
HOW ARE TASKS ALLOCATED TO INDIVIDUALS?	· SQUADS DIVIDE TASKS AMONG THE SQUAD MEMBERS · SOME TASKS ARE ASSIGNED BY SENIOR MANAGEMENT TO TRIBE LEADS AND CHAPTER LEADS
HOW ARE REWARDS PROVIDED TO MOTIVATE PEOPLE?	· AUTONOMY, LEARNING AND KNOWLEDGE SHARING MAKE WORK INTERESTING · SENSE OF BELONGING TO THE ORGANIZATION · OPPORTUNITIES FOR DEVELOPMENT
HOW IS INFORMATION PROVIDED SO PEOPLE CAN TAKE THE RIGHT DECISIONS?	· SQUADS, CHAPTERS, TRIBES AND GUILDS HAVE THEIR OWN MEETINGS · VISUAL MANAGEMENT TOOLS ALONG THE LINES OF AGILE/SCRUM · OFFICE LAYOUT STIMULATES COLLABORATION

Table 7: Core elements of the Spotify model

PROBLEMS SOLVED	· LOW SPEED · INNOVATION NOT BASED ON CLIENT NEEDS · INSUFFICIENT USE OF KNOWLEDGE AT AN OPERATIONAL LEVEL · LACK OF CROSS-FUNCTIONAL COLLABORATION
DISADVANTAGES	· CONTINUOUS DYNAMICS, LACK OF STABILITY · LOW OPERATIONAL CONTROL
SUITABLE FOR?	· FAST-MOVING ENVIRONMENTS · COMPLEX PROBLEMS WITH UNCLEAR SOLUTIONS · PROJECTS WITH HIGH LIKELIHOOD OF CHANGING PROJECT REQUIREMENTS · ISSUES WHERE CREATIVE TEAMS ARE LIKELY TO OUTPERFORM COMMAND AND CONTROL · ORGANIZATIONS WITH STREAMLINED IT ARCHITECTURE OR MODULAR PRODUCT DESIGN
NOT SUITABLE FOR	· ORGANIZATIONS FACING STABLE ENVIRONMENTS · ORGANIZATIONS WITH A HIERARCHICAL AND/OR PLANNING ORIENTED CULTURE · ROUTINE OPERATIONS · PROCESSES WHERE FATAL ERRORS CAN BE MADE
KEY INGREDIENTS	· END TO END PROCESSES (DEVOPS) · SQUADS: AUTONOMOUS, MULTI-FUNCTIONAL, CO-LOCATED TEAMS · FOCUS ON THE WHAT, NOT THE HOW · CLARITY OF INFORMATION · COLLABORATIVE CULTURE · MAINTENANCE OF TECHNICAL COMPETENCES · COMMUNICATION BY PRODUCT OWNER WITH TEAMS
RISKS	· LOSS OF COHERENCE · SELF-EVALUATION OF SQUADS MAY MAKE THEM COMPLACENT · LACK OF ATTENTION TO CROSS-TRIBE ISSUES · INCREASE IN PROJECT PORTFOLIO
LEADERSHIP	· MISSION/VISION · BEARER OF THE CULTURE

Table 8: Information leaflet Spotify model

focused on client needs. Even though there is room in Spotify for people to have their own pet projects that they can work on during 'hack time' or 'hack days' in which they can pursue their own interests, innovation is mainly driven from this client perspective. A further problem solved is that many organizations do not make adequate use of the knowledge of people on an operational level. Best use is made of the available knowledge by having teams self-organize and decide who does what. Finally, the Spotify model stimulates cross-functional collaboration in several ways: in squads, by using open office spaces and in building a strong culture.

The model comes with some downsides, too. The organization is in a constant state of flux. Dynamics are necessary in a fast moving environment but continuous change may come at the cost of focus and can be exerting for the individual employee. Another disadvantage is that operational control is low. The risk that somebody puts features online that do not work is higher than in other organizations. The risk of being too late should therefore be higher than the risk of making the occasional mistake.

"The Spotify model is about creating minimal viable bureaucracy with high autonomy and high alignment"

> Joakim Sunden

The organizational form developed by Spotify is particularly relevant in an environment where fast product development is necessary. The speed with which Spotify releases new features on its site is a key competitive advantage that enables it to compete with companies like Apple that are far larger (Spotify's staff runs only into the hundreds). The organizational form is also well suited for complex problems with unclear solutions[5]. Such problems require experimentation. Sprints make it possible to test many different solutions to a problem without having to make major investments in one. When solutions to a problem are already known, the model is less applicable. Projects with a high likelihood of changing project requirements also fit well into the Spotify model because it allows for changing project requirements along the way. The fact that solutions are not clear also means squads must engage in creative problem solving. When creative teams are likely to outperform command and control ways of working, the Spotify model is an option. Finally, an important precondition for the model to work is a streamlined IT architecture or, for production companies, a modular product design. When there are too many non-standardized interconnections between IT systems or between product modules, teams will not be able to work on them autonomously.

Organizations facing stable environments will find less merit in using the Spotify model. The need for change in such organizations is low and organizing for predictability is probably a safer bet. For similar reasons, organizations with a hierarchical and/or planning oriented culture will find it difficult to work in the Spotify model. Even though hierarchy is not absent in the Spotify model, the model is much less hierarchical than more traditional organizations. If either management or employees or both are more comfortable working in a hierarchy, this model is not for them. In keeping with the previous points, the Spotify model will do little to improve routine operations. The factory floor in a mass production factory, the accounting or the purchasing department will not benefit from tribes and squads. Finally, processes where fatal errors can be made do not lend themselves to this model. Rocket launches, operating theatres and air traffic controllers will do better with command and control accompanied by elaborate procedures.

Keeping in mind that speed is one of the main objectives, the main ingredients of the Spotify model help to realize a faster time-to-market. A first ingredient is the presence of end-to-end processes. When the same team is responsible for developing the software and for running it (called DevOps: develop and operate) the number of handovers between teams is reduced. This increases speed and lowers the number of mistakes. Again, this requires streamlined IT or, in hardware, interface designs that enable teams to work independently on their module[6]. Next autonomous, multi-functional, colocated teams (squads) are the mechanism that ensures speeding up deployment. Making the teams autonomous, co-located and formalizing meetings according to the standard scrum approach, saves considerably on coordination time, thus freeing up time for actual work. Similarly the focus on what has to be done and not how, is a time saver that lowers the amount of time spent on discussions about the best approach to solve problems. Next, clarity of information is achieved through visualization. This makes clear to everybody what the status is of the various sprints. This not only reduces the need for meetings to share that information, but also opens up possibilities for collaboration. People can see where help is needed. The collaborative culture also helps to reduce time used for meetings. In a strong collaborative culture people do not feel the need to be continually informed about the progress of their peers. Instead, they trust their judgment and competency to carry out the tasks they were assigned. The confidence is further enhanced by the fact that maintenance of technical ompetences is ensured via the role of the chapter lead. The attention on competence development is essential for making this model work in the long run. Doubts about competences undermine the collaborative culture. Finally, the model hinges on the communication between the product owner and the teams. This ensures focus on the right issues, adaptation to changing insights and prioritization of the work done.

The Spotify model faces four risks. First, loss of coherence because it is hard to keep an overview of who does what. Teams may develop things that are not in line with the company strategy. Second, as squads self-evaluate their work, there may be a tendency to aim too low or to be easily satisfied. Third, issues that cut across tribes may not get the attention they deserve because nobody is responsible for them. Fourth, it is possible that product owners formulate so many demands that the project portfolio explodes in size. Spotify accepts these risks and solves them in daily management. The Dutch bank ING on the other hand implemented a more structural solution by adding additional control mechanisms to deal with these risks. They implemented Quarterly Business Reviews in which tribes coordinate their work and they use Objectives and Key Results (OKRs). OKRs are a method of target setting that focuses on setting the bar high to avoid team complacency (more on these mechanisms can be found in chapter 9 on Internal governance)[7]. In addition, organizations require a strong focus on the big issues to avoid getting bogged down in a swamp of minor projects[8].

Because of the risk of focusing too much on the operation, the leadership in organizations using the Spotify model has an extra duty to formulate a strong mission and vision. Such a mission and vision not only help to maintain coherence in an organization that is highly decentralized, they also alert the organization to strategic opportunities and threats.

The top leadership also needs to be the standard bearer of the culture. In an organizational form that is so light on formal structure and control processes, culture becomes a glue to hold the organization together. Ensuring that a culture develops and remains alive to support the organizational form is therefore not something that can be done on a Friday afternoon, but needs to permeate the actions of the leadership.

[1] Kniberg H. & Ivarsson, A., (2012). Scaling @ Spotify, Spotify white paper, https://dl.dropboxusercontent.com/u/1018963/Articles/SpotifyScaling.pdf. Spotify also made available some highly informative YouTube videos about their way of working: Spotify Engineering Culture part 1: https://www.youtube.com/watch?v=Mpsn3WaI_4k&list=PL8kOOe_U2cOQQ8zPDFRbecezdjT0S4znF and Spotify Engineering Culture part 2: https://www.youtube.com/watch?v=X3rGdmoTjDc.

[2] Barton, D., Carey, D., & Charan, R. (2018). One Bank's Agile Team Experiment. Harvard Business Review, 96(2), 59-61.

[3] Birkinshaw, J. (2018). What to expect from agile. MIT Sloan Management Review, 59(2), 39-42.

[4] https://hrblog.spotify.com/

[5] Rigby, D. K., Sutherland, J., & Noble, A. (2018). Agile at Scale. Harvard Business Review. 96(3), 88-96.

[6] Rigby et al. (2018) ibid.

[7] Barton, D. et al.(2018) ibid.

[8] Ross, J. (2018). Architect your company for agility. January 10, https://sloanreview.mit.edu/article/architect-your-company-for-agility/.

"Many companies can't use the Spotify model and way of working because their IT architecture won't allow it"

"Dependencies are one of the major challenges in the Spotify model; the more dependencies you have, the less effective the model becomes"

> Henrik Kniberg

CASE STUDY:
ING'S AGILE TRANSFORMATION JOURNEY

An interview with Nick Jue, CEO ING Germany
As CEO of ING in the Netherlands Nick Jue presided over ING's transformation towards an agile organization, largely inspired by businesses such as Spotify, Google and Netflix. He is now also implementing the agile way of working at ING in Germany. In this interview he discusses the transformation process that started in 2013 and the results it has delivered.

Why is ING implementing the agile way of working?

Being agile is not an end in itself. It is about delivering on changing customer needs. It is our way of getting closer to the customer and of fulfilling their wishes much faster. Customer needs and expectations have changed significantly in recent years and we operate in a very competitive market.

We used to have an extensive network of branches where most of the customer interaction took place. Now with the mobile phone, and big players like Amazon, Uber and Airbnb people are used to a specific kind of service - and they want the same type of service from their bank. Everything has to be fast and convenient. For example, if they forget their password, clients now get an email in two seconds with new login information. Until very recently, ING in the Netherlands still restored passwords via letters. People don't accept that anymore. They expect the bank to deliver as fast as Internet firms do. The market has become more diversified with new competitors. We´re not the only ones thinking about financial services. Our competitors are not just the traditional banks anymore. Fintechs and big tech firms also see opportunities in the banking world. And they are much faster and more flexible than us, the big banks.

This is why I came up with the picture of an elephant running a race with greyhounds. Our ambition was to train the elephant to be as agile as a greyhound. We believe big banks still have advantages though. We wanted to keep the strength, the knowledge and the experience. We can invest larger amounts than the fintechs. Still, we do have to become more flexible and faster to meet their competition.

How did you start the change process? Where did you get your ideas?

Spotify: Organization and way of working (Tribes, Squads, Chapters, Guilds)
Netflix: Portfolio and performance management (Quarterly Business Review)
Google: Employee engagement

We mainly learned from others. Looking outside the box is decisive for a successful agile transformation. We visited non-banking companies who operated in an agile way:

Spotify, Netflix, Google. The inspiration helped tremendously in opening our eyes to new ideas. We did not directly copy them, because our business has specific requirements. But we learned from them and took what we could use and put it together to work for us. From Spotify we learned about the organization structure. We took their idea of working in tribes, squads and chapters. However the Spotify model did not meet our requirements for performance management. For that, we took inspiration from Netflix: We used their process of quarterly business reviews. In this quarterly process tribes look at their successes and failures and set their goals for the next three months. This ensures tribes are aligned with our overall strategy. Another important element was introduced via Google, namely: How do you hire people? We realized that we needed to change much of our staff to fit the agile organization. So we implemented parts of their hiring process in which the boss doesn't hire his own staff. Instead we worked in hiring teams to get a broader view of people.

How does that hiring process work?

Let me give you an example. If I needed a new CFO at ING Netherlands, I used to interview three or four candidates myself and selected the one that I thought was the best fit. Now there is a four-step process. First, two board members other than me interview the three or four candidates. Next, another team of two interviews them. Then a team of managers from the finance organization interview the candidates. Finally, an HR team interviews them. So four interviews in total. After that, these teams put their findings together and they decide on the best candidate. Only then do I speak to that candidate. And I can say yes or no to that person, but I cannot propose another person. A big advantage of this process is that the acceptance of the new candidate is better from day one. I would always hire the best candidate, people in the finance department would be happy because they had selected their own boss and the team members in the board also picked their own colleague. An added bonus is that this way of hiring people leads to more diversity. We always talked about diversity, but we never reached more than 20% women, for example. The tribe leads in the Netherlands are now 50/50 male/female. And in Germany we see a similar picture.

So you pieced ideas together from different organizations and blended them to fit ING's needs. What were other important steps in the implementation process?

A key element was cleaning up our product portfolio. Just before we started with the agile transformation we had a merger. As a result we had no less than seventy saving products, making ING a very complex organization. After the transformation we had only five saving products. We also made the products much simpler. We wanted customers to be able to do business within only three clicks. That meant we had to scan all our processes from a customer point of view and clean up every step – to make it as easy and convenient as possible. Another element was a relentless focus on reducing handovers between departments. For example, we fully digitized the repayment process for mortgages in the Netherlands. Repaying mortgages in the past required an email to the bank, than a contract was sent out that had to be returned. Now clients can do it via the phone. Fewer handovers means a more agile organization.

You chose to move fast and took a radical approach to implementation. Why didn't you opt for a more incremental change approach?

Partly that is because of the change we needed. **We needed to think boldly and act disruptively**. If you say: Save 5% on cost, you will only do incremental things. You do not fundamentally rethink your processes and organization. If you say: We have to save 50%, you have to fundamentally rethink what you are doing. Because of the changes in the business environment and our cost/income ratio we needed to be disruptive. A second element is that I believe agile transformation has to involve the whole organization in order to succeed. In ING, everybody knows about agile. Other banks also do agile. All of them. But they have a single department that works agile and that can run into problems in collaborating with non-agile departments. We think you have to do it with the entire organization. That means all roles, functions and responsibilities fundamentally change. *Classic hierarchical structures will vanish. We had seven to nine management layers in the past. Now there are three: the board, tribe leads and chapter leads.* There is much less hierarchy. Alongside the reduction in the number of managers, their role has changed significantly, too. Management is still important, but management now challenges ideas of their employees, they are sparring partners, they help them to grow.

That sounds like a big change in mindset. How important is mindset for an agile organization?

I believe the mindset accounts for 70% of a successful transformation. People have more autonomy and more responsibility.

We use the global Orange Code to foster the mindset (orange being the ING color). It underpins our agile way of working. It consists of three points:
- You take it on and make it happen
- You help others to be successful
- You are always a step ahead

What are the consequence for the organization? What does it look like?

The most important part of being agile for me is to put IT and the business together and give them end-to-end responsibility. They are one team and they work on one customer purpose. This is done in the area we call Delivery. It includes all units that develop and implement products and services for customers. In Delivery we largely followed the Spotify model and we set up tribes, chapters and squads. Squads are autonomous teams of seven people plus/minus two with different areas of expertise. They manage themselves and bear full responsibility for a specific purpose. Such a squad can include marketing, IT, designers - basically every skill they need to get the job done. Depending on the project, there may be more IT or more marketing, but end-to-end responsibility is always important and we always include business people.

But with all these small squads, how do you ensure knowledge is built up and transferred?

The risk is that lessons learned stay in the teams. That is where the chapters come into play. They consist of people from different squads but with the same expertise. We have chapters for product management but also for data analytics, for example. They learn from each other. And last but not least we have the so called Tribes: A Tribe provides a larger framework and it consists of several squads whose goals are related. So rather than thinking from the products that we offer, we try to have the whole customer journey in one tribe with one customer purpose.

You mentioned in the beginning the goals you wanted to achieve. What are the tangible benefits of the agile transformation that you have achieved?

The old way of working was too slow. Multifunctional teams are faster, because they can control the entire process. Formerly, a product manager would develop a new product and after two or three months he had an idea about what the product should look like. Then the IT people would put it on the backlog and if we were lucky it would be ready after six months. But often it never came out of the backlog and did not get implemented at all. We now bring new products and improvements in services to market much faster than we used to. Speed is essential in this market to beat the competition. It has become a competitive advantage for us.

The new way of working is also much nicer for the team members, because they see the progress they make in daily stand ups and sprints of two weeks. For me, the agile structure solves many problems. It has broken through the existing silos and new team constellations have become possible. We have a flatter organization structure and employees have more responsibility. That gives them greater motivation because they can work more autonomously. Was it easy? No. Did everything work at once? I would also say no. But we now reap tangible benefits. A final benefit is financial. The transformation required an enormous investment. This was not just monetary, but also time. But it paid off. We experienced increased productivity and our results in retail banking in the Netherlands doubled from 1.1 billion euros in 2012 to 2.2 billion in 2017. Staff numbers declined significantly. Digitalization helped with that enormously. In 2017, our cost to income ratio was 43%, five years earlier it had been above 60%. We have achieved this despite a substantial increase in regulatory costs, which are outside our control.

Summing up, what would you say are the
top three things for the successful agile
transformation in ING?

First, be ready to let go. Trust your experts and give them full responsibility. Give them a clear framework to work in, but then let go. Second, be disciplined. Being agile means sticking to the rhythm and routines. Agile is a very disciplined way of doing things: There is a daily stand up, a two week sprint etc. Performance management is daily as well: You have to show what you have delivered in the stand up. Maintaining discipline takes effort, but it does pay off. Third, make the change as fast as possible. People will be very uncertain when a transformation starts. The only thing that comes close to a medicine against uncertainty is clear communication and making the change fast.

"Classic hierarchical structures will vanish. We had seven to nine management layers in the past. Now there are three: the board, tribe leads and chapter leads."

> Nick Jue

EXCURSION :
AGILE TRANSFORMATION: WHY, WHAT, HOW?[1]

How to transform an organization into an agile organization? Unfortunately there is no one size fits all solution. The transformation path is highly dependent on the context and the specific circumstances organizations face. For that reason, a thorough diagnosis of the reasons for transforming towards agile and of the current state of an organization is a first and very important step towards transformation.

HOW LIKELY IS IT THAT YOU HAVE TO TRANSFORM?

With the growing popularity of agile, it sometimes seems that an agile transformation is inescapable for any organization. This, of course, is not necessarily true. Some organizations may face circumstances that require them to become agile, whereas others face different conditions and may perhaps find other solutions more useful.

Some organizations are more susceptible to agile transformation than others. Organizations that deliver services and largely work with data or informational products are most likely to gain benefits from going agile. That is why the agile wave started in software and moved on to banks, insurance and entertainment (movies, gaming, music). Another category of organizations are those that deliver a service based on a physical product. Lease corporations, telecoms and commerce are examples here. Even though they handle physical goods, much of their competitive advantage is rooted in gathering data and improving their services based on such data.

The idea in brief
- **The starting position of the organization determines what the transformation process looks like**
- **A thorough diagnosis of the goals of the transformation and the current situation of the organization is necessary to design a custom made transformation process**
- **This process may differ from starting small to one big bang**
- **It always involves: shifting from project to product mode, implementing short cycles, leadership transformation, building content skills in people, involving support functions**

Asset heavy industries like shipping and construction will benefit less from becoming agile.

WHY TRANSFORM?

It may seem like stating the obvious that organizations need to be clear why they want to transform into an agile organization, but when a management concept becomes fashionable, organizations all too often start implementing in the fear of being left behind. The goals organizations want to achieve determine where and how to start. In practice, organizations roughly have one or more of the next five drivers to explore enterprise agility:

- *Cost and efficiency.* Delivering more with less is a perennial quest for organizations.

Agile working can help to reduce overhead and cost.
- *Speed and customer focus.* Faster response to customer demands and reducing time to market of new services is another relevant driver.
- *Simplification.* The simplification of services helps to reduce risk and improve reliability. It also makes it easier to adapt to changing circumstances.
- *Attracting talent.* An organization that is successful with agile may find it easier to attract the right talent, to retain existing talent and to increase its attractiveness as an employer for millennials.
- *Innovation.* Agile may help to identify new growth areas and to become more innovative and thus head off disruption.

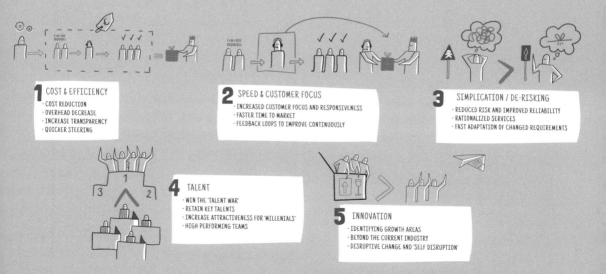

1 COST & EFFICIENCY
- COST REDUCTION
- OVERHEAD DECREASE
- INCREASE TRANSPARENCY
- QUICKER STEERING

2 SPEED & CUSTOMER FOCUS
- INCREASED CUSTOMER FOCUS AND RESPONSIVENESS
- FASTER TIME TO MARKET
- FEEDBACK LOOPS TO IMPROVE CONTINUOUSLY

3 SIMPLICATION / DE-RISKING
- REDUCED RISK AND IMPROVED RELIABILITY
- RATIONALIZED SERVICES
- FAST ADAPTATION OF CHANGED REQUIREMENTS

4 TALENT
- WIN THE 'TALENT WAR'
- RETAIN KEY TALENTS
- INCREASE ATTRACTIVENESS FOR 'MILLENIALS'
- HIGH PERFORMING TEAMS

5 INNOVATION
- IDENTIFYING GROWTH AREAS
- BEYOND THE CURRENT INDUSTRY
- DISRUPTIVE CHANGE AND 'SELF DISRUPTION'

These drivers may of course occur in combination and they are not mutually exclusive. Their priority determines where to start with an agile transformation. When innovation is the most important, other things need to be looked at than when speed is a prime driver of transformation.

CAN YOU TRANSFORM?

A second important element is to understand how ready an organization is to move towards agile. Each organization will have a different point of departure. The next five elements are relevant to look at.

MATURITY LEVELS

TRANSFORMATION STATUS

YOUR OWN TRANSFORMATION STATUS

ORGANISATIONAL CHARACTERISTICS

PEOPLE TRADITIONAL VS. AGILE
1. TRADITIONAL LINE → 2. MATRIX → 3. RUN & CHANGE INTEGRATED → 4. FULL NETWORK ORGANISATION

PROCESSES MANUAL VS. ANIMATED
1. FULLY MANUAL → 2. SEMI AUTOMATED → 3. FULL AUTOMATION SUPPORT → 4. FULLY AUTOMATED

TECHNOLOGY 'SPAGHETTI' TO MODULAR SERVICES
1. MONOLYTH ARCHITECTURE → 2. MODULES AND SERVICES → 3. SERVICE ORIENTED ARCHITECTURE → 4. LOOSELY COUPLED MICRO SERVICES ARCHITECTURE

OUTSOURCING IN HOUSE VS. OUTSOURCED
1. RETAINED ORGANISATION → 2. SIGNIFICANT SOURCING ALLIANCES → 3. NON-CORE SERVICES ARE OUTSOURCED → 4. FULLY IN-HOUSE

APPETITE FOR REORGANISATION
1. ALL IN THIS TOGETHER → 2. GET WITH THE PROGRAM → 3. NO CULTURE WITHOUT CASUALTIES → 4. VIVA LA REVOLUCION

VALUE PROPOSITION 'FIT FOR RENEWAL'
1. SMALL POTENTIAL TO INNOVATE → 2. INCREMENTAL INNOVATION POSSIBLE → 3. RADICAL INNOVATION → 4. PARADIGM SHIFT

First, people and organization may be more oriented towards the traditional hierarchical structure than towards agile working. A fully hierarchical organization is further removed from agile than one that has experience with projects or team-based work. Organizations that work with responsibilities that are low in the organization also have a smaller step to make than those in which management takes most of the decisions.

Second, the processes of the organization determine how big the step towards agile is. Agile depends crucially on automation. The more processes involve manual tasks, the more work has to be done before the agile transformation is complete. When processes are highly automated, it is easier to fully embrace agile.

Technology is a further issue to study. One of the reasons why new organizations are able to start working in an agile way is that they do not have an IT legacy. They can build simple systems from scratch. Existing organizations often have a substantial legacy of complex systems that are connected to each other in ways that resemble a plate of spaghetti. That makes it difficult to create autonomous teams, because teams will not be able to make changes in IT systems without affecting other teams. When, on the other hand, modularization and the use of microservices is widespread, teams can work independently.

The effect of outsourcing on agile transformation is a further relevant factor to understand. When an organization has outsourced many of its activities, the transformation process requires considerable coordination with partners which may slowdown the process. With all activities fully in house, an organization has more control.

The appetite for reorganization also determines how the implementation of agile will run. Many organizations are exhausted from series of change projects that have been unleashed upon them. Others see new opportunities and are energized to make a next step. Naturally this determines their ability to change rapidly.

Finally, the potential for renewal of the organization's value proposition affects the transformation process. With limited potential, there is no need to make big steps quickly. A focused search for where improvements can be made may be sufficient. If the potential is high, for example because an organization has fallen behind other organizations, a larger scale transformation is called for.

The analysis of these factors is unlikely to point in one direction of change. Each organization will have a unique mix of them. Out of that a transformation approach needs to be distilled that best fits the opportunities and constraints an organization faces.

Some organizations may adopt a big bang approach in which the transition is made in a very short period. Others may take a much longer time horizon. Some may involve the whole organization, others may start with a small number of teams. Each of these may be right, depending on the organization's needs and readiness.

WHAT TO TRANSFORM?

Even though the size and speed of the transformation may differ for each organization, there are some elements that always need to be included in the transformation process. The extent may differ, but any agile transformation should at the bare minimum touch the next five elements:

* *Shifting from project to product mode.* In IT this is realized by creating DevOps teams. Formerly organizations split the functions of developing new software (build) and running the day to day operations (run). In agile, the ideal situation is that everything related to a product is managed by one team, that has end-to-end responsibility. Put differently: if you build it, you run it. Rather than having separate development and maintenance projects, a DevOps team has an overview of everything that happens around its product and therefore it is better able to set priorities for its product as a whole. The risk that things are built that cannot be put into operation or that

too many change projects are defined, is minimized. A next step is BizDevOps, which includes the business in the team as well, instead of only the IT people.

* *Short cycles.* Agile organizations work in shorter cycles. Annual planning changes into quarterly planning and the project portfolio is updated regularly to reflect changing circumstances. This helps to bring new functionality to the market quickly. It also lowers the chance that a project that has become less relevant is still finished.

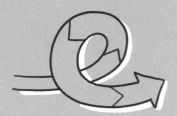

* *Leadership transformation.* Steps need to be made to change management behavior. Even though starting with an agile way of working is a good way forward, in the

end the behavior that fits it needs to be internalized in the leadership. Moving from 'doing' to 'being' may require training, but also hiring other people. A key element is that management needs to shift from a directive/hierarchical management style to a coaching/facilitating style.

- *People.* In the people area, traditional functions need to be replaced by new ones. Traditionally, organizations focus on rewarding management skills. In an agile organization the content skills become more important.

- *Involve support functions.* The changes in the previous four areas also affect support functions. Departments focusing on HR, planning and finance have to develop tools and processes that match the requirements of the new agile organizations. Budgeting cycles for example need to fit the shorter cycles agile requires. New functions need to be defined and remuneration practices need to be adapted. In the financial sector, risk management is a dominant department that needs to be taken into account when practices change.

HOW TO TRANSFORM?

As the transformation process is highly contextual, a detailed prescription on how to manage the transformation cannot be given. Some guidelines, however, seem to be emerging. One of them is that the development of people and IT needs to go hand in hand. Investing in people ahead of IT will lead to frustration because people want to go further than IT allows. Investing in IT ahead of people is a either a waste of resources or may lead to people not being able to work with the systems that are provided to them. Hence the first guideline is to continuously monitor the people-IT fit.

Another element is that many organizations tend to focus on implementing a certain agile framework, like SAFe or the Spotify model. Even though such frameworks may help to guide a transformation process, in themselves they should not be put center stage. Frameworks rarely create enthusiasm and they tend to focus more on the what than on the why. During implementation, focus on and agreement about the agile principles an organization wants to follow should therefore take precedence over the use of frameworks. Only when there is agreement on the principles, people can start looking at (combinations of) frameworks that fit those principles. Use frontrunners to experiment. Front runners are agile units that are launched ahead of other parts of the organization. This allows an organization to iterate on their agile design and to see how ways of working need to be adapted before scaling to other parts of the organization. They can also act as a showcase of what agile can achieve.

Define the common and the optional practices. Agile requires some common practices that are shared by all teams in the organization. Clarity about what the common, non-negotiable practices are is a prerequisite for agile transformation. However, over-standardization must be avoided. As teams differ, they need some wiggle room. Forcing all kinds of standards on teams that do not fit their needs, has to be avoided. Organizations need to strike the right balance between standardization and customization.

"There is no one-size-fits-all model or approach to scale Agile across organizations"

> Ad van der Graaff, PwC

---

¹ This chapter is based on interviews with PwC consultants.

4 HOLACRACY

Another form of organizing that has gained popularity over the past ten years is Holacracy. Holacracy's main strength lies in improving vertical bottom-up communication, radical decentralization of decision-making and in ensuring clarity about everybody's role and responsibilities. Both these elements are not the strength of traditional hierarchies. The Holacracy form is basically the same as sociocracy, developed in 1970 by the Dutch entrepreneur Gerard Endenburg. The better sounding label Holacracy was coined in 2005 and it adds an American twist by requiring companies that want to implement it to sign a holacratic 'constitution'[1].

Holacracy rests on the original four principles defined by Endenburg to build the sociocratic organization: decision-making by consent, a hierarchy of circles in which every member of the organization participates, double linking between circles, election of persons by consent[2]. Decisionmaking by consent involves the absence of argued objection. Consensus means everybody has to agree to a decision, whereas consent means nobody has a serious objection to a decision. The second principle is the presence of circles. A circle is a unit of organization members with a common work objective, who decide based on consent. A circle can decide anything within the limits of its authority. There are different hierarchical layers of circles, which are linked in two ways. A higher circle elects somebody to represent them in the next lower circle and vice versa. This system of double linking ensures vertical information flows not only from the top down, but also from the bottom up. The election of persons takes place according to the consent principle.

The idea in brief
- **Radical decentralization of decision-making is achieved by grouping employees in a circle**
- **The circle divides roles among individuals**
- **Each employee can decide anything within her role, unless it affects somebody else's role**
- **In that case a 'tension' exists which gets resolved via a structured meeting process in the circle, using consent decision-making**
- **A circle and its next higher circle elect people to represent them in the other circle to ensure cross-circle alignment and a good vertical flow of information**

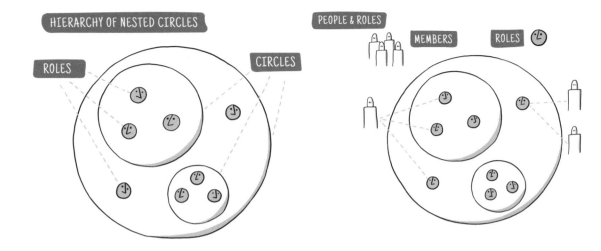

These four organizational principles are applied in the context of the organization's purpose. As with all other forms of self-organization, the purpose of the organization is an important guideline for individuals in their decision-making. To embed the purpose in the organization, each circle defines its own purpose that operationalizes the overall purpose on a circle level. Similarly, for each role a purpose is defined. For example, mortgage advisor Viisi defines its purpose as 'We want to make the world of finance better, more sustainable and more long-term oriented'. One of their circles is called Realising Dreams. The purpose of that circle is to deliver the best mortgage advice as efficiently as possible to as many clients as possible in the target group (which is higher income individuals). One role in the circle is maintaining texts for advice via telephone meetings. The purpose of this role is to ensure optimal standard texts for telephone advice. This role is assigned to one individual, who also fulfils other roles[3].

Figure 5 shows the main way of working in Holacracy on the level of circles. Circles distribute work to be done across clear roles. Each individual in the organization usually has more than one role and can take any decision by himself that he thinks is necessary to perform the role. That is: as long as these decisions do not infringe on the roles of others. If this condition is not fulfilled, somebody else will not be able to fulfill his role adequately, a situation called 'sensing a tension'. In tactical meetings the circle decides on day-to-day issues that need to be coordinated. Normally, a tension will be resolved there. Sometimes however the tensions are too big or they cannot be resolved. In that case the way roles are distributed across the individuals may have to be clarified or improved. This is done in a governance meeting. The advantage of this system is that circles can do their own governance: there is no need for a manager to make these decisions. The circle elects a facilitator to guide them through the elections. They also elect a secretary who administers the decisions, schedules meetings and interprets governance.

Essential in the system on the circle level is the consent principle and a fixed way of organizing and running meetings. For example, in a meeting everybody is expected to give an opinion but there is no open discussion in which everybody joins simultaneously. Consent emerges from seeking opinions in several rounds of questions.

Despite what many people think, Holacracy is still a hierarchical structure[5]. In fact, it can be applied in a traditional organization with management layers and different units without requiring change in that structure. The governance processes however are entirely different and contain many nonhierarchical elements. Starting with the hierarchical element though, a Holacracy still has top management (called the anchor circle) that distributes power in the organization to its next lower circle, which in turn sets conditions for its lower circles. A next higher circle is called a super-circle.

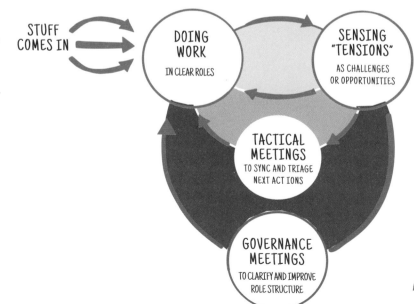

STUFF COMES IN

DOING WORK
IN CLEAR ROLES

SENSING "TENSIONS"
AS CHALLENGES OR OPPORTUNITIES

TACTICAL MEETINGS
TO SYNC AND TRIAGE NEXT ACTIONS

GOVERNANCE MEETINGS
TO CLARIFY AND IMPROVE ROLE STRUCTURE

Figure 5: How circles work[4]

The system of double-linking operates between a circle and its super-circle. A person elected by a super-circle to represent that super-circle in a lower circle is called a lead link. This lead link is, among other things, accountable for ensuring the definition and assignment of roles created in a governance meeting, defining priorities for the circle and allocating resources across projects, but only if asked to do so by a circle member. This role comes closest to a traditional middle management task, but whereas a traditional middle manager can initiate any action at any time, the lead link cannot. Most actions are dealt with within the circle. A rep link represents a lower circle in a higher circle and has to make sure that tensions experienced by his circle that find their source in the super-circle are resolved, so that his circle can get on with their work. Ideally the circle size is six to eight persons, but smaller and larger circles exist[6].

In short, even though the structure is still hierarchical, the other processes are non-hierarchical. The circles are largely self-managing and the double linking system also ensures two-way information flows which so often are absent in traditional hierarchies. The self-managing nature of the circles also means that managers cannot overrule anyone who takes a decision within his role. For example, if you have a role in which you can spend marketing budget and you spend it on newspaper advertising, a manager that thinks advertising online is better cannot undo your decision. The only way

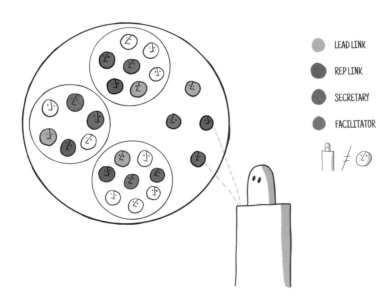

in which such a decision can be challenged would be if somebody else experiences tension on his role because somehow newspaper advertising makes it difficult for him to do his job right.

Note, however, that where self-organization occurs it is guided by many strict rules that are set out in the Holacracy constitution which codifies the way of working in a very strict manner[7]. Even though the principles behind Holacracy are rigid, the organizations that build on it are supposed to be flexible. A circular structure can change continually, adapting to new circumstances because on the circle level people can adapt their way of working themselves. Another interesting feature is that the system focuses on the work that has to be done. Struggles about how power is divided are replaced by discussions about how best to execute work. The team solves the problems that occur.

The Holacracy form has no specific reward structure attached to it. In some cases salaries are determined in joint meetings but this is not a requirement for Holacracy to work. A system of badgebased compensation has been developed that fits well with Holacracy. It revolves around defining skills that are linked to a certain monetary compensation. Excursion 8 contains more information about badge-based compensation. Viisi on the other hand gives people a fixed salary that increa-

ses every year and does not have bonuses[8]. Other rewards for employees are mainly to be found in having meaningful work and control about how goals are achieved (though not which goals)[9].

A further relevant point is that all the roles, circles and tasks may make it difficult for people to keep an overview of who is responsible for what. The number of roles may easily run into the hundreds. For that reason specific software has been developed to administer the different roles, called Glassfrog. Figure 6 shows a screenshot of mortgage advisor Viisi's Glassfrog account. It shows the circles Viisi has defined. Glassfrog makes it possible to click on each circle, drill down into subcircles and even look at the level of individuals and their roles. Such information systems are indispensable for a Holacracy to work especially because they help to keep track of all the roles in the organization.

A telecom company called Voys makes use of holacratic principles and lists as a key ingredient to make it work the tools they use to ensure information sharing and communication: Slack for internal communication, Asana as to-do manager, Google Drive for document management, Klipfolio as dashboard on TV, Glassfrog to give an overview of the structure, Orakel as knowledge bank, GRID360 and Tinypulse for feedback, Freedom as their own online telephone exchange[11]. So even though

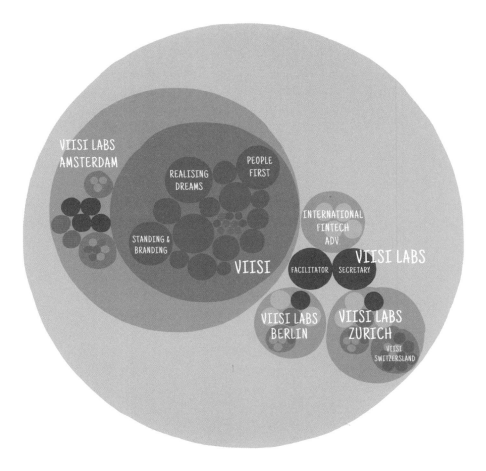

Figure 6: Viisi's circle structure in Glassfrog[10]

the roots of Holacracy predate the information era, Holacracy can be applied more easily and on a broader scale because of the presence of web-based tools. Table 9 summarizes the core elements of the Holacracy form of organizing.

The key problems Holacracy solve relate primarily to the challenges many organizations have in really making use of all the knowledge, expertise and information present in the organization (see table 10 for Holacracy's information leaflet). This problem is solved by giving employees more authority, enabling them to share their knowledge in meetings and ensuring information flows from the bottom up. In addition, Holacracy ensures that problems that arise from unclear roles and accountabilities do not persist but are dealt with in governance meetings and/or

HOW ARE TASKS DIVIDED?	· HIGHER CIRCLE DETERMINES TASKS FOR LOWER CIRCLE · LOWER CIRCLE, AIDED BY THE LEAD LINK, SPLITS THE TASKS INTO ROLES · GOVERNANCE MEETING CAN SPLIT THE ROLES DIFFERENTLY
HOW ARE TASKS ALLOCATED TO INDIVIDUALS?	· CIRCLE DETERMINES WHO GETS WHICH ROLE BASED ON CONSENT; EACH ROLE COMES WITH RESOURCES AND DECISION-MAKING AUTHORITY · GOVERNANCE MEETING CAN CHANGE THE ROLE ALLOCATION · LEAD LINKS ARE ELECTED BY THE SUPER-CIRCLE · CIRCLE ELECTS REP LINK, FACILITATOR, SECRETARY
HOW ARE REWARDS PROVIDED TO MOTIVATE PEOPLE?	· PEOPLE HAVE CONTROL OVER HOW GOALS ARE ACHIEVED (NOT WHICH GOALS) · MEANINGFUL WORK · IN SOME CASES SALARIES ARE DETERMINED IN JOINT MEETINGS OR VIA BADGE-BASED COMPENSATION
HOW IS INFORMATION PROVIDED SO PEOPLE CAN TAKE THE RIGHT DECISIONS?	· SOFTWARE IS USED TO MAKE CIRCLES AND ROLES VISIBLE TO EVERYONE · INFORMATION FLOWS VIA DOUBLE LINKING · INFORMATION EXCHANGE IN MEETINGS

Table 9: Core elements of the Holacracy model

addressed in a super-circle. Traditionally it is the role of managers to solve such issues, but Holacracy makes it the responsibility of all the organizational members. That means problems are solved faster. Holacracy also reduces the amount of time spent talking about how work must be done and getting consensus about that rather than doing the actual work. It is up to the person holding a specific role to decide how to fill in that role. Combining these elements results in a more agile organization that improves continuously.

PROBLEMS SOLVED	· LIMITED USE OF EMPLOYEES' KNOWLEDGE · LIMITED BOTTOM UP COMMUNICATION · UNCLEAR ROLES AND ACCOUNTABILITIES · LOSS OF TIME GETTING CONSENSUS ABOUT HOW WORK MUST BE DONE
DISADVANTAGES	· MANY RULES NEED TO BE FOLLOWED; COMPLEX SYSTEM · MAINTENANCE OF RULES · SOCIAL ASPECT OF MEETINGS GETS LOST
SUITABLE FOR	· ORGANIZATIONS WHERE OPERATIONAL OPTIMIZATION IS IMPORTANT · ORGANIZATIONS WHERE PEOPLE CAN LIVE WITH LIMITED EXPLICIT CONTROL
NOT SUITABLE FOR	· ORGANIZATIONS WHERE ACCOUNTABILITY CANNOT BE DISTRIBUTED · ORGANIZATIONS WHERE THE INDIVIDUAL AND THE ROLE CANNOT BE SEPARATED · ORGANIZATIONS WHERE MANY LINKAGES BETWEEN CIRCLES EXIST
KEY INGREDIENTS	· HIERARCHY OF CIRCLES AND ROLES · DOUBLE LINKS · DECISION-MAKING BY CONSENT · ELECTION OF PERSONS · AUTHORITY LOW IN THE ORGANIZATION · IT SUPPORT · PURPOSE DRIVEN
RISKS	· TOO MANY MEETINGS · ROLE PROLIFERATION · PROJECT PROLIFERATION
LEADERSHIP	· IMPLEMENT AND MAINTAIN THE CONSTITUTION · EXECUTE ROLE IN THE ANCHOR CIRCLE · COACHING THE ORGANIZATION: EXPLAINING WHY

Table 10: Information leaflet Holacracy

A major disadvantage of Holacracy is the fact that it has many rigid rules that have to be followed. The Holacracy constitution is very prescriptive and does not offer a 'light' version. You go all in or you don't do it at all. It is a complex system with its own terminology and procedures[12]. Maintaining all those rules over time requires a continuous effort and may lead to some people getting tired of the processes. To be honest: people also tire of processes in a traditional hierarchy. The rigid meeting structure leads to efficient meetings but the social element of meetings gets lost. There is no time to chat. Maintenance of the social aspect of the organization requires separate attention.

In theory, Holacracy can be useful for many organizations. The system works very well in organizations where operational optimization and continuous adjustment to changing circumstances are important. The system also works well in organizations where people can live with limited explicit control, for example professional organizations. Not everybody is able to self-organize and especially when traditional organizations move towards Holacracy, some people may not be able to cope[13].

The use of Holacracy is more difficult in organizations where accountability cannot be distributed. Governments with democratic control for example will have difficulty with distributed accountability because it is in the nature of their system that one person must be held accountable by an elected body. Organizations where the individual and the role cannot be separated are also less likely to use Holacracy. When unique talents form the basis of an organization's existence the freedom to allocate roles and change roles across individuals is limited.

Finally, organizations where linkages between circles are important will have difficulty with the Holacracy form. If circles cannot operate separately but overlap in the work they do, the need to coordinate between circles may lead to an overload of horizontal links and boundary conflicts. It is the explicit responsibility of management in a Holacracy to ensure horizontal links between circles are created when necessary. When too many of them are needed, the number of meetings will increase and the organization may actually slow down instead of speed up.

The core idea that makes Holacracy work is that everybody can be responsible for managing the organization and that organizations need to make use of all information present in the workforce. The system of hierarchy of circles and roles, double links, decision-making by consent and election of persons ensures authority lies low in the organization. IT support to keep an overview of all the roles and to administer all the processes simplifies the management of the holacratic organization. Most holacracies use the dedicated software of Glassfrog. Finally, the role of the overall purpose which is cascaded down to circles and roles provides an important glue that holds the organization together.

A risk of the Holacracy model is that it ends in too many meetings. In a smoothly functioning Holacracy the number of meetings will be limited. Implementation of Holacracy at Zappos however showed that this does not always happen[14]. The number of meetings proliferated. The holacratic system may also raise quite new discussions. For example the fact that only an argued objection means there is no consent, shifts the debate to the question what constitutes an argued objection. The system therefore also rests on norms and behavior that prevent such discussions from arising. Holacracy also has a facilitator role which has the responsibility to help circles solve such problems.

A second risk of this way of working is role proliferation. Roles assigned to people tend to be small, meaning that individuals have multiple roles. This may lead to fragmentation, compensation and hiring problems[15]. Fragmentation because each role has its own targets and it may be difficult for an individual to focus and set priorities. The fact that everybody has a unique set of roles also makes it difficult to set a benchmark for compensation. However, an upside is that

with so many roles, there is ample opportunity for individuals to create a set of roles that fit them like a glove. A third risk is that there tend to be many tensions in organizations. If each of these has to be resolved this will lead to a large number of projects in the organization. There is no mechanism to jointly prioritize projects and this may result in a growing backlog of unfinished projects. The use of Scrum may help to solve the issue as this fits well with the holacratic way of working[16].

Like any organizational form, Holacracy requires a matching leadership role. The key role of top management in holacracies is to implement and maintain the constitution. Holacracy identifies a ratifier role for this: the top management signs (ratifies) the Holacracy constitution and thereby pledges to uphold its principles. They also need to exercise their roles in the anchor circle and coach the organization in explaining why Holacracy is the way forward for this organization. The Holacracy constitution is strong on structure and processes, but it is silent on the behavior required of managers. The way they fulfill these roles however is highly relevant for the rest of the organization. Knowing which decisions to make and which to leave to the rest of the organization is difficult in any organization, but even more so in a Holacracy.

A note on implementation[17]

The first step in implementing Holacracy is of course to think about why Holacracy could work for you and what you want to achieve with it. It helps to have a thorough understanding of Holacracy and the Holacracy constitution. Next, the new organization structure needs to be defined. A way to do this is for employees to document which tasks they do and which priorities they set, over a number of weeks. Subsequently these tasks can be logically grouped into roles and the roles into circles.

Basically the existing organization structure is the point of departure. When this is done, you can start using the meeting structure: elect a facilitator and a secretary. Undoubtedly it will turn out that changes in roles and circles are necessary. Make everything transparent, for example by using Glassfrog and creating a project board. An (external) coach may be helpful to help people to find their new role. It usually takes some time for everybody to find out what they want and can do in the new organization.

---

[1] Robertson, B. J. (2015). Holacracy: The revolutionary management system that abolishes hierarchy. Penguin UK.

[2] The following description is based on Endenburg, G. (1998). Sociocracy as Social Design: Rationale of a new social design for society, Eburon; Romme, A. G. L. (1995). The sociocratic model of organizing. Strategic Change, 4(4), 209-215; Romme, G. (1996). Making organizational learning work: Consent and double linking between circles. European Management Journal, 14(1), 69-75.

[3] www.viisi.nl. Viisi uses Glassfrog to maintain overview over all roles and circles. Its Glassfrog account is accessible online for everyone to see.

[4] Source: Holacracy.org

[5] Romme, G. (2015). The big misconceptions holding Holacracy back. www.hbr.org, 10 September.

[6] Agile Scrum Group. (n.d.). Wat is Holacracy?, white paper, www.agilescrumgroup.nl.

[7] The constitution as well as much other interesting material can be found at https://www.Holacracy.org/constitution.

[8] Van Ede, J. (2019). Holacracy bij Viisi. Procesverbeteren.nl.

[9] Bernstein, E., Bunch, J., Canner, N., & Lee, M. (2016). Beyond the Holacracy hype. Harvard Business Review, 94(7), 38-49.

[10] https://app.glassfrog.com/organizations/3929/roles/7987651

[11] Voys. (2016). Het Voys handboek. https://www.voys.nl/boek/.

[12] Agile Scrum Group. (n.d.) ibid.

[13] Van De Kamp, P. (2014). Holacracy—A radical approach to organizational design. In: Dekkers, H., Leeuwis, W. & Plantevin I. (eds.). Elements of the software development process. University of Amsterdam, 13-26.

[14] Romme. (2015). ibid.

[15] Bernstein et al. (2016). ibid.

[16] Agile Scrum Group. (n.d.). ibid.

[17] This section is based on Agile Scrum Group. (n.d.). ibid.

"Holacracy is a social technology for governing and operating an organization, defined by a set of core rules distinctly different from those of a conventionally governed organization."

> Brian Robertson, Holacracy

CASE STUDY:
SPARKS FLY AT BOL.COM

An interview with Harm Jans, Director People & Organization Development at bol.com
Bol.com is the number one online retailer in the Netherlands and Belgium with nine million active customers. It offers products in a wide range of categories delivered directly to people's homes. Since its launch as an online bookseller in 1999, bol.com has grown exponentially and expanded to offer more than 18 million products in 22 categories such as music, film, electronics, toys, jewelry, watches, baby products, gardening and DIY. In 2011 it launched a marketplace that gives customers access to products from other retailers, including second-hand goods. In 2012 food retailer Ahold/Delhaize bought bol.com for EUR 350 million. Currently bol.com employs about 1,700 people.

Harm Jans is part of bol.com since 2008 where he started as Product Owner in Logistics. He held various leading positions in their Logistics domain. Inspired by Holacracy in 2015, Harm laid the foundations for what today at bol.com is known as "Spark".

His Spark initiative ignited rapidly and turned into a movement across logistics, customer service and commerce at bol.com. Currently as Director People & Organisation Development Harm leads the Spark movement across bol.com, changing the way people work together to offer customers the best online shopping experience. Today at bol.com, 1,300 people follow Spark as their way of working in more than 150 circles.

What was the reason to start adopting Holacracy at bol.com?

In 2005 bol.com was a small organization with less than 50 employees, many of them with a strong background in IT. Looking back, bol.com was an early adopter of agile principles and practices. Back in 2008 our IT department started following agile principles and practiced scrum as a way of working.

In the following seven years, IT within bol.com grew from eight to 60 cross-functional development teams, requiring us to think about how to scale agile effectively. In 2015, the tribe and squad model from Spotify was an inspiration for us to scale agile in IT. Today our development teams are built around 'fleets' (e.g. features such as shop, search, browse, catalogue, payments, etc.), which are clustered into 'spaces' (e.g. platforms such as shopping experience, retail platform, fulfilment platform). All teams, fleets and spaces have a high level of autonomy with regard to what to build and how they build, run and maintain software. They follow the "YBIYRIYLI" mantra – you build it, you run it, you love it. IT teams build, but also run and maintain software DevOps.

Outside of IT we also faced the challenge to support our rapid growth. Not only our physical operations (fulfillment center), but also our commercial organizations was growing fast. We hired many experienced people from established well known fast moving consumer good companies and retailers for their knowledge on scaling the supply chain, distribution and operations planning. These people not only brought knowledge and experience on logistics and operations.

They also brought "traditional" ideas with them on organizational governance, trying to translate them to the world of bol.com. Whereas within IT we were able to scale agile successfully keeping our unique DNA, we felt that outside of IT our growing organization became more hierarchical and bureaucratic. Our people slowly became less engaged. We knew we are at our best when we work in small, autonomous, cross-functional teams with challenging goals and enough room for fun. Therefore, we were desperate to explore flatter operating models for the whole organization, which distribute decision-making power effectively and place accountability at the lowest possible level in the organization.

In 2014, we learned about how Zappos CEO Tony Hsieh adopted Brian Robertson's Holacracy model and radically reorganized the company. We believed there were many similarities between Zappos and bol.com.

What were some key considerations regarding the implementation of Holacracy at bol.com?

When we started to think about how to implement Holacracy at bol.com, we knew

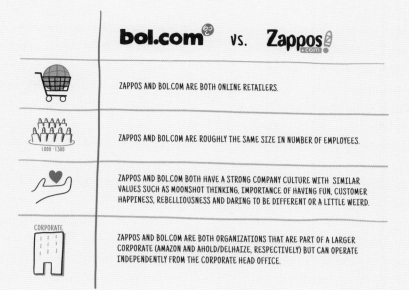

bol.com vs. **Zappos**

ZAPPOS AND BOL.COM ARE BOTH ONLINE RETAILERS.

ZAPPOS AND BOL.COM ARE ROUGHLY THE SAME SIZE IN NUMBER OF EMPLOYEES.

ZAPPOS AND BOL.COM BOTH HAVE A STRONG COMPANY CULTURE WITH SIMILAR VALUES SUCH AS MOONSHOT THINKING, IMPORTANCE OF HAVING FUN, CUSTOMER HAPPINESS, REBELLIOUSNESS AND DARING TO BE DIFFERENT OR A LITTLE WEIRD.

ZAPPOS AND BOL.COM ARE BOTH ORGANIZATIONS THAT ARE PART OF A LARGER CORPORATE (AMAZON AND AHOLD/DELHAIZE, RESPECTIVELY) BUT CAN OPERATE INDEPENDENTLY FROM THE CORPORATE HEAD OFFICE.

that we had to tailor it to our specific environment. Brian Robertson refers to Holacracy as an operating system for an organization – "once Holacracy is in place, you can start playing with it by installing organizational apps". We knew that, in order to give it a chance at success in bol.com, we had to be very pragmatic with the Holacracy operating system. People within bol.com have a rolled-up-sleeve and down-to-earth mentality. They were not going to buy-in on Holacracy if we would ask them to first read the 40 page Holacracy constitution with all the rules, structure and processes of the organizational operating system. Therefore, at bol.com we simplified the Holacracy constitution and brought it back to a single page, summarizing the core principles. We also wanted to give a more positive twist to Holacracy, which according to the constitution relies on the discovery of 'tensions'. In Holacracy a tension describes a person's feeling that there is a gap between the current reality and a potential future. Within bol.com the words 'Holacracy' and 'tension' might have carried a negative connotation. We decided to abandon these terms and replace them by the word 'Spark' instead.

What are the core principles behind Spark at bol.com?

We adopted the basic principles behind circles, sub-circles, the role of the lead link and elected roles such as facilitator, secretary. However, we abandoned the role of the ratifier, rep link and the concept of cross linking in Spark to keep things more straightforward and simple. Within bol.com the hierarchy of functional departments is being replaced with a hierarchy of purpose and objectives. Each circle is given a clear purpose, strategic goals and operational accountabilities by its super-circle. All members of the circle collectively have the freedom to decide how to reach the strategic goals and how to organize roles within the circle. We more or less follow the operational processes and tactical meetings as described under the Holacracy constitution. We refer to tactical meetings as Spark meetings. All circles run weekly Spark meetings (maximum 60 minutes) with the following structure:

- Check-in round: every member of the circle briefly shares what is on their mind.
- Checklist review: check across all members on completion of recurring role related tasks.
- Metrics review: the circle reviews progress against strategic objectives of the circle.
- Project updates: short updates on agreed initiatives in the circle with room for clarification.
- Sparks: all members of the circle raise Sparks (ideas and issues) and indicate what they need from other members of the circle to move forward. The objective is to create actions, not to have in depth content discussion on Sparks during the Spark meeting.

- Ping-Pong: decision making on new or changing roles in the circle and on cross functional business proposals
- Closing round: all members review the meeting and provide feedback.

We do not follow all the rules of the governance processes and meetings that are in the Holacracy constitution. For example, we allow teams to combine governance and tacticals into the Spark meetings. We tend to be somewhat more flexible in the creation or removal of circles. Decisions that affect the governance of a circle within bol.com are dealt with in the Spark meeting during the Ping-Pong step.

How did you start with implementing Spark?

Unlike Zappos, we decided to start small with Holacracy. Zappos changed its organization top-down almost overnight offering their employees an ultimatum to either commit to Holacracy or leave the company and take a severance package. As a result 18% of the people within Zappos left the organization. At bol.com, we wanted to create a more bottom-up movement where our employees would pick up 'Spark' intrinsically motivated but also at their own pace.

In 2015, I started our first Spark experiment within Logistics across two teams who were responsible for the teams responsible for innovation in bol.com pick-up and delivery services. Everybody involved in the Spark experiment became a Spark ambassador causing the start of a true movement. Suddenly various other teams asked for coaching in adopting Spark and it quickly became the new de facto standard way of working within Logistics & customer service.

When did the concept of Spark crossover from Logistics & customer service to other parts of bol.com?

In 2017, our Commerce division approached me with the idea to leverage the concept of circles and Spark to reorganize their functional departments (merchandising, sourcing and marketing and pricing) into small cross-functional teams, focused on a specific product category. The leaders within Commerce wanted the commercial part of bol.com to feel like a small company again. We launched a program called "Score" and created 42 cross-functional commercial store teams (circles). The 42 cross-functional store teams are part of six clusters (super circles) with a shared purpose and strategy. For example, we now have store teams on television, sound, laptops, phone, tablets. They are part of the cluster electronics.

Each store team owns their specific product category and runs the commercial operations for that category as autonomously as

possible. We aim to make this more fun and feel like working for a small company within bol.com. Within their cluster, they share a purpose and strategic goals. They prioritize changes to the bol.com platform with IT and share best practices between teams. All the people are still in their functional departments as well, but the functional departments are shifting their focus from running the business to professional mastery and supporting the teams with process automation and better tools.

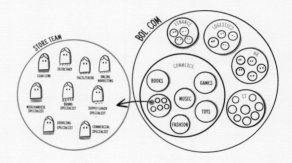

Were there any differences in bringing Spark to Commerce vs. Earlier teams?

The rollout of Spark in Logistics & customer service was highly experimental and a bottom-up movement that gradually spread like an ink stain in the organization. The people within Logistics & customer service are highly analytical and work data-driven. The rollout of Spark in Commerce was more top-down. Compared to Logistics & customer service, the people within Commerce tend to be more entrepreneurial. As a coaches during the transformation in Commerce, we identified that people within Commerce have different needs. So we left-in flexibility for the store teams to co-create and tailor Spark to their environment. Both Commerce and Logistics & customer service follow the basic principles behind Spark but it has a slightly different look and feel.

How does objective setting for circles take place at bol.com?

Each circle is responsible for updating its strategy three times per year. At bol.com, we use the OGSM (Objectives, Goals, Strategies,and Measures) framework. This framework defines our objective in qualitative terms and shows which measurable goals have to be achieved. The strategies show how to achieve those goals and the measures are indicators that show us whether we are on track to meet our objectives. This helps us to define clear actions and accountabilities once every four months. The lead link of each circle is accountable for this process but all members of the team can give suggestions. Updated goals, strategies and measures are reflected in Glassfrog and integrated into the weekly Spark meetings so they are available for all members of a circle.

Do you still have a line organization at bol.com next to Spark?

Yes, our people need to navigate in both Spark (circles) and the functional organization. Most of our people are members of one or two circles. Today our functional departments are still in charge of budgets and resources. Lead links of circles often have the responsibility to address budget and resource related issues with the heads of functional departments, which can still be frustrating and time-consuming. The functional organization is also considered to be a stable fallback for people who work in circles that fail to find an effective way to work together using Spark.

We have not yet gone all-in on Spark but are slowly reaching the tipping point where everybody is working more in circles instead of their functional departments. Our workplaces are flexible and we allow people to decide themselves together with their line manager and lead link when they physically sit together with their functional department and when they work within their circle. We recently started experimenting with giving store teams budget and freedom to spend it. We see that circles take accountability for spending budget in an appropriate manner delivering value to bol.com, we may scale that practice to other circles as well.

How has your personal role changed within bol.com?

During the rollout of Spark towards Commerce, I experienced that it became increasingly hard to combine my role as lead link in Logistics and coach towards other parts of the organization. Bol.com decided to create a Way of Working (WoW) team that is responsible for continuously improving Spark and OGSM and for coaching all the circles on these ways of working. The WoW team keeps track of internal Net Promotor Scores (NPS) from the circles on Spark as a way of working. A Net Promotor Score is a measure that shows whether there are more people wanting to promote Spark than people opposing it. Satisfied people promote Spark actively within bol.com and if teams are happy, Spark will continue to grow. NPS also has a self-improving effect. If NPS is low, we look for what the drivers are and we set out strategies to improve them.

What is the future of Spark at bol.com?

Departments such as Finance and HR are just starting to adopt Spark. Our model is very much open and anybody within bol.com who wants to start using Spark as a way of working within his or her team is free to do so. Our WoW coaches will coach them and help them translate Spark to their environment. We will continuously monitor the effectiveness of Spark in existing circles looking for good practices or ideas on how to improve it within bol.com. More specifically, we are looking to align our agile at scale operating model in IT, based on Fleets and Spaces, with the circles and Spark way of working outside of IT. Finally, the success of Spark within bol.com has also triggered interest at Ahold/Delhaize corporate head office. In 2019, we started the first Spark experiments at Ahold Delhaize. Who knows where this may end!

"Holacracy at bol.com; from Spark to fireworks!"

"Showing that a framework for self-organization and giving more autonomy led to more effective projects and happier teams was an early success story that fueled the movement"

> Harm Jans, bol.com

EXCURSION :
SELF-ORGANIZATION AND ITS LIMITS

Self-organization has become one of the hottest themes in organization design over the past decade. Many of the new organizational forms rely on self-organization in one way or another. What has not been helpful in practice however is that the discussion around self-organization has become somewhat politicized, with some people believing it is a cure for all organizational ills and others remaining highly sceptical about what self-organization can achieve. In our view, the only relevant question is: when does it work and when does it not work?

WHAT IS IT?

But first: what is it? The term self-organization is used in many different circumstances but the common denominator seems to be that coordination of activities occurs without the interference of a higher power. A reduction of hierarchical coordination in favour of horizontal coordination is a common thread in all writing about self-organization. Some people go further and believe organization members can also set their own goals and strategy, but in most cases of self-organization there still is management that sets the vision ('why' we do things) and the strategy ('what' has to be done), but lower levels in the organization can decide who will perform which activity when and in what way ('how'). As management usually also defines which departments, teams or dimension in the organization are most relevant[1], a more correct term may be selfmanagement or self-coordination. The organizational context is set already, but the day-to-day management no longer requires the presence of a fulltime salaried manager. As self-organization seems to be the term most often used, we will follow that convention here.

WHY IS IT SO POPULAR?

The shift from hierarchical organizing towards self-organization can be traced back to a number of developments (see table 11). The first one is that the competitive advantage of firms relies less than before on economies of scale and efficiency and more on innovation

---

The idea in brief
- **There are logical economic reasons why self-organization gains popularity**
- **However, it is not the right solution for all organizations**
- **A checklist helps you to find out whether all conditions for implementing self-organization are met**

and speed. In many, though not all, cases hierarchy slows down the speed at which a company can act. Coordination meetings and approval procedures take time. Reaping economies of scale also requires stability and repetition. That is the exact opposite of what innovation requires.

Markets changed as well. Markets tended to be relatively stable and predictable, but now they change at a very high speed. That requires organizations to be nimbler. Managers can adaptorganizations to unpredictable market circumstances by devolving decision-making power so that changes can be affected faster.

Third, self-organization is enabled by lower cost of information. When the traditional hierarchy emerged, the costs of gathering, processing and disseminating information was very high. As a consequence only a small elite group of managers had access to relevant information and determined which information was gathered and how it was processed. Nowadays information can be gathered from a variety of sources, processed cheaply and spread at next to no cost. Everybody in an organization can see problems and opportunities and act upon them, without a manager having to tell them to. Employees are also better able to make their own decisions because the level of education has increased dramatically over the past hundred years. People are better able to distinguish temporary versus lasting effects, to synthesize information

	TRADITIONAL HIERARCHY	SELF-ORGANIZATION
SOURCE OF COMPETITIVE ADVANTAGE	ECONOMIES OF SCALE AND EFFICIENCY	INNOVATION AND SPEED
MARKETS	STABLE	UNPREDICTABLE
COST OF INFORMATION	HIGH	LOW
LEVEL OF EDUCATION	LOW	HIGH

Table 11: Assumptions behind hierarchy and self-organization

from various sources and to predict which actions will have which effects. Highly trained personnel is much less scarce than it used to be and many less educated people are now able and willing to organize their own work.

HOW TO MAKE IT WORK?

Self-organization sounds deceptively simple. However, it requires much more than simply doing away with middle management and telling everybody they are now empowered to make decisions. In fact, the implementation of self-organization requires a thorough and detailed understanding of where an organization stands and whether self-organization is possible at all. There are a number of preconditions for it to succeed (see the checklist in Box 2).

PRECONDITIONS TO SUCCEED

- *Internalized vision.* Self-organization does not mean that anything goes. Organizations still have goals to achieve and decisions to make. To guide goal setting at lower levels in an organization and decision-making, top management needs to define and communicate a vision on the organization and its markets. This is a starting point for teams to make their decisions. Defining a smaller number of strategic initiatives is usually a good way of doing so, which avoids often woolly formulated vision statements. People also need to internalized the vision.

- *Clearly delineated tasks and accompanying mandates.* Self-organizing teams need to have clearly specified tasks to achieve. The more difficult it is to specify such tasks, the more difficult it will be for team members to define activities and subtasks they need to carry out and the more they will need a higher ranking manager to help them. Mandates need to be given commensurate to the task.

- *Information enabling individuals to make decisions.* The self-organizing team needs to have access to all information they need to make decisions relevant to execute their task.

- *Tools and knowledge to support making those decisions.* Having the right information is useless if you don't know what to do with it. Teams therefore also need the right support infrastructure to make decisions. This may be knowledge, a skill set or spreadsheet that helps them compare alternatives. People need to be capable of making decisions and this requires a rather high level of knowledge and skills.

- *Common building blocks.* To ensure alignment within an organization some common building blocks will have to be in place. Without them, there is a considerable risk of everybody going in a different direction.

BOX 2: CHECKLIST: CONDITIONS FOR SELF-ORGANIZATION[2]

 · DOES YOUR ORGANIZATION HAVE A CLEAR VISION THAT IS INTERNALIZED BY PEOPLE WORKING IN THE ORGANIZATION?

 · ARE TASKS CLEARLY DEFINED AND ACCOMPANIED BY AN ADEQUATE MANDATE?

 · DO INDIVIDUALS HAVE ACCESS TO INFORMATION THAT HELPS THEM TO MAKE DECISIONS?

 · DO THEY HAVE THE TOOLS AND KNOWLEDGE TO INTERPRET THAT INFORMATION?

 · ARE THERE COMMON BUILDING BLOCKS IN THE ORGANIZATION THAT ENSURE ALIGNMENT?

 · ARE THE ERRORS THAT PEOPLE IN YOUR ORGANIZATION MAKE NON-FATAL?

 · CAN EXISTING MANAGERIAL WORK BE ALLOCATED TO TEAMS?

 · DOES TEAM BEHAVIOUR SUPPORT SELF-ORGANIZATION?

 · IS KNOWLEDGE-SHARING ACROSS TEAMS SAFEGUARDED?

 · IS THERE LOW INTERDEPENDENCE BETWEEN TEAMS?

 · IS THERE HIGH INTERDEPENDENCE WITHIN TEAMS?

 · IS FEEDBACK ORGANIZED ON A TEAM LEVEL?

 · DO MANAGERS TRUST TEAMS TO SOLVE THEIR OWN PROBLEMS?

 · DO PEOPLE WANT IT?

Common building blocks may be processes everybody has to follow, training to standardize skill sets or administrative procedures that have to be used. This seems to fly in the face of self-organization, but again: self-organization does not mean everybody can do what they want.

- *Non-fatal errors.* Self-organization is less

 suitable for organizations where errors can be fatal and catastrophic. In those cases, hierarchy to approve decisions or fixed protocols makes more sense. When errors have minor consequences and can easily be corrected, selforganization is an option.

- *Allocation of management tasks to teams.*

 Existing managerial work does not disappear. Planning needs to be done, budgeting has to be taken care of, quality control assured and human resource management tasks remain. To name a few. These tasks need to be allocated to the teams and hence teams need to be ready to take them on. The fact that management tasks need to be done by teams is one of the big disadvantages of self-organization. Not all teams are capable of executing these tasks. The team members that are, may end up doing all the managerial work. And then we are back where we started.

- *Effective team behaviour.* Teams should be able to make decisions among themselves and refrain from escalating problems to

 managers too quickly. An important behavioural element is that it needs to become second nature for people to ask for advice before making bigger decisions. This improves the quality of decision-making, but it is not necessarily something people are used to doing. A team coach may be provided to help improve team behaviour or a team lead may be appointed to ensure teams function properly.

- *Knowledge sharing.* The big weakness of

 self-organization lies in the risk that each selforganizing team will reinvent the wheel. Reinventing the wheel is bound to happen without an incentive or coordination mechanism in place to ensure that best practices or solutions developed in one team are used by other teams. And if that doesn't happen the question is why those teams would be in an organization at all. A well-known case in self-organization is the Buurtzorg organization in the Netherlands, in which local teams of nurses provide care for people living in their region. The nurses decide themselves how they do so. When in their work they come across a care issue they have little expertise about they access Buurtzorg's social network to find someone in the organization that can help them. The social network is excellent and nurses access it several times a day to give updates or to search for information.

- **Low interdependence between teams.** For self-organization to work, teams need to be able to function as independently as possible from each other. If they are not independent, the number of coordination issues between teams is high. In self-organizing organizations coordination takes place via 'teams-of-teams', a team that coordinates across teams. As long as the issues before these teams are limited in number and importance that works fine. If not, hierarchical management may actually be a better solution. Alternatively, the organization needs to redesign its processes in such a way that team independence can be realized.

- **High interdependence within teams.** Teams only make sense when people's tasks depend on each other. If everybody can do their job on their own, there is no need to introduce a team based way of working.

- **Feedback on team level.** In keeping with the team based way of working, feedback must be giving on a team level. If feedback is only given individually or on a department level, teams will miss out on information necessary for them to adapt their way of working.

- **Managerial trust.** It takes time for self-organization to really start working. The hard thing for managers is to not interfere in the process. Teams will make their own mistakes, but they also need to be able to correct them themselves. Managers have to give teams space to learn and may need to sit idle while they are desperate to intervene, but having trust in the teams to work out solutions for themselves is the best option to get self-organization going.

- **Finally of course: teams must want it.** No preconditions, process or brilliant IT system can compensate for a lack of motivation of people to work along the lines of self-organization. For new organizations it is relatively easy because they can select people that fit this way of working right from the beginning. Existing organizations may have a harder time changing. It may be a good step to not force self-organization upon existing staff and let them get there at their own pace.

If these conditions are not fulfilled, it may be hard to get self-organization of the ground. One element we have not yet mentioned is a clear view on what self-organization must achieve. What is the problem it solves? Experience suggest that cost cutting is sometimes used as the reason to transition to self-organization, but that attempts to implement self-organization for that reason appear to be unsuccessful. Also, there is no evidence that self-organization automatically leads to lower absenteeism because of better health, more job satisfaction or less stress. The opposite has also occurred: people taking on so much responsibility that stress increased.

Again this shows that self-organization is not to be entered lightly. In many cases it makes sense on paper, but whether it works out in practice is another matter. Implementation is, as always, a key to success. Why do you want self-organization? Are the above mentioned conditions fulfilled? Can you implement it? Our checklist shows there are many limits to self-organization. For that reason it is not the right solution for all organizations and/or organizations need to think about the transition path they need before they are able to realize a higher level of self-organization.

HOW TO STILL EXERCISE CONTROL?

Does self-organization mean that management no longer has the means to steer the organization in a certain direction? It does not. Management can still exercise considerable control, especially because it still determines the main structure of the organization. In most cases it also still controls the 'why' and 'what'. By setting a vision that contains the strategic priorities and ensuring that vision is embedded in the organization, there is still considerable influence over the direction the organization takes. Management also has control over resources[3]. It can put more teams on tasks it finds relevant and fewer teams on tasks it considers less important. Or it can assign more people to one team while making another team smaller.

[1] Foss, N. J., & Klein, P. G. (2014). Why managers still matter. MIT Sloan Management Review, 56(1), 73-80.

[2] This checklist is based on several publications including: Ross, J. (2018). Architect your company for agility, January 10th, https://sloanreview.mit.edu/article/architect-your-company-for-agility/; De Man, A.P., & Jansse, W. (2017). Zelfsturing: aanjagers, struikelblokken en contra-indicaties, Blog on Sioo website, 10 april, https://www.sioo.nl/actueel/blog/zelfsturing-aanjagers-struikelblokken-encontra-indicaties/ ; Goodman, P. S., & Haran, U. J. (2009). Self-managing teams. In: Levine, J.M., & Hogg, M.A. (eds). Encyclopedia of Group Processes and Intergroup Relations, Sage Publications; Laloux, F. (2014). Reinventing organizations, Nelson Parker; Rigby, D. K., Sutherland, J., & Takeuchi, H. (2016). Embracing agile. Harvard Business Review, 94(5), 40-50; Sanner, B., & Bunderson, J. S. (2018). The Truth About Hierarchy. MIT Sloan Management Review, 59(2), 49-52; Strikwerda, J. (2017). Strategy Execution: An integrative perspective and method for the knowledge-based economy. Amsterdam Business School, University of Amsterdam.

[3] Schaeffer, M. (2017). Het geheim van bol.com, Atlas Contact.

"The data shows that self-organization works. Transitioning to self-organization and self-management is not a radical experiment but it is the future of work"

> Tony Hsieh, Zappos

5 PLATFORM ORGANIZATIONS: FOSTERING ONLINE ECOSYSTEMS

This chapter focuses on ecosystems around platforms in an online context. A platform is a set of shared assets (technologies, capabilities, standards) that can easily be recombined into diverse applications[1]. Online platforms have become household names. Google, Apple, Facebook, Amazon, Alibaba, Uber, Airbnb: all of them are examples of this form of organizing.

The use of this organizational form is not limited to companies that were born on-line. Traditional companies are increasingly rethinking their business and moving towards platforms as well. Data driven organizations like banks and publishers are at the forefront of this development because their products can be changed into information products relatively easily. But industrial companies have entered the fray as well. John Deere, a producer of equipment for agriculture, connected the equipment it sold to an information platform that helps farmers in their decision-making process by providing all sorts of data. There seems to be ample room in many industries to implement similar ways of working.

The core elements of platform organizations are listed in table 12, focusing on how they are organized on the platform level. That is: how the relationship between the platform owner and the ecosystem of complementors is structured. Complementors are organizations that provide apps, services or products based on the platform. Internally, the owner of the platform will often work via agile processes as discussed in earlier chapters.

The idea in brief
- **A platform organization offers a set of shared assets (technologies, capabilities, standards) that can easily be recombined into diverse applications**
- **Platform organizations require a high level of internal transparency**
- **Complementors are organizations that make use of platforms to develop their own apps, services or products**
- **The ecosystem of complementors participates in the decision-making around the platform**
- **Platform organizations and ecosystems are typical for an online world, but occur offline as well**

HOW ARE TASKS DIVIDED?	• PLATFORM OWNER DECIDES INTERNALLY • COMPLEMENTORS DECIDE ON THEIR OWN SERVICES • PLATFORM AND ECOSYSTEM MAY ENGAGE IN COLLABORATIVE DECISION-MAKING
HOW ARE TASKS ALLOCATED?	• EITHER THE PLATFORM OWNER DECIDES WHICH COMPLEMENTOR IS ALLOWED TO DO WHAT OR COMPLEMENTORS DECIDE FOR THEMSELVES • PLATFORM OWNER IS ACTIVE IN DENYING ACCESS TO COMPLEMENTORS
HOW ARE REWARDS PROVIDED TO MOTIVATE PEOPLE/PARTNERS?	• PLATFORM OWNER: COST SAVING, DATA, REVENUE VIA COMPLEMENTORS, RAPID GROWTH OF THE PLATFORM • COMPLEMENTOR: ACCESS TO CLIENTS, FAST SCALING, LOWER DEVELOPMENT COSTS
HOW IS INFORMATION PROVIDED SO PEOPLE CAN TAKE THE RIGHT DECISIONS?	• ONLINE PLATFORMS PROVIDE INSIGHT IN DATA ON NUMBER OF TRANSACTIONS, INTERACTIONS, COMPLEMENTORS, SITE VISITS, SEARCH TERMS ETC.

Table 12: Core elements of platform organizations

The division of tasks between the platform owner(s) and the ecosystem of complementors is initially determined by the platform owner. The platform owner develops the platform, determines its openness, sets the incentives for complementors that sign up and decides on conditions for complementors to access the platform. The complementors determine which complementary services or products they develop, based on available development tools. For online platforms the magic word is API (application programming interface). An API enables developers to build apps for the platform. Standardized agree-ments written by the platform owner govern the relationship[2].

Obviously, this division of tasks describes the initial situation. Over time the relationship between platform owner and complementors may become more symbiotic in such a way that the complementors may start to guide the platform owner about desired directions for development of the platform and the platform owner may guide complementors more and more about their offerings. The precise division of tasks may become more subject to joint decision-making. Participation of external partners in decision-making becomes the norm[3]. This is logical because the platform owner and complementors engage in co-specialization, meaning complementors cannot redeploy their assets to other uses[4]. This necessitates collaboration.

Following on from this, the allocation of tasks to specific complementors can follow two paths. Either the platform owner decides which complementor is allowed to do what or complementors decide for themselves. Complementors may sign up themselves and simply develop and offer their app in an app store. In that case platform owners do not have an active role in allocating tasks to complementors. They may still have a task in curating their network of complementors, for example by denying access to the platform to complementors who do not follow the rules set out by the platform owner.

Platform owners have a number of incentives to choose for a platform organization. By creating a platform the platform owner can save costs, because the IP of a platform can be more easily leveraged across various applications than when IP is held by business units for their own use. More important than the cost factor however are the opportunities for rapid growth that can be realized by opening the platform up to complementors. These mainly lie in the fact that platforms

can gather more data faster. More data means more services can be offered, more and better algorithms can be developed and customers can be targeted more precisely. Rather than the platform having to invest its own resources, it can use the resources of the complementors to grow. This saves time during the expansion process. Finally, the platform owner also generates revenues via the complementors, who need to share their revenue with the platform owner. Because complementors have many more business ideas than the platform owner could ever have had on its own, this can turn out to be quite profitable for the platform owner. For the complementor, the incentives lie in access to the clients of the platform, fast scaling by using the platform technology and lower development costs because many building blocks of the product or service the complementor wants to offer are already present in the platform.

Regarding information sharing, online platforms have a considerable advantage over offline platforms. Online platforms gather so much data and these data are so easy to disclose that both the platform owner and the complementors have access to an abundance of information to guide their decision-making. Valuable insights can be had into the number of transactions, interactions, site visits, search terms, downloads, time spent on a web page and the like. In some cases

though, information sharing via meetings and face to face communication may remain important, in addition to online communication tools.

Platforms provide enormous opportunities for many organizations, but they are not a cure for all ills and they have a number of specific drawbacks that are unique to them. Companies that want to implement them therefore need to take into account their positive and negative sides. Table 13 provides the information leaflet for platform organizations and their ecosystems.

Ecosystems around platform organizations solve a number of problems faced by many companies. The first one is that companies need to invest in innovation, despite uncertainty over whether the innovation is going to be a success. Platform organizations outsource innovation to the ecosystem and thereby transfer (part of) that risk to the eco-

system. Each app or accessory made by a complementor is an experiment in innovation. The market will guide whether it is successful or not. The platform does not have to invest in the development costs. At the same time, all these innovations show that using complementors gives the platform access to creative ideas that it may not have itself. Platforms make use of the well-known principle of Joy's law, named after one of Sun Microsystem's founders, that implies there are always more smart people working outside your company than within. Open platforms make use of the smart people outside by enabling them to innovate. A final and related problem solved is that knowledge and information are often underused. Much knowledge and information is used for only a fraction of the products, services or problemsthey could be used for. Letting complementors use that intellectual capital extracts more value from it.

PROBLEMS SOLVED	· UNCERTAINTY AROUND INNOVATION · LIMITED CREATIVITY · UNDERUSE OF KNOWLEDGE AND INFORMATION
DISADVANTAGES	· LOSS OF CONTROL OVER TECHNOLOGY · COMPLEMENTORS DEPEND ON THE ACTIONS OF THE PLATFORM OWNER · PEOPLE ARE MANAGED BY ALGORITHMS
SUITABLE FOR	· ENVIRONMENTS WHERE NETWORK EFFECTS EXIST · ENVIRONMENTS WITH POTENTIALLY HIGH BUT UNCERTAIN DEMAND FOR COMPLEMENTARY SERVICES · ENVIRONMENTS WHERE PLATFORM BASED INNOVATION DELIVERS ADVANTAGES OF COST OR SPEED; MODULARITY · ENVIRONMENTS WITH MANY POTENTIAL COMPLEMENTORS TO FORM AN ECOSYSTEM
NOT SUITABLE FOR	· ORGANIZATIONS WHERE OPENNESS IS NOT POSSIBLE · CONDITIONS FOR MODULARITY ARE NOT MET
KEY INGREDIENTS	· ATTRACTIVE PLATFORM FOR COMPLEMENTORS · PARTICIPATION OF THE ECOSYSTEM IN DECISION-MAKING · STANDARDIZED CONTRACTS · INTERNAL TRANSPARENCY · EASY TO USE INTERFACES (API'S) · PROJECT-BASED ORGANIZATION DESIGN
RISKS	· OVERLY OPEN PLATFORMS · OVERLY CLOSED PLATFORMS · SOCIETAL BACKLASH
LEADERSHIP	· DETERMINE SCOPE · DETERMINE TECHNOLOGY DESIGN AND IP · MANAGE EXTERNAL RELATIONSHIPS WITH COMPLEMENTORS · STRUCTURE INTERNAL ORGANIZATION

Table 13: Information leaflet of the platform organization and its ecosystems

The main disadvantages of platforms lie in the fact that the relations between platform owner and complementor grow increasingly intertwined over time. This makes it more difficult for platform owners to unilaterally make changes to their technology, as such changes affect many complementors. This limits the platform owner's ability to change. The flipside is true for complementors: they become increasingly dependent on the platform and therefore lose some degree of freedom. And if a platform decides to make changes, the complementor will at least incur costs to incorporate those changes in its offering. An additional disadvantage for online platforms lies in the dehumanizing aspect of them. For Uber drivers or Deliveroo couriers, algorithms determine their income and for other complementors the way a platform owner assigns work or priority to them is based on algorithms as well[5]. Many will see this loss of human interaction as undesirable. Basic notions of fairness can be undermined when people have no opportunity to debate the fairness of algorithms.

From the previous discussion it follows that it is useful to think about platforms in environments where network effects exist. Network effects help to solve the problems of underuse of knowledge and information, limited creativity and the risk of innovation. After all, the more complementors join the platform, the more knowledge and innovation is used, the more creativity is accessed and the more risk is spread. When network effects create a long-lasting network of users, such client lock-in ensures that the platform becomes increasingly valuable[6]. Naturally, the use of ecosystems also assumes there is a potentially high but uncertain demand for complementary services or products[7]. In addition, it must be clear that platform based innovation delivers advantages of cost or speed.

Modularity is a key concept here. The more the platform is modular, the easier it is to combine modules of the platform with modules from complementors. Such modules may be payment systems, tools to diagnose client behavior or GPS tools that enable a complementor to ascertain the location of their users. This leads to fast and low cost innovation. Each owner of a platform needs to assess whether there are sufficient possible partners willing to invest in creating complementary products or services.

If modularity is not an option, this is a contra-indication for building ecosystems around platform organizations. Platforms are also more difficult to use in circumstances where openness is not desirable. This can be around confidential information or when privacy concerns play a role.

A first ingredient for platform organizations is of course the presence of a platform that is attractive for complementors. Such a platform usually requires complementors to participate in decisionmaking. This enables the platform and the ecosystem to co-evolve their capabilities. Standardized contracts govern the relationship between the platform owner and its complementors. This standardization enables many complementors to sign up to the platform without high administrative costs. Internal transparency is a further key ingredient for platform success[8]. All information needs to be accessible to everybody within the platform organization. This ensures consistency, helps to develop new capabilities and facilitates growth. There is no room for silos which limit information sharing. The platform should also have easy to use interfaces such as API's or a modular design that other parties can easily connect to. It also helps when the internal organization of the platform owner and the complementor are project based or have agile characteristics.

This enables fast combination and recombination of modules that will help the companies to really profit from the opportunities offered by the platform.

Platforms face three types of risk. The first is that a platform may be too open. This may relate to allowing everybody to access the platform and thereby degenerating the content delivered or inducing misbehavior[9]. It may also pertain to allowing everybody to make changes to the intellectual property that underpins it. This increases the risk of fragmentation of the knowledge base. Many different versions of the IP may exist in different organizations. In that case it becomes more difficult to profit from the network effects, because the ecosystem may split along the lines of the different versions. Each version then ends up with a smaller ecosystem. Google runs into this problem because it uses an open source technology as its operating system for its mobile applications (Android). Different versions of Android exist, fragmenting the Google platform. The benefit of using open source however was that it was easy for complementors to sign on to Google's platform, which led to rapid growth of the ecosystem. Apple faced the risk of being too closed and protecting its own operating system too much.

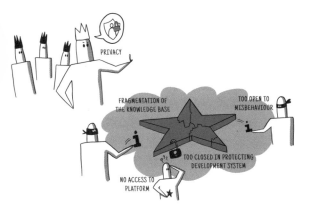

"Unlike traditional pipeline businesses, platforms don't control value creation. Instead, they create an infrastructure in which value can be created and exchanged, and lay out principles that govern these interactions".

> Geoffrey G. Parker,
  Platform Revolution

This made it more difficult for complementors to develop interesting applications. Faced with the growth of Google, Apple was gradually forced to make more and more of its operating system available for developers to build on.

An outside risk to platforms may lie in a societal backlash against them. This is especially true for online platforms. Because online platforms can exercise considerable market power, the fear of abuse of monopoly (and actual examples of it) has led to concerns about them. Antitrust authorities have fined many of the large online platforms. Privacy issues have been raised as well. With people handing over much information about their life every time they search for something or click on a button, platforms amassed a wealth of data. Fears about how these data are used are further fueled by a lack of transparency of the algorithms the platform owners use to extract value from these data. This societal debate is only in its infancy. Organizations setting up platforms now, should be aware that stricter regulations may be implemented in the near future, restricting the value that can be reaped from the data they gathered. The role of leaders in platform organizations has been clearly defined in the literature. The platform owners have five tasks[10]:

- **Set and communicate the vision that energizes the platform organization and the ecosystem;**
- **Determine the scope of the platform: what (not) to do in house;**
- **Determine the technology design and IP: what to include in the platform and how open should the interfaces be;**
- **Manage external relationships with complementors: how to manage them and how to encourage them to contribute to the ecosystem;**
- **Structure the internal organization: one point of attention here is how to reassure complementors that the leader works for the good of the ecosystem, not just for its own good.**

Regarding this last point, the platform owner should ensure the ecosystem of complementors that their future on the platform is secure. Once this faith is gone, complementors will leave the ecosystem. This becomes specifically salient when a platform starts to compete with complementors. Intel implemented some mechanisms to ensure it would be perceived as neutral when it started to compete with its complementors in one of its markets[11]. It established a business unit that would compete with complementors based on Intel IP, but at the same time it made that IP available to the complementors, without giving its own unit a head start. The IP was developed in another department than the new business unit.

The new business unit had its own P&L, but the IP-developing department was not-for-profit. On the one hand this signaled to complementors that Intel believed in the technology by setting up its own business unit, while on the other hand it signaled that complementors would have a fair chance of making money in the market. This was backed up by consistent communication that this was the strategy. In short: the internal structure of the platform owner needs to take into account the neutrality towards the ecosystem of complementors.

Much of this discussion focuses on online platform organizations. The use of platforms is not limited to the online world though. Its potential is much broader. Car manufacturers create platforms around new car models and standardization organizations create platforms of intellectual property that many partners may use.

A main difference between these offline platforms and the online world is of course that data gathering and software development open up other opportunities than are currently possible in the physical world. Yet, with the increasing possibilities of the Internet of Things, traditional companies are applying platform ways of thinking at increasing pace.

[1] *Many definitions of platforms exist. For the background of this definition see Kreijveld, M., Deuten J., & Est, R.V. (2014), De kracht van platformen, Vakmedianet and Thomas, L. D., Autio, E., & Gann, D. M. (2014). Architectural leverage: putting platforms in context. The Academy of Management Perspectives, 28(2), 198-219.*

[2] *Jacobides, M. G., Cennamo, C., & Gawer, A. (2018). Towards a theory of ecosystems. Strategic Management Journal. 39, 2255-2276.*

[3] *Parker, G. G., Van Alstyne, M., & Choudary, S. P. (2016). Platform revolution: How networked markets are transforming the economy and how to make them work for you. WW Norton.*

[4] *Jacobides, M. G., (2018). ibid.*

[5] *O'Connor, S. (2016), When your boss is an algorithm. Financial Times, September 8.*

[6] *Parker et al. (2016) ibid.*

[7] *Gawer, A., & Cusumano, M. A. (2002). Platform leadership: How Intel, Microsoft, and Cisco drive industry innovation. Harvard Business School Press.*

[8] *Parker et al. (2016) ibid.*

[9] *Van Alstyne, M. W., Parker, G. G., & Choudary, S. P. (2016). Pipelines, platforms, and the new rules of strategy. Harvard Business Review, 94(4), 54-62.*

[10] *Gawer, A., & Cusumano, M. A. (2008). How companies become platform leaders. MIT Sloan management review, 49(2), 28-35; Zeng, M. (2018). Alibaba and the future of business. Harvard Business Review. September/October, 88-96.*

[11] *Gawer, A., & Henderson, R. (2007). Platform owner entry and innovation in complementary markets: Evidence from Intel. Journal of Economics & Management Strategy, 16(1), 1-34.*

CASE STUDY:
BOOKING.COM'S PLATFORM ORGANIZATION AND ITS ECOSYSTEMS

Platforms provide infrastructure and rules for a marketplace that bring together producers and consumers to exchange products, services and feedback that create value[1]. While most platforms share the same underlying principles, they are not all the same. Some platforms provide value primarily by optimizing exchanges directly between a consumer and a contributor. Other platforms generate value by enabling producers to create complementary products. There are also platforms that broadcast or distribute products and content to a larger audience. We differentiate between four types of platform-based ecosystems (see table 14)[2].

PLATFORM	DISTRIBUTION PLATFORM	MARKETPLACE EXCHANGE PLATFORM	SOCIAL PLATFORM	MAKER PLATFORM
MAIN PURPOSE	PROVIDE CONTENT AND PRODUCTS FROM PRODUCERS TO USERS	SET-UP TRANSACTIONS BETWEEN PRODUCERS AND USERS	FACILITATE INTERACTION BETWEEN USERS AND PRODUCERS	ENABLE PRODUCERS TO CREATE COMPLIMENTARY VALUE FOR USERS
EXAMPLES	MOVIES (NETFLIX) GAMES (XBOX) MUSIC (SPOTIFY) NEWS (BLENDL) BOOKS (KINDLE) JOBS (MONSTER.COM)	PRODUCTS (AMAZON) SERVICE (UBER) ASSETS (AIRBNB) TICKETS (STUBHUB) HOTELROOMS (PRICELINE) PAYMENTS (PAYPAL)	LIFESTYLE (FACEBOOK) NETWORK (LINKEDIN) DATES (TINDER) MESSAGES (WHATSAPP) REVIEWS (YELP) FILE TRANSFER (DROPBOX)	APPS (GOOGLE PLAY) VIDEO (YOUTUBE) SONGS (APPLE ITUNES) GAMES (NINTENDO) CONTENT (MEDIUM) IMAGES (PINTEREST)

Table 14: Four types of platform-based ecosystems

Distribution platforms are single sided platforms that buy from producers and resell to consumers. Marketplace exchange platforms and social platforms are double sided and often facilitate transactions or interactions between two parties[4]. Maker platforms are also double sided. They enable producers to develop applications to reach multiple consumers. Companies like Google, Apple and Amazon have multiple types of platforms. For example, Amazon has a marketplace platform for merchants to sell products to consumers. It also has a distribution platform with Amazon Prime Video for movies and series and an App Store for developers based on the Android operating system. With Prime Video and the Amazon App Store it competes with Netflix and Google Play.

Across these various types of platform-based ecosystems, there are multiple types of revenue models. The most commonly applied models generate revenue based on subscription fees, transaction fees, commission, advertisement, access, and revenue sharing. Many of the platform-based ecosystems that we see around us have a mixture of these revenue streams. The case study of Booking.com in the travel industry demonstrates a variety of platform based ecosystems and revenue models.

PLATFORM BASED ECOSYSTEMS IN THE TRAVEL INDUSTRY

The travel industry has changed significantly in the past decade. Around the world, people traded in physical travel agencies for the internet to book their vacations. This has led to the introduction of a variety of platform based ecosystems such as Expedia, Booking.com, TripAdvisor and Airbnb. While these platforms operate in the same industry and undertake similar activities, they have different purposes. Their main sources of revenue come from different activities[5].

Expedia is mainly a distribution or reselling platform. Although it generates revenue from both merchant and agency activities, it makes most of its revenue on its platform through the merchant business model. Basically, Expedia facilitates the bookings of hotels, airlines, cars and destinations and acts as the merchant. This means that Expedia buys available hotel rooms in bulk against discounted rates and resells them (often in packaged offerings with airline tickets and car rental services) to travelers.

Booking.com is mainly a marketplace exchange platform. Most revenue from the platform derives from the agency model. Booking.com has contracts with the hotels that it lists and will take a commission on each booking through its site somewhere between 10%-30%. The commission depends on the size, location and reviews of the hotel. Hotels also pay higher commission for a better ranking on the platform. Like Booking.com, Airbnb is also a marketplace exchange platform but it functions slightly different. It makes revenues by charging hosts and guests a service fee per transaction (approximately 5% for hosts and 10% for guests).

TripAdvisor is mainly a social platform where people share reviews on hotels, restaurants and transactions. The most common reason people use TripAdvisor is for decision making and planning of their vacation.

Today, it generates most of its revenue from advertising based on a cost-per-click model. Advertising buttons on the platform redirect users to an online travel agency where they actually book their destination[6].

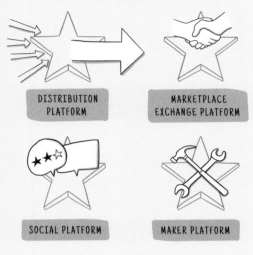

DISTRIBUTION PLATFORM

MARKETPLACE EXCHANGE PLATFORM

SOCIAL PLATFORM

MAKER PLATFORM

SNAPSHOT OF BOOKING.COM

Booking.com, founded in 1996, is part of Booking Holding Group. The Booking Holding Group, also known as Priceline Group, owns a number of other brands that all operate based on a platform business model (including Kayak.com, OpenTable, Rentalcars. com). Booking.com is the largest platform in the Booking Holding Group and one of today's biggest online travel agencies. Booking. com now employs about 17,000 people and its headquarters is in the Netherlands in Amsterdam. The platform has over five million listings in over 100,000 destinations in 150 countries. In 2018, everyday more

than 1.5 million room nights are booked on the platform. Booking.com has long-term relationships with close to 1 million hotels and has 95 million guest reviews on the platform. It is the most visited travel website by traffic with more than 100 million platform visits each month. The platform is accessible worldwide and supported in 42 different languages[7].

When in an interview the CEO of Booking.com, Gillian Tans, was asked if Booking.com was a travel agency or a technology company she had a clear response: 'While travel might be its product, what many people fail to realize is that Booking.com is in fact the third largest ecommerce platform in the world'. With a large team of web developers, and running more than 1,000 A/B tests at any one time, it also prides itself on innovating through continuous experimentation[8].

THE BOOKING.COM CORE PLATFORM

The Booking.com core platform is a two-sided marketplace that facilitates transactions between travelers and hotels. To travelers, the value proposition is variety, guaranteed cheap prices and convenience (see figure 7 for the complete business model). The value proposition towards hotels is the opportunity to sell rooms that would have stayed empty, with high conversion rates and the ability to change availability and prices easily. Hotels that use Booking.com have a global reach and receive market intelligence on various features of their listings. Booking.com promotes listings on search engines and it ensures that the property automatically lists on Google Maps. The partners on the Booking.com platform are not just large hotel chains with multiple properties worldwide. The platform also targets people hosting single room apartments or bed and breakfasts and even more recently, tourist attractions. All partners are part of the Booking.com ecosystem.

CONNECTING HOTELS AND PROPERTY OWNERS ON THE BOOKING.COM PLATFORM

To sign up on Booking.com is relatively easy. The platform has a registration portal where partners provide basic contact information, select the type of property they want to list and follow further instructions to provide details on their listing. They can also disclose specific information on house rules, policies, and overall offerings. During the agreement stage in the registration process, partners get information about the commission-based model. There is no subscription fee for partners on the platform. Once registration is completed, partners have an agreement with Booking.com for using the online reservation platform. They have to pay Booking.com a set commission amount on all confirmed

BUSINESS MODEL CANVAS BOOKING.COM

KEY PARTNERS
- HOTEL / PROPERTY OWNERS
- MAJOR HOTEL CHAINS
- AFFILIATES
- TRAVEL AGENTS
- CORPORATE TRAVEL MANAGERS
- TECHNOLOGY PARTNERS
- META SEARCH ENGINES
- LOBBYISTS

KEY ACTIVITIES
- MANAGE NETWORK EFFECTS
- CUSTOMER EXPERIENCE
- CUSTOMER SUPPORT
- GROW THE PLATFORM
- OBSERVE EXTERNAL FACTORS
- ENHANCE TECHNOLOGY
- GUIDE CUSTOMER JOURNEY

KEY RESOURCES
- NUMBER OF HOTELS
- NUMBER OF LOCATIONS
- GREAT CONTENT
- USER DATA / ALGORITHMS
- USER EXPERIENCE
- GLOBAL NETWORK
- SKILLED STAFF

VALUE PROPOSITION
FOR TRAVELLERS:
- CHEAPEST PRICES
- AMOUNT OF CHOICE
- REDUCTION OF RISK
- CUSTOMER SERVICE
- USEFUL APP
- USEFUL TRAVEL CONTENT

FOR HOTELS:
- INCREMENTAL REVENUE
- ABILITY TO REACT
- GLOBAL REACH
- RISK REDUCTION
- ADDITIONAL WEB TRAFFIC
- MARKET INTELLIGENCE

CUSTOMER RELATIONSHIPS
HOTELS:
- COMMISSIONS
- EASE OF JOINING
- NO BOOKING, NO PAY

TRAVELLERS:
- CUSTOMER SERVICE
- ACCURACY

CHANNELS
- WEBSITE (MOBILE, DESKTOP)
- APP
- PARTNER CHANNELS AD CHANNELS (META SEARCH ENGINES, ETC)
- COMMS CHANNELS

CUSTOMER SEGMENTS
HOTELS:
- PROPERTY TYPES
- ROOM TYPES
- STAR & USER RATINGS
- AMENITIES, FACILITIES
- PROXIMITY
- TYPE OF HOTEL
- LOCATIONS
- TYPE OF INRFASTRUCTURE

TRAVELLERS:
- TRAVEL MOTIVATION
- DEMOGRAPHICS
- BOOKING DETAILS
- EMPLOYMENT
- SPENDING BEHAVIOURS

COST STRUCTURE (FY 16)

OPERATIONAL
- PERFORMANCE ADVERTISING: $3.4B
- BRAND ADVERTISING: $0.29B
- SALES AND MARKETING: $0.43B

- CAPITALISED COSTS: $54.2M

BALANCE SHEET:
- PROPERTY & EQUIPMENT: $347M
- INTANGIBLE ASSETS: $ 2B
- GOODWILL: $ 2.4B

REVENUES (FY 16)
- AGENCY BUSINESS MODEL: $7.98B/$10.7B - 74%
- MERCHANT BUSINESS MODEL: $2B/$10.7B - 19%
- ADVERTISING AND OTHER REVENUES: $0.7/$10.7B - 6.6%

MORE ON: WWW.INNOVATEONTACTICS.COM/BUSINESS-MODEL-CANVAS/

Figure 7: The business model of Booking.com[9]

stays, non-refundable reservations, and partially refundable reservations made on the Booking.com platform. Each month, partners receive an invoice detailing how much commission is due. Partners have full control over their rates and availability of their listing. Booking.com does not add anything to the rates that partners set on the platform; neither does it charge travelers for making a booking. After partners have listed their property, any transaction on the Booking.com platform is a direct agreement between the partner and the traveler. The traveler typically pays the reservation rate to the partner after their stay, or earlier in the case of a non-refundable booking. When a traveler makes a booking through the Booking.com platform, the partner receives an instant confirmation[10].

FEATURES FOR PARTNERS ON THE BOOKING.COM PLATFORM – SUPPORT, CONNECT, PULSE, EXTRANET

Booking.com offers a number of features for partners on their core platform. During the registration process, partners have access to Booking.com 'Support' to ensure that listings are comprehensive and attractive for travelers. Booking.com 'Connect' allows partners to manage all aspects of their business, including anything from updating content to finance to communicating with guests. It has basic functionality such as the ability to turn listings 'off' and 'on', determine availability – (weekends only, seasonal bookings, etc.). The platform also offers features, which allow partners to manage availability of listings around other agency partnerships, preventing double-bookings. As an extension to Connect, Booking.com also offers a mobile app called 'Pulse', which allows partners to get real-time updates on their property's activity wherever they are. Another feature, 'Extranet', gives their partners insights into their property's performance with detailed analytics. Partners can compare their listings, measure them up against industry benchmarks, and identify opportunities on where they can improve.

CONTINUOUS IMPROVEMENT OF THE BOOKING.COM PLATFORM FEATURES USING FEEDBACK FROM PARTNERS

Booking.com uses A/B testing and qualitative research to improve the platform user experience for their partners. A/B testing involves comparing two versions of a feature to see which one delivers a better customer experience. The number of clicks or the amount of time that partners spent on a specific feature can measure the user experience off a feature. Another simple way of understanding the needs and requirements of partners is to spend time with them. Booking.com visits clients regularly, which gives them the opportunity to observe their daily struggles and successes. As part of these visits, they also share new prototypes that they are developing or areas of the platform that they are working on for which they would like their feedback. Combined with visiting partners, Booking.com also works with their partners in co-creation sessions. During these participatory sessions partners can raise specific pain points. Together with Booking.com they come up with creative ideas or solutions that can be tested on a wider audience. Booking.com also organizes Open Lab sessions from their own offices for their partners. These sessions are typically with 4 or 5 different partners throughout the day and last between 45 minutes to an hour. During Open Lab sessions, Booking.com openly shares planned improvements to the platform with partners and quickly gets specific feedback and learnings about the features that they are developing. Finally, shadow sessions with Booking.com customer service agents allows the organization to see for what kind of issues their partners contact Booking.com. In these sessions, their user experience (UX) design and development teams spend an hour with a

A B TESTING

VISITING PARTNERS

OPEN LAB SESSIONS

SHADOW SESSIONS

customer service agent, listening in to phone calls. These sessions allow these teams to hear first-hand the challenges their partners experience with the Booking.com platform[11].

COPYWRITERS AND LINGO

Booking.com employs dedicated copywriters for new features. Copywriters are usually part of a product team made up of developers, designers, and product owners. Copywriters literally copy experiments and A/B testing on the Booking.com platform in other countries with the support of local language specialists. With Lingo, an internal Booking.com tool, copywriters can create a request written in British English and distribute it to language teams for translation, adaptation to local flavors and rapid testing. The entire process of copywriting, translating, and testing is a constant editing cycle. There can be over 40 people looking at the same copy experiment in Lingo across the world all ensuring it is culturally appropriate for their market. If the translated copy does not show the expected result, it means there is room for improvement and the copywriter coordinates another development iteration on the feature[12].

THE BOOKINGSUITE APP STORE

Recently Booking.com also launched an App Store that allows partners to connect and integrate services around their listings on the Booking.com platform with other hospitality software solutions. The App Store is in fact a maker platform where hospitality software solution providers can develop apps for Booking.com partners based on various BookingSuite APIs. The App Store includes a provider portal where solution providers can track performance, manage accounts and data connections, in addition to handling fee collection. Partners can go the BookingSuite App Store and get personalized recommendations for relevant apps based on the type and performance of their listings. All apps in the App Store come with a free trial period. The App Store features hospitality apps in the following categories: online reputation, price optimization, guest communication, property website, upselling and promotions, online check-in, in-stay services[13].

THE BOOKING.COM AFFILIATE PARTNER PROGRAM

Booking.com also has a network with about 17,500 affiliate partners for their core platform. The Booking.com affiliate network consists of third parties ranging from cashback business, airline companies, car rental services, a travel blog, a tourist board, a metasearch site, to anything in between. Any third party can decide to sign up to become an affiliate in the Booking.com affiliate partner program. The Booking.com affiliate partner program gives third parties the opportunity to connect their website to the Booking.com platform. Third parties that become an affiliate integrate Booking.com products and features into their website and in return, earn a commission for each booking made on the Booking.com platform.

THE BOOKING.COM WAY OF WORKING WITH THIRD PARTIES IN THE AFFILIATE PARTNER PROGRAM

Commission for affiliates is calculated using a commission split model and is proportionately linked to the amount of successful bookings made via affiliate partner websites. The more bookings, the higher the commission for the affiliate partner, however every affiliate partner must reach 50 successful bookings at a minimum to earn commissions. Reported revenue sharing proportions are 25% for the first 50 bookings, 30% for 51-150 bookings,

35% for 151-500 bookings and 40% for more than 501 bookings. Booking.com pays affiliates commission by bank transfer or through PayPal between 30 and 60 days after the property has confirmed the guest has completed their stay. Transfers are on a monthly basis with a minimum threshold of 100 EUR. As soon as the commission exceeds the 100 EUR threshold affiliate partners receive the credit-slip (reservation overview) via email.

Booking.com offers a number of products and services to their affiliate partners. The 'map widget' helps visitors of affiliate partner websites look for accommodations around a specific area. The 'search box' helps the visitors of affiliate partner websites to look for their accommodation and is customizable into the affiliate partner website to fit with its specific look and feel. With the 'deals finder' affiliate partners can build a stream of deals for hotels. The Booking.com 'co-brand' feature lets visitors of affiliate partners know that they are on the site of an official Booking.com partner. It helps partners to show that their customers are making their reservation with a trustworthy brand. The 'links' tool (URL constructor) helps create affiliate deep-links to connect their website to any Booking.com page. Deep-links are hyperlinks that connect a page (for example property pages, landmarks, event pages) directly in your site to any page of another website, apart from the homepage. For larger affiliates, Booking.com also offers a variety of APIs to enhance integration of products and services. A strict and mandatory requirement for Booking.com to consider granting API access is an already steady performance of over 500 stayed bookings per month[14].

The case of Booking.com shows the high investments it makes to keep its ecosystem of partners and affiliate partners engaged. The combination of online and offline communication ensures continuous improvement in the quality of the platform. This in turn keeps the ecosystem motivated to work with Booking.com.

"We try to put decision making as low as possible in the organization so we can move quickly. If you have to go all the way to the top to approve every decision, it slows everything down."

> Gillian Tans, Booking.com

[1] Van Alstyne, M. W., Parker, G. G., & Choudary, S. P. (2016). Pipelines, platforms, and the new rules of strategy. Harvard Business Review, 94(4), 54-62.

[2] Moazed, A. (2017). Platform types: explained and defined. www.applicoinc.com, 20 October; Nooren, P., van Gorp, N., van Eijk, N., & Ó Fathaigh, R. (2018). Should We Regulate Digital Platforms? A New Framework for Evaluating Policy Options. Policy and Internet, 10(3), 264-301.

[3] We compiled this table based on Moazed (2017) and Nooren et al. (2018).

[4] Moazed, A. (2016). Platform business model – definition – explanation. www.aplicoinc.com, 1 May.

[5] Nyaga, C. (2018). Expedia, Booking and TripAdvisor compared. www.seekingalpha.com, 25 October.

[6] Uenlue, M. (2018). Business models compared: Booking.com, Expedia, Tripadvisor. www.innovationtactics. com, 30 September.

[7] www.booking.com

[8] Fisher, A. (2018). Booking.com CEO Gillian Tans interview, Authority Magazine, 14 February.

[9] Uenlue, M. (2018). Business model canvas Booking.com. www.innovationtactics.com, 12 December.

[10] www.partnerhelp.booking.com

[11] Butler, J. (2017). End-to-end product thinking: How Booking.com designs for partners. www.booking.design. com, 27 February.

[12] Kemp, E. (2017). Copywriting – The Booking.com Way. www.workingatbooking.com, 16 May.

[13] www.suite.booking.com

[14] www.connect.booking.com

EXCURSION :
SEEING THE WOOD FOR THE TREES IN ECOSYSTEMS

After war and sports, nature is one of the favorite sources for metaphors in business. Predators, preys, symbiosis and extinction events crop up regularly in business vocabulary. The notion of ecosystem was introduced in business literature many years ago, but did not become popular until quite recently[1]. The idea that multiple companies could somehow strengthen each other and be co-dependent is a basic insight behind it.

The idea in brief
- **The term ecosystem is applied to many different forms of collaboration. This excursion provides an overview.**
- **Core elements of ecosystems include the presence of multilateral relationships, the existence of complementors that create products or services that are specific to the ecosystem and the absence of hierarchical control and custom-made contracts**
- **Ecosystems often are based around platforms, but may also focus on a value proposition or knowledge flows between organizations**

INTRODUCTION INTO ECOSYSTEMS

As happens with popular terms, sooner or later they are applied to anything and everything. The term ecosystem has been used for a variety of different phenomena as well. Figure 8 gives an overview of the various uses of the word ecosystem in practice. The chapters 5 and 6 will look at the two newest types of ecosystems in more detail, viz. the online platform based ecosystems and value proposition based ecosystems. The academic literature developed a more strict definition of ecosystems and highlights the following elements[2]:

- **Multilateral relationships.** An ecosystem consists of multiple organizations that depend on each other in a variety of ways.

- **Complementors deliver complementary knowledge, products and services specific to the ecosystem**
  - » Ecosystems are based on a modular design. This enables organizations to deliver complementary knowledge, products or services that can easily be connected to each other
  - » Such organizations are called complementors. Other than suppliers, complementors determine themselves what product or service they deliver to the ecosystem. For example, Twitter comes up with its own ideas and contributes them to the iPhone platform. Also, complementary products/services are integrated by the client, not by a core organization[3]. The individual iPhone user downloads Twitter; Apple does not integrate Twitter standard in its iPhone.
  - » The complementary products are specific to the ecosystem. They cannot be redeployed in another ecosystem. This makes ecosystem partners dependent on each other and requires them to collaborate.

- **The governance is not hierarchical and does not use customized contracts.**
  - » Ecosystems have either no contracts or are governed by standards, interfaces and rules that are similar for all partners in the network (or similar for subgroups of partners that have similar roles).

As a consequence of these characteristics of ecosystems, partners 'co-evolve their capabilities'[4]. This means they are learning from and with each other. The idea is that the stronger the ecosystem is, the stronger each individual organization stands. An ecosystem is healthy when it is productive (i.e. it leads to lower costs and/or creates new products), robust (can cope with environmental change) and creates new niches (new technologies, businesses, products).[5]

PLATFORM BASED ECOSYSTEMS

Following the broader and looser use of the term in practice, the first group of ecosystems is based on a platform. A platform is a business based on a set of shared assets (technologies, capabilities, standards) that can easily be recombined into diverse applications and aims to enable value-creating interactions between partners[6]. Platforms are becoming core building blocks for many organizational forms. They can be online and offline.

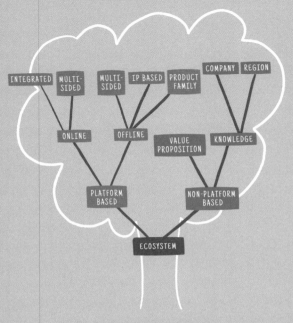

Figure 8: The diversity of ecosystems

it becomes to join them. Indirect network effects exist when having more users on one side of the platform attracts more users on the other side of the platform. An example is the app stores of Apple and Google: the more people use Apple or Google the more interesting it becomes for developers to create apps based on the platform's technology. Uber and Airbnb operate on the same principle: more users attract more suppliers which in turn attract more users and so on. Amazon and eBay are examples as well: the more suppliers bring their products to the auction the more buyers will use the platform. In the platform literature these buyer-supplier platforms are known as two- or multisided platforms.

The newest platforms are online digital, integrated platforms as created by Google, Amazon, Facebook and the like. We label them 'integrated' because they incorporate many of the features of the other forms of ecosystems: they often connect suppliers with buyers, are based around intellectual property, create product families and continually develop new value propositions[7].

Online platforms rely on direct and/or indirect network effects. In the case of direct network effects, more users beget more users[8]. This is typically the case in social networks like Facebook and LinkedIn. The more people are on these platforms the more interesting

Platforms however do not only exist in the online world. Multisided platforms have been known in the offline world for many, many years. Take for example the New York Stock Exchange that provides a platform to trade company shares of which many ecosystem partners (traders, brokers, banks) make good (too good, according to some) money. Platforms may also consist of a set of intellectual property (IP) of which an organization or multiple organizations make use. Disney's content is an example: the characters of Mickey Mouse and Donald Duck can be used in diverse applications from cartoons, to dolls, to toys. Other platforms are based on patents. For example in organizations like

IMEC various organizations contribute and develop IP for their joint and individual use[9]. Yet another common form of platform thinking occurs around product platforms. Often these are modular product platforms where, based on customer demand, various modules can be configured to create a custom-made product[10]. This is common in the car industry, but also in aircraft manufacturing. A product family is a set of different products that are assembled based on such modules. The ecosystem in this case consists of the owner of the platform and its suppliers. Note that in these instances the practical use of the term ecosystem differs significantly from the academic definition provided above: in these cases the core companies determine who supplies what and use customized contracts to govern the relationship with the supplier.

OWNERSHIP AND OPENNESS OF PLATFORM BASED ECOSYSTEMS

Platforms may have one or multiple owners. Multiple organizations or even individuals may own the IP of the platform. The large Internet players are single owners of their platform. The other extreme is open source software which also provides a platform without having a traditional owner. Another characteristic in which platforms differ is their openness. They may be open or closed[11]. Some platforms are exclusively for the use of the owner. These internal platforms are not included in figure 8, because they have

no ecosystem around them. Other platforms are very open in that anyone can contribute to the platform to enrich it and make use of the assets in the platform to build their own product or service. Many platforms are in between with certain parts open for use by other parties. Especially in online platforms, platform owners open up part of their IP for others to build upon. Core IP often remains closed, but interface technology may be opened up, for example for app developers to build their apps[12]. Disney's IP platform is relatively closed. Only under strict licensing agreements will Disney allow others to make use of their platform IP and Disney exercises strong control over how its brand and cartoon characters are used.

The level of openness may change over time, especially for online platforms[13]. These platforms have a tendency to start as closed, but to move towards openness. The reason for this is that once a platform is in place, the opportunities created by network effects are very compelling. Profiting from them, requires opening up. Opening up enables partnering organizations to create complementary services or products around the platform. Complementors may have immediate value for the platform owner, for example when the platform owner receives part of the revenues a complementor generates via the platform. Even when there is no direct value, there may be indirect value in having complementors, just like an amusement park may not own a hotel nearby, but still benefits from the presence of the hotel because guests now stay overnight and visit the park on two consecutive days rather than only on a daytrip.

NON-PLATFORM VALUE PROPOSITION BASED ECOSYSTEMS

A second group of ecosystems refers to organizations collaborating without centering around a platform but focusing on final customers. The past couple of years have seen the rise of value proposition based ecosystems[14]. In these ecosystems a smaller set of partners enter into an alliance to develop a value proposition for one or more customers and jointly agree about which products and services will be delivered under what conditions. This use of the term has become especially popular in IT. An example is the ecosystem that was set up to provide Honda with virtual desktops for their R&D department. This was a demanding and complex project. It required the collaboration of HP, Nvidia, Dassault Systèmes, VMWare and Ansys. These partners agreed on a joint value proposition, joint innovation and joint sales in order to meet Honda's demand[15]. Clearly, for these ecosystems contracts are customized, not standardized.

Another use of the term ecosystem is tied much more to the knowledge flow between companies. This use of the term is partly a relabeling of the long existing literature on learning in alliances and networks[16]. Terms like 'the Microsoft ecosystem' refer to all partners big or small that somehow contribute to make Microsoft a success, including the sales channels. What has changed over the years is that many of these partnerships used to be quite passive. For example a channel partner was just supposed to sell stuff. In the current world, there is much more interaction, knowledge exchange and thinking about joint value propositions between a central firm and its partners.

A final use of the term ecosystem relates to economic activity in a certain area. For example, Silicon Valley consists of all kinds of organizations large and small, public and private, profit and not-for-profit that together make it a thriving region. This use of the term is similar to the notion of clusters that was introduced by Michael Porter many years ago. The use of the word ecosystem for such regional success stories is only a rebranding of the term cluster. Even though this is an interesting and valid perspective, the direct implications for management of this view are limited. They have more interesting implications for governments[17].

ECOSYSTEM MANAGEMENT

Hence, the term ecosystem refers to a broad variety of approaches. Therefor there is not one overall management approach for ecosystems. Below we sketch four key elements that determine the nature of ecosystem management. *The first* is whether an ecosystem is mainly online or offline. Ecosystems around online platforms provide opportunities for monitoring activities on the platform that offline ecosystems do not. Facebook can measure engagement of partners in a way that Toyota cannot do with its ecosystem partners. Strengthening the Toyota ecosystem requires more face-to-face interaction than strengthening Facebook's ecosystem. For the latter having the right API's and developer conferences may be much more important.

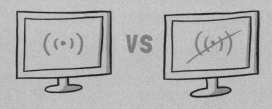

A second element is the presence of a central player. Apple has a highly centralized ecosystem revolving around Apple technology. In open source software on the other hand, the ecosystem is not centralized. Regional ecosystems provide even less opportunity to guide them in a desired direction. Apple will have to consider how it uses its power and influence to shape the ecosystem without destroying it. Its power is a weakness as well as a strength. In regional ecosystems, specialized intermediaries may emerge to act as brokers between

organizations. Venture capitalists, industry associations or governments may play that role and thus help to manage the ecosystem.

The third element determining the type of management that ecosystems require is whether the ecosystem is open to anyone or whether it is closed. In closed ecosystems, entry of partners into the ecosystem may look much like traditional partner selection in alliances. In fact, Toyota's ecosystem is very difficult to get into as suppliers that want to enter have to meet some very high criteria. Appstores have low barriers to entry and therefore need to be managed in a different way with more emphasis on making the conditions attractive to enter the ecosystem and, at least as important, putting mechanisms in place to find and remove undesirable partners.

The final element affecting the type of management is whether IP is open or closed. With closed IP, protection of it and ensuring continuous development of it, are key points of attention for ecosystem managers. With open IP, the challenge is more to avoid the IP becoming diluted or spawning so many different versions that the coherence of the IP gets lost.

Ecosystems that are not based on platforms, have no central player, are closed and have closed IP resemble traditional alliances more than ecosystems that are platform based, have a central player, open access and open IP. In the latter case, different skills may be required than the ones traditional alliance managers have to offer. In the first case, traditional alliance management approaches may still work well.

"In a forest, there is no master tree that plans and dictates change when rain fails to fall or when spring comes early. The whole ecosystem reacts creatively, in the moment".

> Frederic Laloux, Reinventing Organizations

[1] Moore, J. F. (1993). Predators and prey: a new ecology of competition. Harvard Business Review, 71(3), 75-86

[2] Jacobides, M. G., Cennamo, C., & Gawer, A. (2018). Towards a theory of ecosystems. Strategic Management Journal. 39, 2255-2276.

[3] Adner, R., & Kapoor, R. (2010). Value creation in innovation ecosystems: How the structure of technological interdependence affects firm performance in new technology generations. Strategic Management Journal, 31(3), 306-333.

[4] Moore (1993) ibid; Williamson, P. J., & De Meyer, A. (2012). Ecosystem advantage: How to successfully harness the power of partners. California Management Review, 55(1), 24-46.

[5] Iansiti, M., & Levien, R. (2004). The keystone advantage: what the new dynamics of business ecosystems mean for strategy, innovation, and sustainability. Harvard Business Press.

[6] Many definitions of platforms exist. For the background of this definition see Kreijveld, M., Deuten J., & Est, R.V. (2014), De kracht van platformen, Vakmedianet and Thomas, L. D., Autio, E., & Gann, D. M. (2014). Architectural leverage: putting platforms in context. The Academy of Management Perspectives, 28(2), 198-219.

[7] Thomas et al. (2014).

[8] Evans, P.C. & Gawer, A. (2016). The rise of the platform enterprise. The Center for Global Enterprise, www.thecge.net.

[9] Leten, B., Vanhaverbeke, W., Roijakkers, N., Clerix, A., & Van Helleputte, J. (2013). IP models to orchestrate innovation ecosystems: IMEC, a public research institute in nano-electronics. California Management Review, 55(4), 51-64.

[10] Thomas et al. (2014) ibid.

[11] Evans & Gawer (2016); Thomas, L. D. (2014) ibid.

[12] Cusumano, M. A., & Gawer, A. (2002). The elements of platform leadership. MIT Sloan Management Review, 43(3), 51-58; Gawer, A., & Cusumano, M. A. (2002). Platform leadership: How Intel, Microsoft, and Cisco drive industry innovation. Harvard Business School Press.

[13] Van Alstyne, M. W., Parker, G. G., & Choudary, S. P. (2016). Pipelines, platforms, and the new rules of strategy. Harvard Business Review, 94(4), 54-62.

[14] Adner, R. (2017). Ecosystem as structure: An actionable construct for strategy. Journal of Management, 43(1), 39-58.

[15] Hanson, C.B. (2017). Orchestrating partnerships at the speed of light. Strategic Alliance Magazine, Q4, 30-34.

[16] Dyer, J. H. (2000). Collaborative advantage: Winning through extended enterprise supplier networks. Oxford University Press; De Man, A. P. (ed.), (2008). Knowledge management and innovation in networks. Edward Elgar Publishing.

[17] Elfring, T., & De Man, A. P. (1998). Theories of the firm, competitive advantage and government policy. Technology Analysis & Strategic Management, 10(3), 283-294; Porter, M. E. (1990). Competitive advantage of nations: creating and sustaining superior performance. MacMillan Press.

6 VALUE PROPOSITION BASED ECOSYSTEMS

Most companies have company ecosystems consisting of many partnerships (see Excursion 5 for the various ecosystem definitions that exist). These company ecosystems provide another route to agility than multidimensional organizing, Spotify or holacracy. They enable companies to react to changes in demand by bringing together different partners to deliver a new value proposition[1]. This is called a value proposition based ecosystem and is defined as a set of companies that jointly bring a product or service to the market. This chapter analyses them.

The idea in brief
- **Value proposition based ecosystems gather a limited set of firms around one value proposition**
- **This value proposition can be aimed at one or more clients**
- **As the value proposition is likely to change over time, managing the dynamics of these ecosystems is an important skill**

Ecosystems around specific value propositions are set up with an idea about what is valuable for one or more clients. That vision determines which functionalities must exist in the ecosystem. Such value proposition based ecosystems are particularly popular in IT. An example is an ecosystem set up to deliver virtual desktops to Honda[2]. Together, the partners Dassault Systèmes, VMware, NVIDI, ANSYS and HP developed and continually improved their offering.

As it requires more than one partner to realize the value proposition, the division of tasks is based on the partners' joint vision of what is necessary and joint decision-making about the required functionalities (see table 15 for the core elements of ecosystems). Many mechanisms for joint decision-making may exist in multi-partner collaboration, including 'one man one vote', consensus or lead partner decision-making.

The allocation of tasks is the next step and again will be done via joint decision-making. The partner's competences play an important role here. The ecosystem partners will normally be invited to participate based on the fact that they bring something to the table that the other partners do not. Most of the tasks will therefore be divided naturally along these lines. Discussions arise when two or more partners have overlapping competences and hence can both deliver the required competence. A further element to be considered are the rules governing access to the ecosystem. Partners may choose to ask new partners to join the ecosystem to provide further competences, or to provide more of the same competences. The latter can make sense to provide back up for critical competences and thus ensure the ecosystem can always deliver to a client or in the case of rapid growth of the market to ensure this growth can be met. The mechanisms to motivate the partners lie primarily in different profit sharing agreements. The basic models for this are a full profit split (in which all profits generated by the value proposition are put in one pool which is next shared between the partners following a previously agreed mechanism), each partner carrying its own revenues and costs or some performance-related mechanism (e.g. units sold or hours spent or quality delivered)[3]. This usually coincides with target setting on the ecosystem level that brings focus to the efforts of the partners. A final motivation is reputation. In a world of ecosystems, whether a company has a good reputation as a partner or not, is of great importance.

A damaged reputation means the company will not be high on the list of preferred partners to work with. This will lead to fewer invitations to join ecosystems and therefore declining sales.

HOW ARE TASKS DIVIDED?	· PLATFORM OWNER DECIDES INTERNALLY · COMPLEMENTORS DECIDE ON THEIR OWN SERVICES · PLATFORM AND ECOSYSTEM MAY ENGAGE IN COLLABORATIVE DECISION-MAKING
HOW ARE TASKS ALLOCATED TO INDIVIDUALS?	· EITHER THE PLATFORM OWNER DECIDES WHICH COMPLEMENTOR IS ALLOWED TO DO WHAT OR COMPLEMENTORS DECIDE FOR THEMSELVES · PLATFORM OWNER IS ACTIVE IN DENYING ACCESS TO COMPLEMENTORS
HOW ARE REWARDS PROVIDED TO MOTIVATE PEOPLE?	· PLATFORM OWNER: COST SAVING, DATA, REVENUE VIA COMPLEMENTORS, RAPID GROWTH OF THE PLATFORM · COMPLEMENTOR: ACCESS TO CLIENTS, FAST SCALING, LOWER DEVELOPMENT COSTS
HOW IS INFORMATION PROVIDED SO PEOPLE CAN TAKE THE RIGHT DECISIONS?	· ONLINE PLATFORMS PROVIDE INSIGHT IN DATA ON NUMBER OF TRANSACTIONS, INTERACTIONS, COMPLEMENTORS, SITE VISITS, SEARCH TERMS ETC.

Table 15: Core elements of ecosystems

Consequently, the reputation mechanism is one way of ensuring a partner is motivated to contribute to the health of the ecosystem.

Information sharing in ecosystems is done via reporting into governance teams. The extent to which information is shared about sales and costs incurred will differ per ecosystem. In larger ecosystems various cross-company teams may exist that discuss the implications of the information provided and decide on actions to take. Another important feedback mechanism is client feedback. This may show in terms of sales, but in the long run qualitative feedback about client wishes is of much more importance to guide the ecosystem in the development of new, enhanced value propositions.

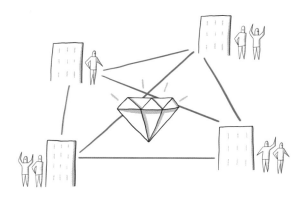

Table 16 shows the information leaflet for using this organizational model. What problems do ecosystems solve? The most important one is that ecosystems help when an individual company is not able to deliver on client demand on its own. This occurs frequently and especially in IT-related industries, where most companies focus on delivering a component of a solution and rarely is one company able to offer a complete solution. By focusing on a limited set of components and simultaneously collaborating in an ecosystem, a company is able to maintain focus, while also delivering complex solutions to clients[4]. A further problem solved is that unexpected changes in the business environment need to be responded to, but that doing so is difficult in long-term stable relationships as occur in companies. Ecosystems make it easier to connect and disconnect partners and thus reconfigure to adapt to market changes. This may ultimately also speed up innovation because combining and recombining the competences of various companies makes it possible to rapidly develop new value propositions.

The price to pay for solving these problems lies in a number of disadvantages that accompany ecosystems. Firms become dependent on other firms for their performance and do not have strong levers of control when their ecosystem partners do not perform. Ecosystems are non-hierarchical: there is no higher power above the partners that can make and enforce decisions. That is why communication intensity in ecosystems

PROBLEMS SOLVED	· INDIVIDUAL COMPANY NOT ABLE TO DELIVER ON CLIENT DEMAND · DILEMMA HOW TO DELIVER INCREASINGLY COMPLEX SOLUTIONS WHILE MAINTAINING CORPORATE FOCUS · RESPONDING TO THE UNEXPECTED · SLOW INNOVATION
DISADVANTAGES	· DEPENDENCE ON PARTNER · LIMITED CONTROL · INTENSITY OF COMMUNICATION
SUITABLE FOR	· CUSTOMERS DEMAND COMPLEX INTEGRATED SOLUTIONS · KNOWLEDGE IS KEY RESOURCE AND IS DISPERSED AMONG DIFFERENT ORGANIZATIONS · CONSIDERABLE UNCERTAINTY EXISTS
NOT SUITABLE FOR	· SIMPLE PRODUCTS OR SERVICES · STABLE MARKETS
KEY INGREDIENTS	· JOINT VALUE PROPOSITION · GOOD VALUE SHARING ARRANGEMENT · COLLABORATIVE BEHAVIOR
RISKS	· INCREASE IN CO-OPETITION · CHANGING PARTNER RELEVANCE · PARTNER EXIT (WHAT IF A PARTNER LEAVES: WHOLE VALUE PROP COLLAPSES) · FREE RIDER BEHAVIOR · BOUNDARY-CROSSING
LEADERSHIP	· MAINTAIN FOCUS · MAINTAIN BALANCE · DECIDE ON ENTRY AND EXIT

Table 16: Information leaflet ecosystems

is high. With various teams collaborating within and across companies, communication is challenging and time consuming.

Ecosystems are especially suitable when customers demand complex, integrated solutions and the knowledge to deliver them is dispersed among different organizations. As one of the strengths of ecosystems is responding to the unexpected, they fit well into environments marked by considerable uncertainty.

The complexity and cost of managing ecosystems makes them less suitable for simple products and services and in stable markets. In such markets, external collaboration in general is not a good option, because stable markets tend to demand efficiency instead of innovation.

A key ingredient for this ecosystem type is of course the presence of a joint value proposition. A joint value proposition serves several purposes. The most important one is that it gives focus to the ecosystem's activities. The value proposition explains why the ecosystem exists and what it aims to deliver. It is the glue that holds the ecosystem together. Next, as the metaphor of the ecosystem suggests, it can only be viable if every individual organism (read: company) can live and contribute to the ecosystem. The arrangement for value sharing that is put in place therefore needs

to ensure two things. First, it needs to deliver a steady stream of cash flow to each partner, so that it can survive financially. Second, the value sharing arrangement needs to provide incentives for each partner to contribute to the ecosystem. Both the pains and the gains need to be shared. Finally, ecosystems also take root in the system of norms and values that support it. Collaborative behavior is re-levant to make them work; a live-and-let-live mindset increases the viability of the eco-system[5]. This includes knowing how to deal with the dynamics of ecosystems. Much may change over time and partners need to adapt to those changes. This ties into the next topic: risks.

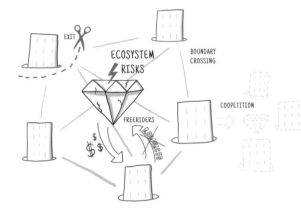

The main set of risks for ecosystems relates to developments over time that may affect the ecosystem. Everything may look great at the start, but because ecosystems operate in a changing environment the relationship between the members of the ecosystem may also change. In many ecosystems there will be an element of co-opetition: partners cooperate in the ecosystem, but they may compete with those very same partners in another ecosystem. When markets change, it is very well possible that competition in one area becomes so fierce that it may hurt the collaboration in another area. Another form of such dynamics lies in partner relevance. Over time one partner may become more or less important in an ecosystem because the client values that partner's contribution more. This can put tension on the relationships between the companies. A final form of dynamics lies in partners exiting. A partner may leave an ecosystem for all kinds of reasons. If that partner delivers a crucial element that sustains the value proposition, the ecosystem will collapse.

Other risks in ecosystems include free-rider behavior and the difficulty of boundary-crossing. Free-rider behavior occurs when one of the partners picks the fruits of ecosystem membership but does not contribute to the ecosystem in the same measure. Setting the right incentives is a way of dealing with this and the reputation effect also mitigates free-rider behavior. But in settings with multiple partners free-rider behavior is not always easy to spot and may go unnoticed for an extended period of time. Boundary-crossing refers to the risk that the members of the

ecosystem are not able to share their knowledge across the boundaries of their organization. This may be due to different levels of knowledges or different types of knowledge bases, that make it hard to transfer the knowledge to a partner organization. This impedes the partners from realizing the potential value of the ecosystem.

For the leadership of companies in an ecosystem the key task is to maintain focus and balance. With multiple companies in the ecosystem, the chance is high that focus is lost because all partners emphasize different elements of the value proposition. Leadership therefore needs to continue to stress the elements that matter for the coherence of the ecosystem. Maintaining balance is another challenge. What is the right balance between the individual interest and the ecosystem interest? It is naïve to think the ecosystem interest always comes first to the detriment of the company interest. It is equally naïve to think the opposite. This balance cannot be struck by employees working in the ecosystem, because the balance between self- and ecosystem-interest depends on many different factors, many of which are outside the scope of the individual employee.

For similar reasons, whether to engage in an ecosystem or not is a leadership decision. Such a decision depends on the broader vision of how a company sees the market developing, the competitive implications and the opportunity costs (could the resources invested have been more productive in another context?).

"It's difficult for any single company to develop all applications and services."

> Ma Huateng, WeChat

[1] Adner, R. (2017). Ecosystem as structure: An actionable construct for strategy. Journal of Management, 43(1), 39-58.

[2] Hanson, C.B., (2017). Orchestrating partnerships at the speed of light. Strategic Alliance Magazine, Q3, 30-34.

[3] De Man, A. P. (2013). Alliances: An executive guide to designing successful strategic partnerships. John Wiley & Sons.

[4] The discussion of the 'problems solved' and 'suitable for' is almost entirely based on Williamson, P. J., & De Meyer, A. (2012). Ecosystem advantage: How to successfully harness the power of partners. California Management Review, 55(1), 24-46.

[5] De Man, A. P., & Luvison, D. (2014). Sense-making's role in creating alliance supportive organizational cultures. Management Decision, 52(2), 259-277

CASE STUDY:
ECOSYSTEM ORCHESTRATION AT INTERNATIONAL SOS

An interview with Sally Wang, Group Vice President Global Strategic Alliances and Partnerships, International SOS

Can you explain what role ecosystems play for International SOS?

At International SOS we help organizations keep their employees safe and healthy. Many organizations send their people abroad for short or long periods of time. While travelling or staying in a country, their employees can face a variety of health, safety & security risks. We offer integrated services and technology solutions to manage those risks. We have been doing this since 1985 when Arnaud Vaissié and Dr. Pascal Rey-Herme founded our organization in Asia to ensure quality health care for organizations with a mobile workforce. Over time that has evolved into an organization with 11,000 colleagues delivering assistance to our clients.

To achieve our goal we employ ecosystems, alliances and partnerships in a mix that enables International SOS to react to a wide range of different situations in an agile way. There is an overall company ecosystem with different types of partnerships. For individual clients or market segments, we select partners from that overall company ecosystems to deliver specific value propositions.

Organizations with many employees abroad need to know their employees are safe and healthy. Safety and health are broad concepts, so to deliver on that we have partnerships ranging from providers to strategic alliances, such as hospitals, airlines, travel agencies, visa agencies, doctors, air ambulances, insurance companies, security companies, technology companies, and many more organizations. This ecosystem ensures that when an individual is in need we can respond to that in the right way at any time anywhere on earth. Our company ecosystem has grown organically over the years. We would like to build customer-obsessed solutions that delight our clients and by doing so maintain our position as market leader.

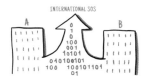

Data: the integration of travel and location data to enable a truly holistic approach to risk management. Example: our partnership with shared economy companies like UBER and Airbnb enables the integration of travel and hotel bookings with traveller tracking tools and analysis.

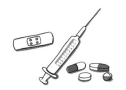

Technology: delivery of superior risk management experiences with measurable results. Example: our partnership with Everbridge provides a seamless multi-modal crisis communication platform.

Capabilities: services that support the evolution of employee care requirements. Example: in partnership with WPO, we are addressing the increasing need for mental health services for a globally mobile workforce.

Thought-leadership: working with experts in their respective fields to address the necessary research and study of how we can improve global employee Duty of Care. Example: with KPMG, we are researching how the future of global mobility will look – starting with the synergy that can be sought from our combined services in this area.

Collaboration: International SOS is the preferred Duty of Care partner to a number of best-in-class mobility service companies. We can collaborate with organizations to develop a truly integrated service offering that helps their clients to meet their Duty of Care obligations, putting the protection of people at the heart of your offering. Example: International SOS is the preferred 'Safety & Security' provider to CWT, a world-leading travel management provider.

Box 3: Partnership types of International SOS

What does the company ecosystem look like?

We have many different types of relationships. Some are transactional and sometimes we acquire companies. Within our ecosystem, we distinguish five types of partnerships we have with companies (see Box 3).

Some partners fulfill only one of those roles, but some tick three or even all of these boxes. These latter partnerships are complex and require more extensive governance. This may include putting in place executive sponsorship, a steering committee, and key performance indicators to align goals and determine progress. Most of my work lies in this area.

Within your overall company ecosystem, do you also form value proposition based ecosystems with a smaller number of partners?

We very often pull multiple partners together from our overall company ecosystem. We regularly go to a potential client with two or three of our partners. Based on our estimate

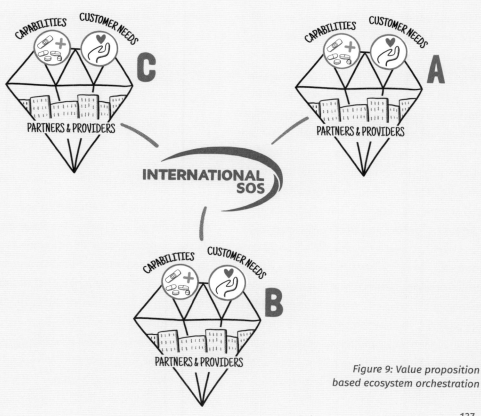

Figure 9: Value proposition based ecosystem orchestration

of what the client is looking for, we may realize that bringing in our partners helps us to serve the client need better. We call this 'value proposition based ecosystem integration' (see figure 9): based on a customer's needs we define the capabilities required to deliver a solution. Based on that we select partners and providers that help us deliver a solution that fulfills the customer's need.

This happens often in the area of data integration. Let me give an example. We need robust travel data to mitigate risks. Clients may have multiple travel agencies via which their employees travel. This does not make it easy to know where their employees are. International SOS collaborates with various travel agencies to integrate their data so we can locate employees. Our knowledge of the employees' location enables us to trigger travel risks mitigation protocols, such as sending a notification to individuals when an incident has occurred like an attack or natural disaster. This helps the client to know whether their employees are safe. Location data are important for that and that is why work with over twenty travel agencies. We also add data from partners in the sharing economy world, other location partners, and our own app to help us locate people. We orchestrate multiple partners to meet that specific client need. Such value proposition based ecosystems may come in different legal forms. Sometimes clients contract each partner individually.

At other times one partner acts as the lead partner and contracts the others to deliver their services. The best option really depends on the situation. In general we have a direct distribution model and we hold the primary contract. In most cases the financial side of such ecosystems is relatively straightforward. Each partner carries their own revenues and costs. Sometimes there are fixed costs to maintain the integration and we usually share those on a 50/50 basis.

With so many partners in the ecosystem, you run the risk of conflict between partners or between the partner and you. How do you deal with that?

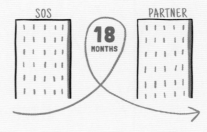

The most important thing is to prevent conflicts from arising in the first place. Before we go to market with a partner we have a very good idea about which partner is going to contract what. We agree on that upfront. This must also be clear to the client. We also define rules of engagement. That includes answers to a number of key questions: Who leads? Who supports? Who invoices the client? Who contracts? What are the incentives for sales on both sides? In the vast majority of cases this is sufficient for our sales people to figure out how to work with a partner.

But we are in a dynamic environment. Over time partners may develop services or solutions that come close to what we offer. And vice versa: we sometimes encroach upon areas where a partner is active. Even then it may be possible to work alongside each other because the solutions are still different, and a sales person can clarify to a client when to use which solution. To decide which solution to offer, we focus on the client perspective. What delivers most value for the client? Sometimes that is our solution, sometimes it is a partner's solution. You win some, you lose some. If you cannot deal with that, it becomes difficult to work in an ecosystem environment.

Finally, a more strategic way of looking at conflict is what I call the 'organic refresh'. We do not change partners often. Most of our partners have been with us for three years or more. Somewhere around 18 months into the partnership it often becomes necessary to adjust the relationship or engagement to changed circumstances. We next sit down with them and review our collaboration. Such a refresh brings new clarity, new energy and mitigates the risk of conflict.

Going to a client with partners raises the question who is going to get which share of the pie. Sales people may not like having to share revenue with partners. Do you have that problem at International SOS?

We don't. We have thought carefully about what drives the behavior of sales people and we recognized the risk you mention. Our solution is to reward sales staff for introducing partners to our clients. So, the incentives for our sales people are aligned with our partner model. We find this works very well. We have a high retention rate with our customers, and they trust our advice.

Introducing a partner that can provide superior service goes a long way with a customer. We really believe that the health of our ecosystem is vital to our business. If we were only to optimize sales in the short run, that would undermine the health of the ecosystem or ignore customer's needs. If, on the other hand, our partners are happy and healthy, we can deliver on our promise to look after the health and safety of our clients. The arrangement must be mutually beneficial.

What do you think are important trends for the future?

Our company is the leader in the industry, we continue to innovative. Digitalization is breaking down barriers, and we will become more open, will add more capabilities to our offering. Within that company ecosystem, we will form individual alliances and value proposition based ecosystems to address specific client needs. The focus on offering the right value to the client is what drives our partnerships.

The growth of the ecosystem also affects the internal organization. To manage all the partners, many people in our organization need the skills to interact with the partnerships we have. Companies like International SOS that work with ecosystems need to make sure that knowledge about collaboration is present across the organization. In traditional alliance management, collaborative knowledge is usually centralized in one department. This can't scale and does not work in ecosystems. So we need to build up a decentralized collaborative capability by coaching and influencing our colleagues on how to work with partners.

"The world has become so vibrant and complex that expertise needs to be locally based, and this is really what I'm pushing for: our company to be more distributed around the world"

> Arnaud Vaissie, International SOS

EXCURSION :
FOURTH GENERATION ALLIANCES

One of the major trends in organizing is that organizations have started to organize across organizations. Ecosystems are only the latest incarnation of a trend that started some decades ago with the rise of strategic alliances. Somewhere in the early 1980s a growth in the number of alliances occurred, accelerating in the second half of the 1990s[1]. The wave of alliances started in the IT and biopharma sector and spread to all industries. In the more than twenty years since alliances started to become popular they have undergone various evolutions. Roughly four generations can be distinguished in the development of alliances[2] (see table 17).

1ST	2ND	3RD	4TH ?
· TILL 1990	· FROM 1990	· 2010-	· 2015-
· JOINT VENTURES; MINORITY HOLDINGS	· CONTRACTUAL BILATERAL, CLOSED	· MULTI-PARTNER, ECOSYSTEM, OPEN	· PLATFORM BASED ECOSYSTEMS
· SCALE, INTERNATIONALIZATION	· INNOVATION, FLEXIBILITY, BUS DEV, SALES	· CROSS-SECTOR INNOVATION, BHAG	· COMBINATORIAL INNOVATION, DATA DRIVEN
· SEPARATE BUSINESS	· OFTEN IN ONE SILO	· INPUT FROM MORE SILOS	· PLATFORM REPLACES SILOS
· NAM	· SENSEO · AF/KL-DELTA	· FUTURE STORE INITIATIVE · TRANSCELERATE · SMART CITIES	· APPLE, GOOGLE · BLUEMIX (IBM) · HUE

Table 17: Four generations of alliances

The idea in brief
- **Organizing across boundaries is a long-term trend**
- **The number of alliances and joint ventures has grown almost continuously over the past decades**
- **Four generations of alliances (joint ventures, closed bilateral alliances, open multilateral alliances and platform based partnerships) can be distinguished**
- **These generations do not replace each other, but co-exist**

The **first generation** has a long tradition and lasted till roughly the 1990s. In this generation alliances were relatively static. Most of them were joint ventures set up by two or more parent companies. Their aim was to create economies of scale, for example by jointly exploiting a large chemical plant, or they aimed at gaining access to foreign markets, by partnering with a local company. Joint ventures can be run as relatively independent from the parents. An example of such a joint venture is NAM, co-owned by Royal Dutch Shell and ExxonMobil, which exploits one of the largest gas fields in the world. Joint ventures have not disappeared and continue to be important to realize company strategy. About 2,500 of them are set up each year[3]. The real growth however has been in the number of second generation alliances.

The **second generation** of alliances is characterized by contractual collaboration, without setting up a separate joint venture. This form became dominant in the 1990s. The goals of these alliances started to shift towards innovation and obtaining more flexibility in the face of a rapidly changing business environment. These alliances also tended to focus on sales and business development objectives[4]. Contractual alliances are easier to adapt than the fixed structures of joint ventures and hence are more suitable to deal with change. In most cases, these alliances are bilateral and closed in the sense that other parties could not join the collaboration. They were often run from within a business unit in an organization. Senseo, a collaboration between Philips and coffee company Douwe Egberts is an example of this alliance generation. Similarly the Air France/KLM collaboration with Delta Airlines falls into this category.

"Great industries are never made from single companies. There is room in space for a lot of winners."

> Jeff Bezos, Amazon

Over the first decade of the 21st century a **third generation** of alliances emerged. These are multipartner alliances, sometimes incorporating a dozen or more partners with different industry backgrounds. They often have an open nature: other organizations can enter the collaboration. Their focus is on innovation across sectors that is often required to obtain Big Hairy Audacious Goals (BHAGs) or to realize innovative value propositions. Smart cities projects for example may require building contractors, IT companies, logistics experts and local governments to collaborate to solve congestion or safety issues in cities. The Transcelerate alliance set up by pharma companies to jointly do research into improving their innovation processes is another example. So is the Future Store Initiative that brought some fifty partners together to create the supermarket of the future. The alliances also have a 'launch first' approach: rather than detailing all the projects the alliance will carry out in advance, companies agree on the problem to be solved and next see over time which specific projects are going to be carried out under the alliance umbrella. The impact of these alliances inside the individual partners also tends to be bigger than in the previous alliance generations because they usually require input from several of the silos inside a company. That increases the internal coordination problem for each partner.

The **fourth generation** of alliances can be seen around platforms and their associated ecosystems. Although platforms have been around for quite some time, the breakthrough to a broader group of organizations is more recent. There is more emphasis around these platforms on combinatorial innovation, that is innovation that comes into existence by combining elements or modules from partners around the ecosystem. Often opportunities are spotted by analyzing data the platforms gather off activity they host. An interesting feature of platform organizations is that the silo problem that plagued earlier alliance generations disappears, because the platform is central to the organization, which simplifies not only the external but also the internal collaboration. The examples include of course the well-known names of Google, Apple, IBM's Bluemix, but in the lighting business Philips' Hue platform shows that fourth generation collaboration is not limited to the usual suspects.

Because collaboration in the fourth generation revolves around online platforms, it is quite different from what happened in the previous generations. In previous generations companies followed extensive partner selection processes before entering an alliance. Many partners in the online platform world simply sign up or a put an app in the app store. Traditional alliances tend to have elaborate governance structures, whereas around online platforms there are no custom made contracts and governance meetings. In the fourth generation, standardized terms and conditions and smart contracts (computer protocols that manage a contract digitally) govern the relationship between the platform owner and the partners. Monitoring of the relationship is also done online, replacing human interaction.

The fourth generation model is particularly relevant around platforms based on blockchain-technology. Organizations like Ethereum are 'zero-trust-platforms' that enable people to engage in transactions via smart contracts and without any personal contact or use of a trusted third party like a bank. These developments are still in their infancy but clearly new ways of collaboration between organizations that go beyond traditional alliances, are emerging.

The human factor in collaboration will diminish as a consequence and many insights from traditional alliance management may lose their validity. However, traditional approaches will remain valid. First of all because the fourth generation of alliances will not replace the previous generations. The previous generations still have their use, because the problems they solve continue to exist. The fourth generation is more an addition to all the mechanisms for collaboration that exist than a substitute for them. Second, so far smart contracts are able to execute repetitive and relatively simple tasks. Online collaboration also facilitates combinatorial innovation in as far as it requires the combination of different standardized modules. When innovation requires more than that, human interaction is still necessary. Much innovation relies on a deeper exchange of knowledge, experimentation and forms of creativity that so far have not been automated.

The fourth generation may even strengthen the previous generation in that the technology that it is based upon may help to lower the high transaction costs more traditional alliances often have. If many of the operational transactions that lie at the basis of traditional alliances can be automated via platforms and smart contracts, this may open up new opportunities, especially for generation 2 and 3.

For these two generations, forming the vision of an alliance and designing the contract still require human interaction, but further implementation may be done online.

"Alliances are difficult precisely because there is no 'boss' in them. They are partnership. And partners are equals, by definition. One cannot give orders to a partner. Hence the secret of a successful alliance is to manage it as a customer relationship."

> Peter Drucker
  The Effective Executive

[1] Hagedoorn, J. (2002). Inter-firm R&D partnerships: an overview of major trends and patterns since 1960. Research Policy, 31(4), 477-492.
[2] The first three phases were defined in De Man, A. P. (2013). Alliances: An executive guide to designing successful strategic partnerships. John Wiley & Sons.
[3] Saada, B. & Gomes-Casseres. B. (2018). Why your next deal may be a partnership. Strategy+Business, 3 December, https://www.strategy-business.com/article/Why-Your-Next-Deal-May-Be-a-Partnership?gko=5b7fd.
[4] De Man, A. P., Duysters, G., Luvison, D., & Krijnen, A. (2012). The fourth state of alliance management study. Association of Strategic Alliance Professionals.

7 OPEN SOURCE ORGANIZATIONS

The open source organization is perhaps the least and at the same time the most traditional of all organizational forms. It is the least traditional because it is completely online. It is the most traditional in that it is an organization of volunteers and voluntary organizations, which may very well be the oldest form of organizing we have. Open source organization is a form of organization in which individuals collaborate on a voluntary basis to develop a product or service that is freely available for all. There is no formal contract between the individuals making up the organization or between the individuals and the organization, but it does have rules to which all must conform. Some of the rules are informal, others are written down in a manual.

The idea in brief

- Open source organizations are organizations in which volunteers develop a resource for the whole world to use
- Their main governance mechanisms are benevolent dictatorship, consensus based democracy and information transparency
- Their strength lies in the high motivation of the volunteers to contribute; their weakness in the lack of formal control mechanisms to ensure alignment
- 'Innersourcing' is the application of open source thinking inside organizations

Open source organizations first emerged to develop open source software in an online environment, where people collaborated to create a joint source code and worked on improvement of the source code or its derivatives. The best known examples are of course Java, Linux and Android, but there are many other examples. Other open source organizations produce services for a broad audience, like the online encyclopedia Wikipedia. The original impetus for open source often was a combination of a desire to develop software that was not created by commercial organizations and by a more idealistic and even hippy-like renunciation of the idea of intellectual property (in this view, ideas should not be owned)[1].

Since its emergence in the open source software movement, the concept of open source has also been applied outside the online world. Most popular attention has gone to the Free Beer movement, that made a recipe for beer brewing. Anyone can use this recipe as a basis for brewing their own beer. To give open source activity a legal foundation, lawyers developed Creative Commons licenses which enable creators to maintain some ownership about aspects of their work they want to control (their 'copyleft' instead of copyright) while simultaneously allowing anyone to build on the ideas in a way they see fit. A Creative Commons license usually requires such users to contribute their ideas to the commons as well.

With these developments and the increasing legal backing behind it, open source ideas have spread far beyond their initial creators and have made a considerable impact. Open source software is widely used by many organizations and the structure of the organizations behind it is therefore worth studying. Table 18 summarizes the key ideas behind open source organizations[2].

Even though open source organizations rely on self-organization this does not imply an absence of management. The division of tasks is usually done by leadership, at least concerning high level tasks. This may be the person who founded the organization or an informal leader who emerged over time. In a minority of cases, like Wikipedia, such task division is not done by a leader but purely left to the self-organizing capabilities of the organization. Around specifically challenging issues, a consensus based democracy may work. In a consensus based democracy, everybody tries hard to reach consensus and only when that fails is the issue put to a vote.

The allocation of tasks to specific individuals may also be done by informal leaders, but it is more common that people nominate themselves to execute a certain task. In open source organizations there may also be managers with a specific task like being responsible for documentation or managing the frequently asked questions list. Such managers may assign certain tasks to certain individuals. The term 'assign' is used loosely here. Because the organization consists of volunteers, managers cannot dictate others what to do. Rather they make a request to someone. Also they do not have the monopoly on the area they were assigned. Their role is more that of coordinator.

As open source organizations are voluntary and not-for-profit, rewards for people are not of a monetary nature. Most participants in an open source organization are intrinsically motivated to work on it, because they enjoy it or strongly believe in its cause. Visibility, recognition and status can also be a benefit for people participating in an open source project. These may lead to an individual being asked to do more interesting work for the organization. In other instances participation in an open source project may increase somebody's market value for employers. The knowledge, skills and network gained through participation may be valuable for commercially operating organizations. A final source of rewards lies in the result of the project. When better software, products or services are available, the participant in the open source organization will benefit from those as well. Everybody adding to Wikipedia also benefits from the existence of Wikipedia when they want to look something up in the encyclopedia.

The flipside of motivation is how to discourage people from contributing. Here open source organizations face a problem: as people are volunteers they cannot be fired, demoted or transferred to another department. In addition, because the organization depends on volunteers, utmost care must be taken in how people are treated to avoid scaring away potential participants. The 'firing' of people therefore consists of gathering evidence and politely asking them to leave[3].

HOW ARE TASKS DIVIDED?	· INFORMAL LEADER (OR LEADERSHIP TEAM) · SELF-ORGANIZATION AND CONSENSUS BASED DEMOCRACY
HOW ARE TASKS ALLOCATED TO INDIVIDUALS?	· SELF-NOMINATION · INFORMAL LEADER · MANAGERS
HOW ARE REWARDS PROVIDED TO MOTIVATE PEOPLE?	· INTRINSIC MOTIVATION · VISIBILITY, RECOGNITION, STATUS · INCREASE MARKET VALUE FOR EMPLOYERS · ACCESS TO BETTER SOFTWARE, PRODUCTS, SERVICES · RISK OF BEING ASKED TO LEAVE
HOW IS INFORMATION PROVIDED SO PEOPLE CAN TAKE THE RIGHT DECISIONS?	· ONLINE VISIBILITY OF TASKS TO BE DONE · RADICAL OPENNESS IN COMMUNICATION · SUPPORTING DOCUMENTS

Table 18: Core elements of the open source organizations

The key to making open source organizations work lies in information sharing. The first element of information sharing is creating visibility about the tasks that need to be done. As self-nomination for tasks is the main mechanism for task allocation, it needs to be easy to see which tasks await completion. Online environments are very helpful in this. The second element is that communication needs to be radically open, meaning that all communication can be seen by all. This enables people to understand why certain decisions were taken and avoids any suspicions that may arise that an inner crowd is determining everything that happens. A concrete example may be that debates on a wiki about an issue are visible to all and get summarized regularly by someone to clarify the different positions. Open source is also supported by explicit rules, manuals and/or governance documents that lay out the way of working of the organization.

The organizational form of open source solves a number of problems, but creates a few new ones (see table 19). One problem solved compared to other organizations is that the extent of customization traditional organizations can deliver is often limited. Open source organizations offer the opportunity for anyone to use the source it created and build onto it whatever they like, so that a fully customized solution is created. Next, the problem how to motivate people is much smaller in an open source organization than in a traditional organization because people sign up voluntarily. There is no need for a person or a system to be put in place to extrinsically motivate employees. The intrinsic motivation also simplifies knowledge exchange as it makes people want to help each other. The role of IT systems in capturing the knowledge is an important enabler to ensure an optimal use of knowledge.

"Huge open source organizations like Red Hat manage the collaboration of hundreds of people who don't know one another and spent no time hanging around the water cooler"

> Margaret Heffernan, Five Business

In the description above of open source organizations, a few disadvantages of this way of working become apparent. It is hard to get rid of non-performers because there are no formal disciplinary measures that can be taken against someone who distracts people from work or slows down the decision-making

PROBLEMS SOLVED	· LIMITED CUSTOMIZATION · LACK OF MOTIVATION · LACK OF KNOWLEDGE EXCHANGE
DISADVANTAGES	· GETTING RID OF NON-PERFORMERS · LACK OF OWNERSHIP · NOBODY IS FORMALLY RESPONSIBLE · BORING TASKS REMAIN UNDONE
SUITABLE FOR	· COMMON SOURCE OF WHICH OTHERS CAN LEVERAGE AND WHICH CAN BE IMPROVED · HIGH INTEREST FOR A SUFFICIENTLY LARGE GROUP
NOT SUITABLE FOR	· PRODUCTS/SERVICES WHERE ONE PERSON'S MISTAKE IS FATAL · CONFIDENTIAL AFFAIRS · WORK THAT REQUIRES SIMULTANEOUS WORK OF A GROUP
KEY INGREDIENTS	· STRONG SHARED VISION · INFORMATION SHARING VIA SUPPORTING INFRASTRUCTURE · SENSE OF COMMUNITY
RISKS	· CHURN · LACK OF SELF-CLEANING CAPABILITY · SPLITS · INTERNAL POLITICS
LEADERSHIP	· BENEVOLENT DICTATOR · FACILITATING

Table 19: Information leaflet open source organizations

process by holding on to untenable positions. Despite the high level of intrinsic motivation, open source organizations can suffer from a lack of ownership. People may feel responsible for their part of the job but may identify less with the organization as a whole, particularly when they work on it only part-time. The fact that everybody is responsible may mean nobody is responsible. Finally as people sign up for tasks based on their own interest the more boring and mundane tasks may remain undone. People need to be alert that they sometimes have to do the dirty work and call others to account on this as well.

Open source organizations require a common source that can be improved by others or leveraged by others to build upon. If such a source is not present, the open source organization is not a suitable organizational form. The source also needs to arouse high interest among a sufficiently large group of people willing to join the network. There is a network effect to open source organizations similar to platform organizations: the more people join, the more interesting the organization becomes to others because the common source and its derivatives improve in quality.

"Copyleft instead of copyright"

It is not a suitable organizational form for products or services that can be irreparably destroyed by one person's mistake. It must always be easy to undo decisions and to repair changes made in the source or its derivative products and services. Open source organizations are also less suitable when part of or the entire source needs to be confidential. Here lies an important difference with many platform organizations. In the latter the platform is a source of income that needs to be protected. Alternatively, platforms may gather sensitive information, for example user information that cannot be shared. In those cases a more closed way of working is required.

Open source is also less logical in situations where groups need to work on issues simultaneously rather than consecutively. Even though technically it could be possible to work on issues with a larger group at the same time, the voluntary nature of many contributions implies that not everybody will be available at the same time. It works better for asynchronous collaboration.

The key ingredients to make this organizational form work include the presence of a strong shared vision that provides direction to all working for it. A clear view of why the organization exists is one way of providing the glue to make it work. A supporting infrastructure for information sharing is another element that keeps the organization together. Standardized tools have been developed over the years to support this. The relevance of simple and transparent communication online will be evident.

Open source organizations do not have onboarding processes: people have to find out themselves how the organization works and why it is organized the way it is. By capturing knowledge in IT systems, providing manuals and showing discussion threads online, newbies are helped to find their way. These explicit mechanisms are not enough though. Any organizational form also requires softer and implicit mechanisms to make it work. In this case, a strong sense of community is required to deal with many of the risks and disadvantages of open source organizations.

If people feel part of a community this greatly eases communication, increases their willingness to do chores and provides a foundation for stability.

As is so often the case, the major benefit of this organizational form is also its major risk: its voluntary nature. The benefit of working with volunteers is that it gives access to a highly motivated, free work force. The downside is that this workforce can leave the organization at any time without giving any notice.

The risk of a high level of churn in the membership is high and this may imply that there is no accrual of organizational memory and skills. Because of the voluntary nature of the organization, it may also lack the self-cleaning capability to rid itself of

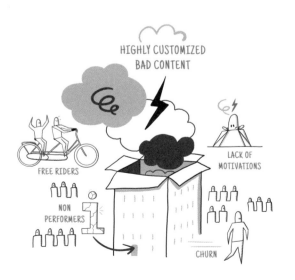

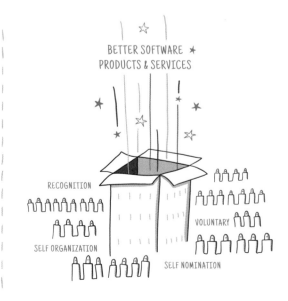

underperformers and free-riders. And if a group of people decides to walk off and start a competing organization or create a sub-branch of the source and work on that, there is no formal way to prevent this. These risks are mitigated however by the fact that the volunteers are not all individuals working for themselves.

IBM for example is a leading company in open source and employs many employees who work on it. Voluntary open source organizations therefore can tap into the resources of well-established companies and that provides them with some stability. A final risk lies in internal politics. In-crowds may emerge that go unchecked by a hierarchical manager or transparent procedures. Such in-crowds may overrule the less powerful contributors to the organization without being held to account.

Leaders in open source organizations have primarily a facilitating task in helping others to solve problems or support them in their decision-making. Their role is often described as that of a benevolent dictator. Only when the organization is not able to come to a consensus, will the leader make the decision. A benevolent dictator can be given this position based on his expertise and his reputation as a person who is reticent with the exercise of power. The benevolent dictator model is often used in the early phases of development of an open source organization. Over time the model may transform into the consensus based democracy model.

To better understand open source it is valuable to compare it to agile and scrum. There are a few differences[4]:

- Agile is developed for teams that meet face to face. It assumes people are based at the same location. Open source assumes teams are dispersed and can work anywhere around the globe.
- This also explains why Agile focuses less on getting good documentation for the software: there is always somebody around to answer your questions. As open source works in dispersed teams, it requires very good documentation.
- Agile and scrum are less scalable but deliver results fast; open source is highly scalable because of its online way of working, but it delivers results more slowly.
- Agile and scrum focus on the internal organization whereas open source is interorganizational.
- Agile has a strong focus on the end user; end user involvement in open source is limited.

INNERSOURCING
There is no reason why the principles of open source organizations cannot be applied in organizations internally and indeed a number of companies have begun to experiment with

what is known as 'InnerSourcing'[5]. IBM claims to have some successes with this approach and Paypal has made very significant steps in this area even founding an organization dedicated to it: InnerSourceCommons.org[6]. It is not a strange idea to use open source internally, because in many organizations projects exist that may not be on the official radar but that employees find important to work on anyway.

The problem with such projects is that in a traditional organization they will have difficulty in flourishing because no formal resources are assigned to them. By freeing up such resources an innersourcing approach may work. The benefit of using open source principles inside organizations is that more teams across corporate silos can collaborate to develop a source. So far the application of this idea is a recent phenomenon and it seems to be limited to the software industry. It will be interesting though to see how this develops and especially if it can help to alleviate one of the problems an increasing number of companies face: how to ensure collaboration between globally dispersed teams?

"Open source shows us that world-class software, like Linux and Mozilla can be created with neither the bureaucratic structure of the firm nor the incentives of the marketplace as we know them"

> Howard Rheingold, Way-New Collaboration

---

[1] If the principles behind open source are still not clear to you, see this wonderful Lego-based explanation: https://www.youtube.com/watch?v=a8fHgx9mE5U. Another great source is opensource.org.

[2] Table 18 is largely based on Puranam, P., Alexy, O., & Reitzig, M. (2014). What's "new" about new forms of organizing?. Academy of Management Review, 39(2), 162-180 and on Fogel, K. (2018) Producing Open Source Software, http://producingoss.com/en/index.html , version 2.3106. Puranam et al. offer a more fine-grained discussion of different ways open source organizations operate as there is considerable variety between them. Fogel's insightful online book is based on his experience in the Subversion project. Particularly helpful for the discussion here were chapters 4 and 8. Another canonical text is Raymond, E.S. (2000). The cathedral and the bazaar, http://www.unterstein.net/su/docs/CathBaz.pdf.

[3] Fogel (2018) ibid. Especially see chapter 6 about handling 'difficult people'.

[4] Ohram, A. (2015), Getting started with InnerSource. O'Reilly Media.

[5] Ohram, A. (2015), Getting started with InnerSource. O'Reilly Media.

[6] http://www.eweek.com/servers/ibm-adopts-open-development-internally; http://paypal.github.io/InnerSourceCommons/

CASE STUDY:
WIKIPEDIA AND THE GOVERNANCE OF AN OPEN SOURCE ORGANIZATION[1]

Wikipedia is a multilingual, web-based, free-content encyclopedia project, based on a model of openly editable content, created and edited by volunteers all over the world. Since its creation in 2001, Wikipedia has grown rapidly into one of the largest reference websites, attracting over 300 million unique visitors monthly. There are approximately 100,000 active contributors working on more than 48,000,000 articles and pages in 302 languages.

The non-profit Wikimedia Foundation provides the essential infrastructure for free content based on open source principles. Wikimedia refers to Wikipedia as one of their 'free-content-projects' which is part of the Wikimedia family including Wikibooks, Wikiversity, Wikinews, Wikidata and many others.

SHORT HISTORY OF THE WIKIPEDIA PROJECT

Wikipedia is a spin-off from Nupedia, a project to produce a free encyclopedia, started by the online media company Bomis in the 1990s. Nupedia had an elaborate system of peer review and required highly qualified contributors, but the writing of articles was slow. During 2000, Jimmy Wales (founder of Nupedia and co-founder of Bomis), and Larry Sanger discussed alternatives on how to make Nupedia more open for the public to accelerate the development of the encyclo-pedia. As a result, in 2001 Nupedia introduced the concept of a 'wiki', allowing members of the public to edit and contribute material. In 2003, Nupedia changed to the present wikipedia.org. The not-for-profit Wikimedia Foundation launched as Wikipedia's new parent organization with the '.org' top-level domain denoting its non-commercial nature.

THE CONCEPT OF A 'WIKI'

A 'wiki' is a website on which users collaboratively modify content and structure directly. A single page in a wiki website is referred to as a 'wiki page', while the entire collection of pages, which are usually interconnected by hyperlinks is the wiki. A wiki is run using a 'wiki engine'. A defining characteristic of a wiki engine is the ease with which wiki pages are created and updated. Generally, there is no review by a moderator or gatekeeper before wiki modifications are accepted.

Wikis are open to alteration by the general public without requiring registration of user accounts, except in limited cases where editing is restricted to prevent disruption or vandalism. Edits can be made in real-time and appear almost instantly online. Wikis have little inherent structure, allowing structure to emerge according to the needs of the users. WikiWikiWeb was the first ever wiki, developed by programmer Ward Cunningham in Portland, Oregon, in 1994. The WikiWikiWeb was a website to discuss software design patterns between developers. Cunningham's idea was to make WikiWikiWeb's pages quickly editable by its users. WikiWiki is a reduplication of wiki, a Hawaiian language word for quick. Cunningham named it WikiWiki from his experience at Honolulu International Airport where a counter employee told him to take the WikiWiki shuttle bus that runs between the airport's terminals.

THE PURPOSE OF WIKIPEDIA

Wikipedia is a collection of wikis, each one having a specific language. The purpose of Wikipedia is to create a web-based, free content encyclopedia of all branches of knowledge, in an atmosphere of mutual respect and cooperation. The goal of a wiki article on Wikipedia is to create a comprehensive and neutrally written summary of existing mainstream knowledge about a topic. The articles on Wikipedia are written collaboratively by volunteers.

WIKIPEDIANS

Editors or contributors, often referred to as Wikipedians, are the people that form the community of volunteers that write and edit the pages of Wikipedia. Some Wikipedians use their real life names as user names, to identify themselves on Wikipedia, whereas others do not reveal personal information. All Wikipedians are supposed to be equal in a discussion about content and regarding any project related matters. Long-standing or awarded Wikipedians have no extra say. All Wikipedians can participate in all discussions on equal terms. There are over 80 million registered Wikipedians across all language editions of Wikipedia. As of April 2019, more than 300,000 Wikipedians have performed an edit in the last 30 days (active users). About half of the active users spend at least one hour a day editing and a fifth spend more than three hours a day.

TERMINAL 1

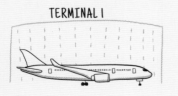

WIKI WIKI SHUTTLE

TERMINAL 2

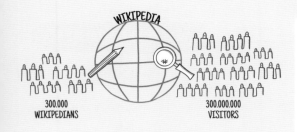

WIKIPEDIA

300.000
WIKIPEDIANS

300.000.000
VISITORS

PRINCIPLES, POLICIES AND GUIDELINES

Wikipedians are encouraged to be bold in editing in a fair and accurate manner with a straightforward, just-the-facts style. Articles should have an encyclopedic style with a formal tone instead of essay-like, argumentative, promotional, or opinionated writing. The Wikipedia community of editors has developed many policies and guidelines to improve the encyclopedia; however, it is not a formal requirement to be familiar with them before contributing. The fundamental principles by which Wikipedia operates are structured under five pillars:

- **Wikipedia is an encyclopedia. It is not a soapbox, advertisement platform, vanity press, dictionary or newspaper.**

- **Wikipedia is written from a neutral point of view avoiding advocacy. Personal opinions, interpretations or opinions do not belong on the platform.**

- **Wikipedia is free content that anyone can use, edit and distribute. No editor owns an article or contribution that they have made.**

- **Wikipedia's editors treat each other with respect and civility. Do not engage in personal attacks or editorial wars.**

- **Wikipedia has no firm rules. There are policies and guidelines but they are not carved in stone and interpretation can evolve over time.**

Pursuant to the five pillars, Wikipedia does not have strict rules. Wikipedia's policies (standards) and guidelines (good practices) are derived from principles, not a code or law, and they are actualized using common sense and editor or contributor discretion. The policies and guidelines are created and revised by the editing community of Wikipedians. They require discussion and a high level of community-wide consensus.

THE WIKIPEDIA ORGANIZATION AND GOVERNANCE

At the top of the human and legal administrative structure is the Wikimedia Foundation (WMF) governed by a Board of Trustees (see figure 10 for the complete structure). Although the Wikimedia Foundation owns Wikipedia, it is largely uninvolved in the creation of Wikipedia's policies and daily monitoring on those policies. The Wikimedia Foundation employs approximately 300 people who work together to provide the basic platform for all their Wiki initiatives.

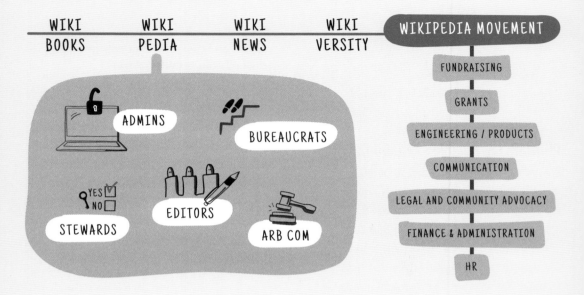

Figure 10: Wikipedia's structure

This includes fundraising, communication, branding and support on their technology infrastructure. The Wikimedia Foundation carries the responsibility for user research, experience design and cross-device support and maintaining and advancing the technology needed to keep Wikimedia projects open, functional, and internationally accessible.

The Wikipedia community itself is self-organizing and self-governed. Editors with varying administrative abilities and their elected administrators are granted considerable discretion over the means used to accomplish Wikipedia's purpose. Some editors are elected or appointed to certain roles to ensure the implementation of the consensus-developed policies and guidelines governing the creation and development of all types of pages. All these roles ultimately derive their own authority from the Wikimedia Foundation. Examples of roles are:

- **Stewards:** Stewards are volunteer editors with complete access to the wiki interface on all Wikimedia wikis, including the ability to change any and all user rights and groups. Stewards are elected annually by the global Wikimedia community. Candidates must have a support / oppose ratio of at least 80% with at least 30 supporting users.

- **Arbitration Committee:** Members of the Arbitration Committee (referred to as ArbCom or Arbs), are volunteer editors that can impose binding solutions on conduct disputes the community has been unable to resolve. They have a very wide latitude in adjudication with the authority to impose general sanctions and/or personal sanctions on editors or groups of editors. Arbitrators are elected annually in one-year or overlapping two-year terms.
- **Bureaucrats:** Bureaucrats, or 'Crats', are volunteer editors with the technical ability to promote other users to administrator. Users are granted bureaucrat status by community consensus.
- **Administrators:** Administrators, also known as admins or sysops (system operators), are editors who have been trusted with access to restricted technical features. For example, administrators can protect and delete pages, and block other editors. Administrators are appointed after a community review process.

GETTING STARTED AS A WIKIPEDIAN ON WIKIPROJECTS

Editors do not even have to log in to read or edit articles on Wikipedia. Just about anyone can edit almost any article at any given time, without logging in, making every user a Wikipedian. Creating an account is free and has several benefits. For example, the ability to create articles, upload media and edit without one's IP address being visible to the public. Wikipedia tries to educate and socialize Wikipedians in a variety of ways. The Wikipedia tutorial is a step-by-step guide explaining Wikipedians on how they can contribute. The Wikipedia Adventure is an interactive guided tour, which covers all the essentials about editing and the expectations and norms of the Wikipedia community. WikiProjects function as a central hub for editor collaboration. They are open groups of Wikipedians who work together as a team, often with the focus on a specific topic area or wiki. A WikiProject is essentially a social construct: its success depends on its ability to function as a cohesive group of editors working towards a common goal.

EDITING & CREATING CONTENT

Wikipedia uses a simple format to allow editors to concentrate on adding content. Page editing is accessible through tabs along the top edge of the wiki page:

- Article: shows the main Wikipedia article.
- Edit: allows users to edit the article.
- Talk: shows a user discussion about the article's topic and possible edits and revisions.
- View history: This tab allows readers to view the editors of the article and the changes that have been made in the past.

Clicking the 'Edit Tab' takes editors to a page with a text box containing the editable text of the wiki article they were viewing. In this box, editors can type the text they want to add, using wiki markup to format the text and add other elements like images and tables. When editors finished editing, they are expected to write a short edit summary in the small field below the edit-box describing their changes. After that they can simply press the publish changes button.

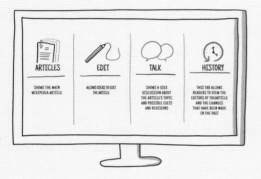

The creation of new articles is only permitted for confirmed and active users, which means those whose accounts are more than four days old and who have done at least ten edits. Confirmed users can draft their article using the Article Wizard function. Contributors that have an idea for the title of an article, but no content for the article itself, can make a request at 'Requested articles' portal. Non-confirmed users and non-registered users can submit a proposed article through the 'Articles for Creation' process, where it

will eventually be reviewed and considered by the community for publication.

REACHING CONSENSUS VIA 'TALK PAGES'

Decisions on Wikipedia are primarily made by consensus, which is accepted as the best method to achieve Wikipedia's goals. Editors usually reach consensus in a natural process. After an editor changes a page, others who read it can choose whether or not to further edit. Any edit that is not disputed or reverted by another editor can be assumed to have consensus. Should that edit later be revised by another editor without dispute, it can be assumed that a new consensus has been reached. In this way, the encyclopedia improves gradually over time. When editors do not reach agreement by editing, discussion on the associated talk page continues toward consensus.

When agreement cannot be reached through editing alone, editors open a section on the associated talk page and try to work out the dispute through discussion. As indicated earlier, all edits are explained by clear edit summaries indicating the reason for the change on the associated talk page. The purpose of a talk page is to provide space for editors to discuss changes to its associated article or WikiProject. Here editors try to persuade others, using reasons based in policy, sources, and common sense. They can also suggest alternative solutions or compromises that may satisfy all concerns. The result might be an agreement that does not satisfy anyone completely, but that all recognize as a reasonable solution. When editors have a particularly difficult time reaching a consensus, several processes are available for consensus building. This includes involving neutral third opinions on the talk page or setting up a dispute resolution on a noticeboard. In more extreme situations, administrators or arbitrators take authoritative steps to end editorial disputes. This may depend on local rules. In some countries (or languages), administrators may end a discussion, whereas in others a discussion can be escalated to an arbitration committee, which next decides the issue. Local Wikipedias may enact different ways of working.

IS IT AS GOOD AS IT SOUNDS?

'Our purpose is to create a web-based, free content encyclopedia of all branches of knowledge, in an atmosphere of mutual respect and cooperation', says the Wikipedia site. The egalitarian way of working sounds great. But is it? A recent conflict in the Dutch Wikipedia gives some insight into Wikipedia's culture[2]. It shows it is not always fun. One of the local administrators was impeached in an impeachment procedure, which is possible according to the rules of the Dutch Wikipedia. This administrator deleted pages without explaining why, which irritated a number of

users. The existence of this power to delete without being held accountable shows Wikipedia is not as egalitarian as it sounds. On paper everybody is equal, in practice some have power over others, even when those officers are elected by the Wikipedians.

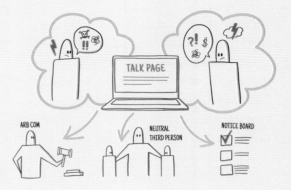

The impeached administrator had a long affiliation with Wikipedia and performed many tasks, but was still voted out. This is not an isolated case. A survey conducted by Wikimedia Netherlands showed that users found the atmosphere in the Dutch Wikipedia suspicious and brawling. Egos and stubbornness are identified as important causes for conflicts in the Dutch version of the encyclopedia.

MAINTAINING THE WIKIPEDIA PLATFORM

Maintenance work is a vital part of keeping Wikipedia running optimally. To assist in the administration of the Wikipedia community and development of the encyclopedia, the community has established a wide range of administration pages. Some administration pages are static in nature and provide information and guidance on certain aspects of maintaining the Wikipedia project. Other pages relate to Wikipedia requests and need continuous attention from volunteers.

For a list of jobs and tasks to be completed, that is easy to understand, there is the 'Task Center'. Maintenance tasks of the most pressing importance are listed at the 'Backlog'. The 'Community Portal' is a central location to find collaborations, tasks, and news about Wikipedia. The Wikipedia 'Signpost' is a weekly, community-written and edited newspaper that covers stories, events, and reports related to Wikipedia. Editors can contribute their opinions to Wikipedia 'Noticeboards' in order to have a say in decisions and help come to consensus on certain issues. Online communication and coordination has thus been turned into an art at Wikipedia.

WIKIMANIA AND MEETUPS

However, not all activities can be managed through pages and clicks on the platform. Wikipedia contributors organize meetups to socialize and collaborate around the common goal of sharing information. Any editor can organize a Wikimedia meetup. Most meetups have at least one experienced Wikipedian present, but editors do not need permission to organize meetups. There are also no requirements for WikiProjects to have a meetup

in a certain way. Wikipedia meetups are both in person and organized as online events. Some meetups are for discussing initiatives of the Wikimedia Foundation, while others have the goal of convening people to edit.

Next to meetups, the Wikimania is the official open annual conference of the Wikimedia Foundation. Topics of presentations and discussions include ongoing projects such as Wikipedia, other wikis, open source software, free knowledge and free content, and social and technical aspects related to these topics.

MOTIVATION AND REWARDS FOR WIKIPEDIANS

Helping others, demonstrating knowledge, and gaining recognition in the community are among the biggest reasons why Wikipedians contribute to the platform. The free and open source characteristics and low transaction costs of participating create a catalyst for collaborative development and encourages participation. Many editors have long toiled, independently and without much recognition on the platform. Respect and gratitude from peers is regarded the best reward an editor can receive and therefore the community and the Wikimedia Foundation has set-up 'Wikipedia Awards'.

The Wikipedia Awards are the honor system of Wikipedia. Traditionally, those considered of the highest esteem are honors awarded personally by Jimmy Wales, founder of Wikipedia. These are the 'Order of the Day' and 'Wikipedian of the Year' which are announced annually on the Wikimania conference. Wikipedians may reward each other for their work and due diligence by awarding them 'barnstars' on their edits and user accounts. In addition to these virtual awards, editors may nominate someone to receive a non-monetary merchandise gift from the Wikimedia Foundation.

Finally, the Wikipedia 'Reward Board' is a page where Wikipedians can offer a reward to editors willing to take on a task. The execution and details of the transaction are the responsibility of the participating parties, and the reward can be monetary, goods like books or cookies, barnstars, or tit-for-tat editing. The Wikimedia Foundation is not hiring contributors and no payments are made by the Foundation. The Reward Board is purely a page for editors to offer rewards to other editors.

"Wikipedia is like a sausage: you might like the taste of it, but you don't necessarily want to see how it's made"

> Jimmy Wales, Wikipedia

---

¹ All the information for this case is taken from www.wikipedia.org in April 2019, except for the information on the Dutch Wikipedia case.
² NRC (2019). De grote Wikipediabewerkingsoorlogen. 5 February, C6-C7.

8 THE DARK SIDE

Organizations invent new organizational forms because they provide better solutions than previous ones. That does not mean they are without problems. In the discussion of new organizational forms we already saw that each form had its specific downsides. There are also some common disadvantages connected to new organizational forms. Hierarchical forms had some general downsides in terms of their limited flexibility, limited freedom for employees and the presence of bureaucratic procedures. Similarly we identified a number of downsides for new organizational forms. We discuss these below. The new organizational forms also affect society more broadly. Sometimes they are at odds with existing habits, rules and laws. Sometimes the law does not keep up with the development of organizational forms. The second part of this chapter discusses some institutional challenges that come with them.

The idea in brief
- New organizational forms have drawbacks on the organizational level and affect society at large
- On the organizational level, data-driven work, continuous change and the focus on norms and values may also lead to loss of privacy, exhaustion and dehumanization of work
- On the societal level questions may arise about the effect of new organizational forms on equality (the (in)equality paradox), corporate governance (the responsibility paradox) and anti-trust laws

THE LIMITS OF NEW ORGANIZATIONAL FORMS

The totalitarian organization and the privacy/performance tradeoff[1].

At the risk of becoming repetitive: new organizational forms are rooted in the enhanced capacity to gather, process and share information. Companies also collect information about employees. By using artificial intelligence and the Internet of Things employers can monitor their employees in many different ways. A chip in the company ID badge can track an employee's movement around the office. Employees can be given smart watches or bracelets to monitor their health or behavior. These devices can also be used to notify an employee a certain task has to be performed. The office can turn into an information panopticon in which privacy is gone and everybody is measured and watched continuously[2].

As with all technology, these developments can be used to the benefit of people and to their detriment. A key issue is how companies use these data and interpret them via artificial intelligence. Algorithms may appear objective because they deliver interpretations based on objective data, but the algorithms themselves are not objective. They are built with a certain goal in mind and may be subject to prejudice. And beyond that there is the human right to privacy and the feeling you don't want to be spied upon by your employer.

The Economist proposes three mechanisms to alleviate privacy problems that stem from using artificial intelligence in the workplace. Employers may make use of employee data but should anonymize the data whenever possible. Employees should be told how employers use artificial intelligence and what data they gather. Employees should be able to request the data employers have on them. The Economist provides a succinct summary of the issue: 'The march of AI into the workplace calls for trade-offs between privacy and performance. *A fairer, more productive workforce is a prize worth having, but not if it shackles and dehumanizes employees.* Striking a balance will require thought, a willingness for both employers and employees to adapt, and a strong dose of humanity'[3].

The disappearing middle management
Even though new middle management functions emerge to replace the old ones, the higher reliance on self-organization in the organizational forms we discussed will probably tilt the balance towards a declining number of middle managers. This is not necessarily a bad thing. However, this implies all employees will have to participate in some administrative duties. It means time that could have been devoted to the 'real' work now has to be devoted to management tasks.

A longer-term issue with middle management disappearing lies in the question who is going to succeed the top managers. Traditional career paths gradually gave people more responsibility and thus created a pool of managers from which the best could be selected. But what if that pool is very small? Will there be sufficient choice? Moreover, with a small pool the opportunities for career growth also decline for those at the bottom of the pyramid. With fewer opportunities to progress, people may believe they are underutilized or underappreciated.

The algorithm says you are fired

The combination of the two previous issues brings us to algorithms. Many functions of middle managers will be replaced by algorithms. In many ways, the programmer will be performing management tasks by specifying what is to be measured and what not[4]. In online platforms like Uber, algorithms already determine pricing and job allocation. Algorithms replacing human judgment may seem to be more objective because decisions are based on data, but in fact it may be highly subjective. The algorithm may not measure specific circumstances that explain a good or bad performance and that a human would take into account. When algorithms become your manager, is that really desirable? This may also create a new divide in organizations akin to the line-staff divide in traditional hierarchies: the line-data analyst divide in which line managers try to get their business knowledge and priorities into the heads of

the data analysts and vice versa. Companies already use algorithms to select

personnel. Algorithms are used to filter CVs or to analyze videos candidates make as part of an interview process. The first selection of applicants can be done without human intervention. There are of course tremendous benefits because this limits the influence of human biases based on a candidate's appearance, gender or skin color. But the algorithm is written by someone with a certain view of what is important and hence is also biased. Opening up algorithms to external scrutiny may enhance their credibility.

Permanent Beta

One of the main differences between the traditional hierarchical organization and the new organizational forms described in this book is that the hierarchy was organized to provide stability whereas the new organizational forms are in a constant flux. The new organizational forms fit better in a constantly-changing business environment. Various organizational forms use various mechanisms to achieve the change. To name a few: broader information sharing to enable staff to react to change more quickly (multidimensional organization), involving employees in the governance of the organization to ensure the structure adapts rapidly (Holacracy), ensuring new wishes can be incorporated in products and services at any time (Spotify and Holacracy) or changing partner constellations (in the various forms of ecosystems).

This means the organization is never finished. The term Permanent Beta has been coined to describe a situation in which something is under continual development. This term certainly applies to these organizational forms. Just like hierarchy came with the boredom of stability and high costs of change, the permanent beta organization comes with a loss of stability and a risk of pursuing the hype of the day. The new organizational forms try to remedy this by giving employees support with a clear vision, a strong culture or fixed processes. But the risk of getting tired of change or loss of identification with an organization or team looms large. For those people who like to work towards a concrete goal, it may be as hard to work in a new organizational form as it was for an entrepreneurial type to function in a hierarchy.

Norms and values as totem poles

The emphasis on norms and values to fill the control gap in new organizational forms also raises issues. The first is the risk of groupthink in which the focus on norms and values is so strong that other ways of thinking are no longer tolerated. Social pressure to conform may exist just as much in new organizational forms as in traditional hierarchies, except that the tools to create conformity are not rules and procedures, but norms and values. In itself that is not a bad thing because organizations require conformity to some norm, but it is easy to predict that what happened to rules and procedures may also happen to norms and values. The focus on norms and values may end up where the planning & control cycle ended up: going through the motions around the corporate totem pole[5]. The planning & control cycle was an excellent idea, but after having been through a couple of them, they quickly lose their appeal. Discussions about norms and values may suffer a similar fate. Others have noted that the increased emphasis on norms and values creates the opportunity for in-crowds to emerge that informally guide the organization[6]. Such in-crowds may accumulate much power in the absence of formal procedures that provide checks and balances. Informal power structures unchecked by rules may work out well for the in-crowd, but can be quite vicious for those who are not part of the inner circle.

Information overload

The availability of a plethora of information also comes with a cost[7]. The quantity of information can be bewildering even for a person who is highly capable of interpreting information and turning it into action. The idea that transparency is always good and that everything should be shared openly comes at the price of stress and loss of time when sifting through information to find the one nugget that applies to you. And when you finally found that nugget the next piece of information pops up on your screen.

So much information is shared under the heading of transparency that sometimes the opposite is achieved: nobody can see the wood for the trees. Sometimes transparency can lead to conflict or unintended consequences. In various countries transparency led to an increase in top management salaries: every top manager could point to a peer who earned more than he/she did. That strengthened their negotiating position. In companies, there are many other ways in which good intentions may turn out to achieve their opposite.

Systems as straitjackets

If going through the motions about norms and values can become boring, so can going through the motions of the more procedural new forms of organization. Holacracy and Spotify in particular run this risk. Motivation may dwindle when the umpteenth circle meeting or daily scrum is held. More threatening though is that there is a sizeable number of advocates of these forms who believe there is only one right way to implement them and that there is no room to diverge from this one right way. Then these organizational forms become straitjackets; the model becomes a goal in itself. Such a belief is obviously fraught because it wrongly assumes that there is one best way of organizing. Adopting, evolving and applying organizational methods in a conscious way is more effective than a rigid belief in one true faith of organizing.

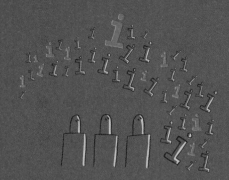

Best practice sharing

Even though many new organizational forms pay much attention to sharing knowledge and experience, there are also important limits in this area. An important one is that much focus of knowledge sharing is on the team level and not so much across teams. That may lead to myopia in the way teams work and impede the transfer of management best practices across teams. In Spotify, chapters and guilds are tasked with managing this, but their focus is more on the direct craft of the employees than on the more abstract principles of management.

THE INSTITUTIONAL CHALLENGE

A second set of problems occurs around the institutions within which new organizational forms operate. Laws, habits and cultures are not always adapted to the new reality of organizational forms. Many of society's institutions are rooted in the industrial era and not in the information era. The fact that there is a lack of regulation in some areas is something organizations can take advantage of, but they should be aware that the possibility of a backlash exists. Sooner or later new rules and habits will emerge that may not only enable but also constrain their future development. Below, we explore the impact on institutions in the areas of labor relations, corporate governance and antitrust.

Labor relations: the (in)equality paradox

Depending on the new organizational form, there are three relevant labor relations issues. The first one relates to new types of employment that exist around platform organizations, the second one relates to the disappearance of the middle class. Together with the third issue, more egalitarian internal labor relations, they constitute an equality paradox: whereas inside organizations relations may become more equal, on a societal level inequality may increase.

To start with the first one, platform organizations run into the issue that existing laws worldwide only distinguish between being an employee and not being an employee. Many people working in the gig economy however fall between these two categories. They earn a substantial part of their income via the platform. They may even be granted jobs via the platform and their performance may be reviewed via the platform. An important defining characteristic of an employee is that an employee receives instructions from an employer. But does an Uber algorithm that tells you to pick up a passenger count as such? Despite the fact that these new jobs have some characteristics that are present in traditional labor contracts, Uber drivers also are independent entrepreneurs determining their own working times and maybe having other jobs on the side.

The big gig economy platforms like Uber, Deliveroo and Foodora have come under increasing scrutiny. They are criticized for setting rates unilaterally, undermining the usual structure of wages in countries and not paying attention to working conditions (safety, health). In some cases this has already led to protests by people signed up to the platform who claim they are exploited. New countervailing platforms are emerging very much like the traditional unions that balanced the power of the large corporations in the twentieth century. An example is Faircrowd. work where platform workers can unite. It has already had some success in getting some platforms to accept codes of conduct vis-à-

vis their platform workers. At the same time parliaments are looking into the matter and considering new legislation in this area. Slowly, new institutions are evolving.

A second impact of new organizational forms on society lies in the decline of hierarchy[8]. Hierarchical organizations offered large swathes of the population a way of rising from the working class into the middle class, because it presented so many opportunities for career advancement. When companies become smaller and implement self-organization, as has happened over the past decades, the number of middle class jobs decreases and opportunities for promotion become scarcer. This may lead to rising inequality in society. In the USA this trend is strengthened by the fact that many social benefits like pensions and health insurance are provided by employers. People lose access to those as well. The disappearance of larger corporations may have as an unexpected consequence that inequality increases.

The previous two observations are interesting when combined with the notion that labor relations inside organizations may actually become more equal. The increased emphasis on self-organization implies that employee participation in an organization becomes more normal. The power balance between employee and employer may become more equal, especially when employees have unique talents and are highly educated. It remains to be seen to what extent these relations will become less adversarial than they used to be. In the Netherlands, organizations that implemented sociocracy (see chapter 4) are already exempt from the requirement to install a worker's council, because their participation is adequately ensured by the sociocratic processes. The interesting thing, however, is that the higher equality inside organizations, because of self-organization, may coincide with lower equality on a societal level, because of the rise of platform workers and the disappearance of middle management jobs. We call this the (in)equality paradox.

Corporate governance: the responsibility paradox

Ever since the Dutch East India Company introduced the idea of tradeable shares to the world, thereby putting shareholders at a distance from the operations of the company, shareholders have had to deal with the question how to monitor managers. The pos-sibility that managers would use the funds entrusted to them for their own benefit was not imaginary: the Dutch East India Company repeatedly duped its shareholders. Over time, numerous rules and regulations developed to solve this corporate governance issue, carefully balancing the rights of shareholders, employees, managers and the company itself. Different countries developed different systems, depending on their preferences.

New organizational forms raise a number of new questions. Many of them revolve around the role of top management. The scope for top management to steer companies may become increasingly limited. Three factors are the root cause of this:
- Societal pressure
- Self-organization
- External collaboration

Societal pressure refers to the fact that there is a trend for companies to not only look at creating shareholder value, but to also contribute to broader societal wellbeing.

Whether this is a good or a bad trend can be debated, but the point is that it limits top management in setting the goals of their organization. Others have argued that the goal of the organization should still focus on the shareholder, but not so much the shareholder's financial returns as his total welfare. Shareholders could be given voting rights to decide what a company policy should be[9]. Such a proposal would limit top management discretion even further. The increase in self-organization does the same thing. The more self-organization is implemented, the more difficult it becomes for the CEO to intervene in the organization, because that will often run counter to the culture necessary to make self-organiza-tion work. Hierarchical interventions in non-hierarchical organizations always remain possible, but are likely to remain rare. Finally, we have seen that new organizational forms have many external relationships, so much so that over half of the business may depend on external partners. Again, this means that much of what affects the performance of an organization is not under top management control.

So far the fiction that the CEO or top management team is accountable for everything that goes on in the firm, has worked relatively well, in part because a set of behaviors existed that made that fiction workable. But with an increased pressure from society for good corporate behavior, a high level of self-organization and an extensive ecosystem, the scope for top management to steer a company becomes very narrow. Managers are held accountable by society for many things beyond their control, like the working conditions at their suppliers and decisions made by people in self-organizing teams. The combination of increasing demand for accountability with a declining control by managers over decision-making leads to a responsibility paradox[10].

Anti-trust and the data challenge

Especially for online platforms the laws of competition change. Because of indirect and direct network effects, markets are subject to tipping, meaning only one player remains[11]. The more people join, the more interesting the platform becomes for other people to join until there is a (near) monopoly. In such a market, traditional antitrust policies like breaking up a company in two or more different companies does not work: because of the network effect one of those companies will probably rapidly grow into a monopoly again.

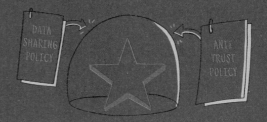

In addition, the large platforms have an information advantage that enables them to monitor what is going on in their business[12]. They may spot new competitive threats early on and take action against them. They may adapt their algorithms in such a way that they can lower prices instantly when a cheaper competitor enters the market and so eliminate the competition.

Proposals to deal with anti-trust issues range from making data sharing mandatory (like banks that must make their customer data available to fintech startups to give the latter a chance to compete), to opening up algorithms so they can be publicly scrutinized for any anticompetitive or discriminatory practices to increasing data portability, enabling individuals to take their data with them to other platforms[13].

"Decentralization also hurts. When each team is on its own, its ability to learn becomes limited. Each team turns into its own little silo"

> Katy Sherman

---

[1] This section is largely based on The Economist. (2018). AI Spy: The work place of the future, March 28.
[2] Berner, M., Graupner, E., & Maedche, A. (2014). The information panopticon in the big data era. Journal of Organization Design, 3(1), 14-19.
[3] The Economist (2018) ibid.
[4] Davis, G. F. (2016). Can an economy survive without corporations? Technology and robust organizational alternatives. The Academy of Management Perspectives, 30(2), 129-140.
[5] De Bruijn, H., Van der Voort, H., Van Wendel de Joode, R., Warmelink, H. & N. Willems (2014). Nieuwerwets organiseren, Van Gorcum.
[6] Spicer, A. (2018). No boss, no managers: the truth behind the 'flat hierarchy' façade. The Guardian, 30 July.
[7] Cable, D., & Birkinshaw, J. (2017). Too much information? London Business School Review, 28(3), 6-9.
[8] Davis, G.F. (2016). The vanishing American corporation. Berrett-Koehler Publishers.
[9] Hart, O., & Zingales, L. (2017). Companies should maximize shareholder welfare not market value. Forthcoming in Journal of Law, Finance, and Accounting.
[10] Davis, G.F (2016). ibid.
[11] Shapiro, C., & Varian, H. R. (1998). Information rules: a strategic guide to the network economy. Harvard Business Press.
[12] Ezrachi, A., & Stucke, M. E. (2016). Virtual competition. Harvard University Press.
[13] The Economist has been especially vocal in raising these issues. See The Economist. (2017). Data is giving rise to a new economy. May 6th, 13-16. Also their special reports on Fixing the Internet (June 30th 2018) and Trustbusting in the 21st century (November 17th 2018) contain much relevant information.

EXCURSION :
SELF-ORGANIZATION AND THE REVENGE OF MIDDLE MANAGEMENT[1]

One of the characteristics of new organizational forms is that the role of middle management declines because of the increased use of self-organization. The disappearance of middle management is seen as a main benefit of self-organization by those who believe middle management is synonymous with bureaucracy without any added value. We can debate whether that characterization of middle management is justified, but it is more interesting to see if the idea of the disappearance of middle management is true. In some cases the disappearance of middle management is clearly visible. Especially in the United States there have been substantial cuts in the middle management layers[2].

The idea in brief
- **New organizational forms require fewer middle managers**
- **However, new middle management roles emerge too**
- **Traditional middle management tasks do not disappear, but are often executed by self-organizing teams**

It seems to be true that the traditional, official functions disappear. However, there are two counter tendencies. The first is that new functions emerge that can be classified as the new middle management. The second is that the activities middle management performs do not disappear entirely, but are performed by other people.

To start with the new functions table 20 lists some that are mentioned in this book. Some of these are relatively light, others are relatively heavy jobs just like the term 'middle management' covers a wide variety of jobs. A first conclusion from this table is that to some extent middle management jobs are replaced by other functions or partly relabeled as something new. In new organizational forms there is still a need for some form of hierarchy.

The fact that the death of hierarchy is overstated finds its cause in issues such as the need for accountability and the simple logic that some tasks are more complex than others[4]. People who are able to execute those more complex tasks will be placed in other

ROLE	DEFINITION
TEAM COACH	SUPPORTS SELF-MANAGING TEAMS IN THEIR COLLABORATION
SCRUM MASTER	ENSURES CORRECT APPLICATION AND RENEWAL OF SCRUM METHOD
CHAPTER LEAD[3]	IN THE SPOTIFY MODEL, OVERSEES COACHING AND PERFORMANCE MANAGEMENT; RESPONSIBLE FOR TRACKING AND SHARING BEST PRACTICES
TRIBE LEAD	IN THE SPOTIFY MODEL, ESTABLISHES PRIORITIES, ALLOCATES BUDGETS, AND COORDINATES WITH OTHER TRIBES TO ENSURE KNOWLEDGE SHARING
PRODUCT OWNER	DETERMINES WHICH ACTIVITIES HAVE TO BE DONE IN WHAT ORDER TO DEVELOP A CERTAIN FUNCTIONALITY
LEAD LINK	IN HOLACRACY: REPRESENTS A HIGHER CIRCLE IN A NEXT LOWER CIRCLE
RELEASE TRAIN LEAD	IN SAFE: COORDINATES WORK THAT HAS BEEN PRIORITIZED
VALUE STREAM LEAD	IN SAFE: DETERMINES WHAT TASKS HAVE TO BE DONE AND COORDINATES WITH OTHER VALUE STREAM LEADS
ALLIANCE MANAGER	RESPONSIBLE FOR ALIGNING AND MONITORING A FORMAL COLLABORATION BETWEEN TWO OR MORE ORGANIZATIONS
ECOSYSTEM MANAGER	RESPONSIBLE FOR CREATING A GOOD ECOSYSTEM CLIMATE AND FOR CONNECTING MEMBERS OF THE ECOSYSTEM AROUND CERTAIN VALUE PROPOSITIONS
BENEVOLENT DICTATOR	IN OPEN SOURCE: PERSON WITH THE FINAL SAY IF OTHERS ARE NOT ABLE TO AGREE AND IS EXPECTED, BECAUSE OF PERSONALITY OR EXPERIENCE, TO USE THAT AUTHORITY WISELY

Tabel 20: New roles in new organizational forms

positions in the organization. However, that does not mean that the functions of hierarchical layers remain unchanged.

There are a number of differences between traditional and new middle management roles. They may not all apply to the same extent in all organizational forms, but here are some of those differences:

- **From directing to facilitating.** The new middle manager is less a person who directs people telling them what to do, but more somebody who helps self-organizing teams to function effectively. They don't decide but help others to make decisions. By doing so, they are no longer part of the decision-making process itself and therefore they play a more neutral role than in a traditional setting.
- **From integral to expertise based.** In traditional hierarchies somebody became a middle manager based on experience and on the assumption that she had a number of capabilities that were broad enough to solve a diverse number of problems. New organizational forms find that so much specific knowledge is necessary to make sensible decision nowadays that this is no longer a reasonable assumption. Therefore the middle management function is cut up and allocated to different persons, each with their own unique expertise, being recognized in their organization as an authority in that specific area.

- **From formally appointed to elected or informal leadership.** Traditional middle managers are appointed by higher management. Even though this still occurs in new organizational forms, there are cases in which middle managers are elected or emerge as informal leaders on the job.
- **From owner of resources to influencer.** Traditional middle managers had all the resources at their disposal to execute the assignment top management had given them. In new middle management roles, the middle managers depend on others to give him at least part of the resources and hence need to have considerable influencing skills in obtaining them. Having to rely more on influencing than on formal power to get a job done is becoming increasingly normal.
- **From lasting till temporary.** The new middle manager often fulfills a temporary role. That can be in a project or a temporary team.

In addition to new middle management roles emerging, traditional activities carried out by middle managers do not always disappear but often are reassigned to other individuals. The new middle managers do not have to execute all traditional activities in addition to their new roles as coaches and influencers. Obviously it differs per organization what these activities are, but some that are frequently taken away from middle management are planning work, having annual performance reviews with employees, monitoring budgets and translating top management vision to the rank and file. Often these are the tasks middle manager do not particularly enjoy.

These activities are reassigned to self-organizing teams. They do not always like that. A regular complaint of self-organizing teams is that it would be nice if somebody else would do these chores. When performance reviews are done within a self-organizing team, it is not always easy to give feedback to a colleague, let alone ask for a colleague to leave the team. Many people do not like planning or budgeting either. So self-organization does not deliver only benefits, there is also a price to pay.

Does middle management take revenge for its disappearing role in new organizational forms by coming back in a different form, but without the chores they used to have?

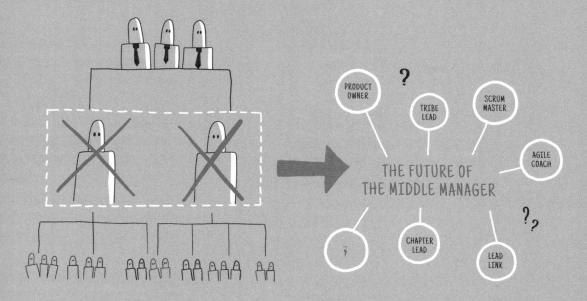

[1] An earlier version of this text was published by Ard-Pieter de Man as a blog on www.sioo.nl on 25 January 2018.
[2] Davis, G. F. (2016). The vanishing American corporation: Navigating the hazards of a new economy. Berrett-Koehler Publishers.
[3] The definitions of chapter lead and tribe lead are taken from Barton, D., Carey, D., & Charan, R. (2018). One Bank's Agile Team Experiment. Harvard Business Review, 96(2), 59-61.
[4] Jacques, E. (1990). In praise of hierarchy. Harvard Business Review, 68, 127-133.

9 INTERNAL GOVERNANCE: REPLACING PLANNING AND CONTROL?

An organization consists not only of a structure which shows which departments, teams or tribes exist. It also requires an internal governance structure to tie together all those departments, teams or tribes. This chapter gathers some thoughts around internal governance that are scattered throughout the book and adds descriptions of some new techniques companies use to govern their organization.

We use the term internal governance to describe a system that ensures that:

- priorities are set and choices are made;
- resources are allocated to those priorities;
- incentives are set in such a way that people are motivated to work on realizing the priorities;
- monitoring takes place that ensures that an organization adjusts to changing circumstances so that the organization retains strategic and operational control;
- delegation of authority and mandates, ensuring the right decisions are taken at the right time by the right people;
- responsibilities and accountabilities are clear;
- activities are coordinated.

The idea in brief
- **Traditional organizational forms have extensive systems in place to ensure alignment of the organization with their strategy**
- **Likewise, new organizational forms have put in place mechanisms to ensure alignment**
- **These mechanisms however are less rooted in a 'planning & control' mindset than in an 'experiment & iterate' mindset**
- **We present several mechanisms that operationalize this latter mindset**

TOWARDS EXPERIMENT & ITERATE

The general idea behind many new governance mechanisms is that the traditional approach assumes a high level of predictability, making planning & control possible. When situations are unpredictable, experimentation and iteration may be more suitable than traditional planning & control to help companies discover a way forward. Table 21 shows some differences between a traditional planning & control mindset and a mindset based on experiment & iterate.

The planning & control cycle is a core element in the governance of traditional organizational forms. However, the cycle makes assumptions about the business environment that have lost their validity for an increasing number of companies. It assumes the market and the competitors are known; that market circumstances are not wildly different from one year to the next so extrapolation of trends proves a good guide for the future; that data are available to analyze markets and that markets are stable and changes predictable. When these assumptions are met, companies can commit resources to projects or departments for the longer run. Tools and processes to govern the organization can follow the plan-do-check-act (PDCA) cycle, that is based on analyzing problems, selecting a solution, gathering data to analyze whether the solution will be effective and next implementing the solution.

Other popular tools in this strand of thinking are building a business case and using scorecards with key performance indicators to move companies forward.

But in how many markets are the assumptions behind planning & control still valid? More and more competitors emerge that were not even on the radar a year ago. New markets form through interesting combinations of technologies. Different visions of how a market will develop may be reasonable without having the data to decide which vision is the best. Rather than analyzing data, testing assumptions may be necessary to find out which vision seems the most relevant. Change is frequent and unpredictable. In such an environment, the long-term commitment of resources makes less sense. Instead, managers will want to continuously track whether they need to adjust their resource commitments, based on new information that becomes available. Learn and fail fast is one of the popular mottos here. Tools like discovery driven planning, quarterly business reviews (QBRs) and objectives and key results (OKRs) fit better in such a world. Rather than PDCA, companies should be inspired by the Observation-Orientation-Decision-Action (OODA) mindset. The OODA approach was developed in the US Airforce in the late twentieth century. It is very well suited to situations that meet the assumptions

	PLANNING & CONTROL	EXPERIMENT & ITERATE
ASSUMPTIONS	MARKET AND COMPETITORS ARE KNOWN	NEW PLAYERS CREATE NEW MARKETS IN UNEXPECTED CORNERS
	EXTRAPOLATION OF TRENDS PROVIDES A REASONABLE GUIDE TO THE FUTURE	DIFFICULT TO JUDGE THE VALIDITY OF DIFFERENT VISIONS OF THE FUTURE
	DATA ARE AVAILABLE TO ANALYZE THE MARKET	MARKET DATA ARE UNAVAILABLE OR INCOMPLETE; TESTING OF ASSUMPTIONS NECESSARY
	STABILITY OR PREDICTABLE CHANGE	FREQUENT AND UNPREDICTABLE CHANGE
PRACTICES	LONG-TERM COMMITMENT OF RESOURCES TO PROJECTS OR DEPARTMENTS	LEARN AND FAIL FAST; COMMIT AND ADJUST RESOURCES WHENEVER NEW INFORMATION BECOMES AVAILABLE
	PDCA, PLANNING & CONTROL CYCLE, BUSINESS CASES, SCORECARDS/KPIS	OODA, DISCOVERY DRIVEN PLANNING, QBRS, OKRS

Table 21: Planning & control vs Experiment & iterate

behind the experiment & iterate approach. It describes how we gather data as best we can (observe), next make a mental picture out of those data (orientation), decide what to do based on that mental picture (decide) and then act. Unlike the PDCA approach, OODA does not require full information, nor a clearly defined goal. You work with what you have and adjust according to how things play out.

HOW CAN THE NEED FOR FORMAL GOVERNANCE BE REDUCED?

Before discussing the tools companies use to operationalize the experiment & iter-

ate approach, it is important to note that in some new organizational forms the need for extensive formal systems of governance has been reduced because organizations apply a number of techniques that reduce the coordination load. These include:

- *Modularization.* The power of modularization to reduce coordination loads has been recognized for some time and some new organizational forms make good use of it[1]. Modularization occurs when a product consists of components that interface with other components and can easily be recombined. When a product or

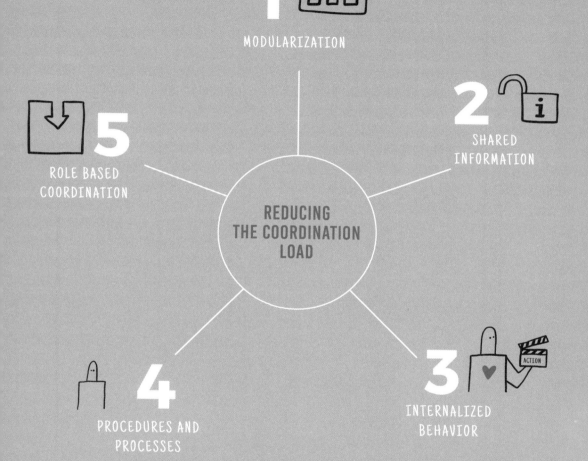

1 MODULARIZATION

2 SHARED INFORMATION

REDUCING THE COORDINATION LOAD

5 ROLE BASED COORDINATION

4 PROCEDURES AND PROCESSES

3 INTERNALIZED BEHAVIOR

an IT infrastructure is modularized, teams can work on individual modules without having to worry that their work may affect the work of others outside the team, as long as the interfaces between component are not affected. In the Spotify model, the IT infrastructure meets this requirement. Similarly, around platform organizations each ecosystem partner can work on his or her own service, product or app quite independently.

- *Information sharing.* The decreasing costs of information gathering and sharing enable decentralization of decision-making. More people can have access to relevant information and hence act accordingly, without a manager telling them what to do. The information monopoly of management has disappeared leading to shorter decision-making processes. Similarly, information gathering can take place more easily and therefore it is easier to monitor and adjust organizations.

- *Internalized behavior.* Many tools and processes for internal governance aim at guiding the behavior of employees in the direction a company wants. The assumption behind this is of course that employees may engage in behavior that does not fit with the organization's aim. The gap between desired behavior and factual behavior can be caused by negative personality traits such as a tendency to shirk and freeride[2]. Or people may be willing to contribute to the organization's goal, but don't know how or are limited by all kinds of organizational barriers to contribute positively. One of the best ways to align individual behavior with company goals is to hire people that already have internalized the behavior that fits the organization. For that reason, hiring processes in new organizational forms often are quite different than those in traditional organizations. Better selecting the people that have the best fit diminishes the need to put formal governance mechanisms in place that ensure alignment between individual and organizational goals.

- *Procedures and processes.* In many organizations, control processes have become embedded in procedures and processes that replace formal control procedures or managerial oversight. The processes are such that once implemented the need for additional planning and control mechanisms decreases. Lean and agile working are examples here. They are based on extensive processes and rituals in which many traditional coordination activities are embedded. Likewise, the Holacracy constitution prescribes in quite some detail how an organization should operate. Other forms of self-organization are also rooted in procedures and processes and are certainly not based on the idea that anyone can do as they like[3].

- *Role based coordination.* Some new organizations use roles instead of functions. Functions may consist of various interrelated roles and therefore it may not always be clear what can be expected from someone who has a certain function. This leads to continuous discussion about who is allowed to do what. This results in loss of time. Clarifying roles and allocating them to individuals creates clarity and avoids useless discussions[4]. Holacracy made this a core principle and goes furthest in making use of role based coordination, but clarity about roles is applied widely in other new organizational forms as well.

NEW TECHNIQUES TO GOVERN

In the remainder of this chapter we highlight some governance, planning, control and budgeting approaches that fit with new organizational forms. These may be applied individually or in combination. There is not one optimal approach: each organization will have to find out what works in their specific situation.

Discovery driven planning

Traditional planning cycles have a number of features that make them less suitable for planning around innovations and ventures. First of all, traditional planning follows a long cycle and does not allow for rapid integration of new insights into an innovation. Second, traditional planning assumes a certain

amount of knowledge about the future and the market. Innovations however are always based on untested assumptions. These assumptions are only tested by moving forward with the innovation. Only then does new information become available about how to adapt the innovation. Discovery driven planning is a method based on this latter idea that planning should be seen as testing of assumptions[5]. On a regular basis, ventures need to see whether at certain checkpoints their assumptions hold true. This type of thinking has also inspired ideas about Minimum Viable Products and rapid prototyping that are developed in the lean start-up movement[6]. The key issue in both these methods is that there is no certainty about what will work, that experimentation is therefore necessary and that new insights need to be incorporated fast.

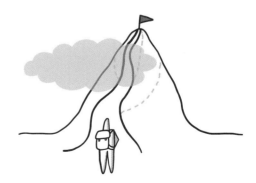

Meetings: QBRs and Obeyas

Meetings play an important role in organizations. They help to align, coordinate, report and prioritize. Interestingly, despite the widespread aversion to meetings, many new organizational forms require more, not fewer, meetings. The higher frequency is necessary to ensure continued alignment in a fast paced and decentral organization and to adapt to changing circumstances. More meetings do not have to translate into a heavier burden if the meetings are productive and short. The meetings in new organizational forms tend to have higher energy levels than those in traditional organizational forms, because they use more interesting formats than sitting around a table to stare at documents and PowerPoints. They may also be shorter. The daily stand up in lean/agile teams are a case in point: they are conducted often, they are short and they are held standing.

In agile organizations the Quarterly Business Reviews (QBR) are a meeting form that ensures alignment between all business domains. The process runs as shown in figure 11. Boards and senior staff prepare a QBR by aligning around the strategic goals for the next quarter. Product owners, teams and sector or domain leads use that as input to write a QBR memo, which shows what they plan to do. Next they comment on each other's memo's to ensure they are aligned. Coordination is ensured where necessary. In a 'big room

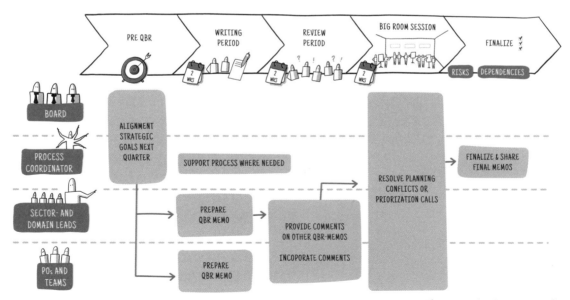

Figure 11: The QBR process[7]

session' planning conflicts are resolved and where necessary the Board sets priorities. Final memos are shared after the meeting. QBRs mitigate the risk that teams lose track of the overarching strategy. Big room planning sessions are derived from Toyota's Obeya concept. Obeya means big room. In a big room, organizations visualize their core processes and goals using tables and charts. This enables managers to have standing meetings in the room to discuss relevant issues and get insight quickly into what is going on. Even though physical presence of everybody involved helps, some organizations use online Obeya's to help manage a globally dispersed organization.

An example of how to conduct a big room session is provided by Lego Digital Solutions[8], where 150 people meet for one day every other month in order to plan the next Product Increment. During that day teams run through a prioritized product backlog that is prepared before the meeting. Each team has a white board showing what its plans are. Any risks they see for a particular development project are put on a risk board. As everybody sees the risk board, some risks identified by one team can be resolved by another. The management needs to review the remaining risks at the end of the day and decide what to do with them. There also is a dependency board that uses post-it notes to show where teams depend on each other to develop a

certain product feature. After the meeting this dependency board is used twice per week in a scrum of scrums meeting to discuss where dependencies create problems. All this forms input for draft plans for teams. Those are presented but not in a plenary session. Instead there are 5-7 minute presentations by one team member that take place simultaneously by all teams in the room. The other team members listen to those presentations by other teams that are most relevant for their work and give feedback. This leads to final plans for each team. Any remaining problems need to be solved by management, but because everybody is in the room, many issues get resolved before a manager needs to get involved.

BUDGETING AND RESOURCE ALLOCATION

Budgeting is another area that is reconsidered to better fit the needs of new organizational forms. To be clear, even in organizations that rely extensively on self-management, the budgeting cycle that allocates resources is an important mechanism management can use to exercise influence. They may give more budget and resources to what they find more important, for example by allocating more time to some issues than to others[9].

In the Spotify structure as implemented by ING, budgeting is straightforward. Each tribe has a fixed number of people and that deter-

mines the budget[10]. The tribe lead determines how the budget is used during the year. This is a dynamic process: more resources may be invested in issues that arise during the year and fewer to issues that have become less important. Those shifting priorities are set in the QBR.

Beyond budgeting aims to get rid of the of the often rigid fixed budgets and rewards based on them[11]. It identifies a number of principles that fit well with new organizational forms, like avoiding fixed annual budgets[12]. It does not prescribe other budgeting mechanisms, but focuses on the principles budgeting mechanisms should meet. For example, budgeting should fit the business rhythm not the annual calendar and budgets must be made available when needed, not through detailed annual allocations. Following such principles can lead to different outcomes for different organizations. Some companies may use rolling forecasts in which,

for example, each three months new projections for the next year are made and budgets updated to reflect changing conditions. Others may choose to reward teams based on their performance relative to success against the competition, instead of rewarding them for meeting a budget. Each of these outcomes may meet the principles of beyond budgeting. The point is that there is no one size fits all way of budgeting, but that budgeting needs to be tuned to each specific business.

Target setting: from KPI to OKR

For a long time, Key Performance Indicators (KPIs) were the most important mechanism of target setting in business. They often ended up in a balanced business scorecard, which would combine targets in a variety of fields: financial, learning and innovation, a company internal perspective and a customer perspective. When implemented correctly, the scorecard would be the end of a strategy-setting process[13]. With the importance attached to speed in new organizational forms, the scorecard and the process needed to create it, became too slow. Over time, other problems with KPIs emerged, like the fact that managers start focusing more on the KPIs they

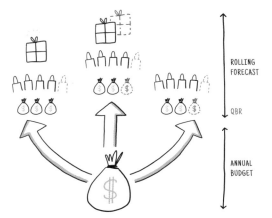

ROLLING
FORECAST

QBR

ANNUAL
BUDGET

have to meet than on realizing the company vision. Still, many organizations have a need to set targets.

The concept of Objective and Key Results (OKR) was developed as a next iteration of KPIs. It apparently emerged at Intel in the 1970s, and in 1999 it was introduced at Google. After Google's success, an increasing number of companies has begun to imitate it. Table 22 shows the differences between the two. First of all, each quarter a qualitative objective is established that is inspirational and that a team can act upon individually. It is a vision for what the team will do during the next quarter. In addition, about three quantitative measures are set. The advantage of this combination of qualitative and quantitative measures is that it has a wider appeal. Some people are motivated by qualitative measures whereas others are spurred on by quantitative targets. The qualitative element also clarifies why something has to happen, rather than only what must be done.

The quantitative targets should be somewhat of a stretch, in that a team should have a 50% chance of meeting them. This in contrast to KPIs which usually have a much higher chance of being met. The stretching targets ensure teams are working at their full potential and keep thinking about how they can improve. That is also the reason why OKRs, other than KPIs, normally are not connected to bonuses and performance reviews. If they were, employees would always fear they

KEY PERFORMANCE INDICATOR	OBJECTIVE AND KEY RESULTS
EXCLUDES VISION	INCLUDES VISION (OBJECTIVE)
ONLY QUANTITATIVE	QUANTITATIVE (OBJECTIVE) AND QUANTITATIVE (MOST OFTEN THREE)
HIGHER THAN 50% CHANCE OF MEETING THEM	50% CHANCE OF MEETING THEM
TIED TO BONUSES AND PERFORMANCE REVIEWS	NOT INTENDED TO BE TIED TO BONUSES AND PERFORMANCE REVIEWS
SET ANNUALLY	SET QUARTERLY; CHECK PROGRESS WEEKLY
DERIVED FROM STRATEGY (TOP DOWN)	SET VIA A DESIGN PROCESS (TOP DOWN AND BOTTOM UP)

Table 22: KPIs vs OKR[14]

would not meet their targets and therefore would set their targets too low.

KPIs and OKRs also differ with respect to the processes followed in two ways. OKRs are set on a quarterly basis whereas KPIs are set annually. A shorter timeframe means OKRs can be adapted to changing circumstances faster than KPIs. Also progress towards OKRs is checked weekly, whereas KPIs tend to follow an annual cycle. Next, KPIs are set top down, because they are derived from strategy only. The process of setting OKRs on the other hand is inspired by design-thinking techniques. It starts with employees proposing objectives for the next quarter. The best ones are brought into an executive team meeting with the CEO in which the best objectives are chosen and key results defined. The process contains top down and bottom up elements. Once OKRs are set, halfway through the quarter organizations check, for example by grading, whether they are on track. The discussion about this helps to focus on what can be done, rather than continuing to work on things that turn out to be impossible.

SPOTIFY RHYTHM

Spotify Rhythm is an approach used by Spotify to create focus in the organization[15]. The key element in it is the definition of company bets: large projects or cross-organization initiatives to which resources are allocated. Spotify arrives at bets via a top down and a bottom up process. The top down process consists of:

- Identifying company beliefs: the CEO develops a vision for what Spotify can do for the next 3-5 years
- Definition of a North Star & two-year goals. These are targets the lead team sets for Spotify, two years out.
- Company bets. They last 6-12 months and drive towards the two-year goals. There are also functional and market bets within single functions or markets. They either also work towards the two-year goals or are very important for that specific function or market.

The bottom up process follows a Data-Insight-Belief-Bet (DIBB) process that forces people to make their reasoning explicit about why they believe a certain bet is necessary. It works like this:

- Data. For a specific problem: which data do you have? For example, facts may show that people listen more music via mobile and less via desktops.
- Insight. What is your interpretation of those data? An insight could be that mobile is overtaking desktop.
- Belief. Based on that insight, what beliefs have you formed about the problem? For example, we need to focus more on mobile.
- Bet. What bets should we make based on that? A bet could be to hire more mobile developers.

When all bets are identified, Spotify stack ranks them so that it is clear which one is number 1, 2 etc. This leads to a clear priority setting, to which resources can be allocated.

DECISION-MAKING: EXPERTISE AND ADVICE

Higher levels of self-management cannot be achieved without decentralizing decision-making. Decentralized decision-making requires the decision-maker to have the expertise to make a certain decision and to have the right information to make a decision. The use of information technology means that the latter condition is fulfilled in many more instances than before. In addition the principle that the best qualified person should take the decision is also gaining ground. Expertise based decision-making replaces hierarchy based decision-making.

Such decision-making may be augmented by obligatory advice processes that require anyone that has to make a decision to consult others who have expertise in the area and those who are affected by the decision[16]. In Sociocracy, the precursor of Holacracy, the principle of consent was developed that basically means that a staff member can proceed with a decision when nobody has an objection to it. If a person does have an objection, that objection only needs to be listened to if the decision would make it difficult for that person to fulfill her role. Whereas consensus often leads to watered down compromises because everybody has to agree to a decision, the consent principle tends to lead to clearer decisions because people only have to not disagree.

FROM EXTRINSIC TO INTRINSIC MOTIVATION

Motivating people is another element in internal governance that has been slowly changing over time. For quite some time the focus has been on motivating people extrinsically by rewarding or punishing them. Setting targets, attached to bonuses and salary increases has been a standard way of motivating people.

More recently a shift has taken place from extrinsic to intrinsic motivation. This search for alternatives occurred partly because of the negative effects of bonus cultures that became evident during the financial crisis of

2009. The change however also is rooted in new organizational forms' need for additional control mechanisms. The decentralization of decision making that occurs in many new organizational forms also implies a risk that employees do not act in the organization's best interest. In a hierarchical organization this could be managed by direct managerial oversight and incentive setting, but in non-hierarchical organizations these mechanisms do not apply.

Another way of closing this control gap is via intrinsic motivation. In order to ensure people are intrinsically motivated to contribute to the organization, a number of tactics can be used. None of these tactics are new, but they have increased in importance, found wider application or have been improved. Examples include:

- More emphasis on purpose[17]. In order for people to identify with an organization, an appealing purpose explaining why an organization exists works better than setting a financial target.
- Selecting the right people. To put it in black and white terms: in traditional organizations the approach is to hire smart people and next mold them into what the organi-

zation needs whereas in new organizational forms people are selected that already exhibit a high degree of fit with the organization. For more about hiring processes see Excursion 8.
- Culture, norms and values. Norms and values have always played a role in internal governance. Recently, organizations have invested more in making those norms and values explicit. Partly this is done to meet society's demand for good corporate behavior, but if that is the only drive this is not likely to succeed. Those organizations that see a real need for it for governance reasons may achieve both better governance and societal respect.
- A coaching management style that focuses on helping colleagues to develop themselves and helping them to solve problems, rather than making decisions for them, may also play a role in giving people more ownership of their work.

GAMIFICATION

The newest member of the governance family is gamification. Some companies experiment with games to focus their employees on the right things. For example, a retailer mays ask its shop floor staff to set a target for selling a product. If the target is met, they get a reward. Shops may also compete with each other. An app can show which shop performs the best and where your own shop stands in the ranking. Such mechanisms are still in their infancy. Ethical implications may lie in increasing stress, pitting people against each other and increasing work pressure. On the brighter side, it may provide focus and fun.

"By clearing the line of sight to everyone's objectives, OKRs expose redundant efforts and save time and money"

> John Doerr

[1] Sanchez, R., & Mahoney, J. T. (1996). Modularity, flexibility, and knowledge management in product and organization design. Strategic Management Journal, 17(Winter), 63-76.

[2] Williamson, O. E. (1975). Markets and hierarchies. The Free Press.

[3] Laloux, F. (2014). Reinventing organizations: A guide to creating organizations inspired by the next stage in human consciousness. Nelson Parker.

[4] Bechky, B. A. (2006). Gaffers, gofers, and grips: Role-based coordination in temporary organizations. Organization Science, 17(1), 3-21.

[5] McGrath, R. G., & MacMillan, I. C. (1995). Discovery driven planning. Harvard Business Review, July/August, 44-54.

[6] Ries, E. (2011). The lean startup: How today's entrepreneurs use continuous innovation to create radically successful businesses. Crown Books.

[7] PwC. (2018). Enterprise Agility. Internal document.

[8] Kniberg, H., & Thyrsted Brandsgård, E. (2016) Planning as a Social Event. https://crisp.se/wp-content/uploads/2016/12/Agile@Lego.pdf.

[9] Schaeffer, M. (2017). Het geheim van bol.com, Atlas Contact.

[10] Barton, D., Carey, D. & Charan, D. (2018). One bank's agile team experiment, Harvard Business Review, March/April, 59-61.

[11] Hope, J., & Fraser, R. (2003). Who needs budgets? Response. Harvard Business Review, 81(6), 132-132.

[12] https://bbrt.org/the-beyond-budgeting-principles/

[13] Kaplan, R. S., & Norton, D. P. (1996). The balanced scorecard: translating strategy into action. Harvard Business Press.

[14] This table was distilled from Wodtke, C., (2016). Introduction to OKRs, O'Reilly Media, Inc.

[15] Kniberg, H. (2016). Spotify Rhythm: How we create focus. Presentation for Agile Sverige, 1 June.

[16] Laloux, F. (2014). ibid.

[17] Among the early advocates of purpose are Bartlett, C. A., & Ghoshal, S. (1994). Changing the role of top management: Beyond strategy to purpose. Harvard Business Review, 72(6), 79-88; Ghoshal, S., Bartlett, C. A., & Moran, P. (1999). A new manifesto for management. MIT Sloan Management Review, 40(3), 9.

EXCURSION :
THREE HR TRENDS THAT SUPPORT NEW ORGANIZING

New organizational forms usually demand new HR policies as well. There is considerable variety in how organizations approach compensation, hiring, careers and promotion. How organizations deal with compensation is a case in point:

- In the multi-dimensional organization of IBM, a more traditional system exists with salaries tied to function levels and the presence of bonuses. The new element is that the bonuses for some managers are no longer exclusively based on individual performance but also on the overall company performance.
- Netflix eschews bonuses altogether but has a policy to pay at the top of the market.
- For Holacracy a system is developed based on 'badges' that show the skills an employee has. The various badges and skill levels are next linked to a certain compensation.
- In some organizations relying on self-organization employees can set their own salaries or discuss their bonuses within their team or unit. The team next has to agree jointly on who receives what bonus.

The Netflix approach to HR has received much attention, because the concrete HR policies are so different[1]. Employees decide for themselves how much time they take off, there are no expense reports that need to be signed off by a boss, there are no annual salary rounds, no annual performance reviews and overall the number of rules in the company is limited. Much more interesting than these policies is the thinking that lies behind them.

> *The idea in brief*
> - **New organizational forms require new human resource (HR) policies that support them. There are three of them**
> - **Trend 1: an increased emphasis on developing the skills of employees**
> - **Trend 2: more use of vision and values as a coordination mechanism**
> - **Trend 3: increasing objectivity in human resource processes**

"Netflix' motto is Freedom & Responsibility".

But: it believes this can only be realized by hiring top talent and creating the right context for them. When these two things are in place, there is no need to have elaborate control procedures. Control only becomes necessary when a company grows fast and hires people that are not excellent. When people are excellent at their job and have excellent values, there is no need to curtail their freedom. They can self-manage and will even be more productive when they do so. Supporting this idea, Netflix identified nine values people should possess: judgment, communication, impact, curiosity, innovation, courage, passion, honesty and selflessness (see table 23). Each of which is clearly described in a way that makes clear which behavior is required. To get the right people there is no debate about salaries: if you want the best, you pay top of market. What top of market is, may differ substantially between individuals. Fixed salaries connected to jobs therefore do not exist: the market determines.

Next to great people, good context is the second element Netflix pays attention to. Good context refers to ensuring that all employees have a good understanding of the strategy and the company results. They have to understand how the way they set priorities in their work affects the realization of the strategy and the outcomes. For that reason Netflix also works with a more traditional approach of setting metrics and defining goals. It also is radically transparent about them and about the decision-making around them. Much time is invested in getting everybody aligned around the strategy and goals. How teams want to achieve the goals is up to them.

With the right people and the right context in place, there is no need to put in place many control mechanisms. People will act responsibly and do the right things, because they are excellent. It is interesting to note Netflix is a public company listed on the stock exchange and in 2018 had some 5,000 employees. The idea that a public company cannot do without many controls because it has to follow all kinds of guidelines does not hold. And with 5,000 employees the model is scalable.

Clearly the Netflix model is not universally applicable and Netflix does not claim it is. The original Netflix HR document is actually very clear about when it does not work. First of all, it only works if everybody is a responsible top performer. As not everybody is a responsible top performer, it will not work in companies that have a less excellent workforce. Second, the model assumes that errors made by employees are not fatal and can be repaired rapidly. If that is not the case, the low level of control may be risky. The original Netflix document outlining their policies mentions manufacturing or medicine as areas where very costly mistakes can be made and where a control focus on preventing errors may be a better choice. In creative environments however the opposite is true.

Netflix has the luxury of being able to select its staff from the world's top talent pool. For that reason alone, its' HR policies cannot be copy-pasted to all other organizations. Still,

JUDGMENT

· YOU MAKE WISE DECISIONS DESPITE AMBIGUITY
· YOU IDENTIFY ROOT CAUSES, AND GO BEYOND TREATING SYMPTOMS
· YOU THINK STRATEGICALLY AND CAN ARTICULATE WHAT YOU ARE, AND ARE NOT, GOING TO DO
· YOU SMARTLY SEPARATE WHAT MUST BE DONE WELL NOW, AND WHAT CAN BE IMPROVED

COMMUNICATION

· YOU LISTEN WELL, INSTEAD OF REACTING FAST, SO YOU CAN BETTER UNDERSTAND
· YOU ARE CONCISE AND ARTICULATE IN SPEECH AND WRITING
· YOU TREAT PEOPLE WITH RESPECT REGARDLESS OF THEIR STATUS OR DISAGREEMENT WITH YOU
· YOU MAINTAIN CALM POISE IN STRESSFUL SITUATIONS

IMPACT

· YOU ACCOMPLISH AMAZING AMOUNTS OF IMPORTANT WORK
· YOU DEMONSTRATE CONSISTENTLY STRONG PERFORMANCE SO COLLEAGUES CAN RELY UPON YOU
· YOU FOCUS ON GREAT RESULTS RATHER THAN ON PROCESS
· YOU EXHIBIT BIAS-TO-ACTION, AND AVOID ANALYSIS-PARALYSIS

CURIOSITY

· YOU LEARN RAPIDLY AND EAGERLY
· YOU SEEK TO UNDERSTAND OUR STRATEGY, MARKET, CUSTOMERS, AND SUPPLIERS
· YOU ARE BROADLY KNOWLEDGEABLE ABOUT BUSINESS, TECHNOLOGY AND ENTERTAINMENT
· YOU CONTRIBUTE EFFECTIVELY OUTSIDE OF YOUR SPECIALTY

INNOVATION

· YOU RE-CONCEPTUALIZE ISSUES TO DISCOVER PRACTICAL SOLUTIONS TO HARD PROBLEMS
· YOU CHALLENGE PREVAILING ASSUMPTIONS WHEN WARRANTED, AND SUGGEST BETTER APPROACHES
· YOU CREATE NEW IDEAS THAT PROVE USEFUL
· YOU KEEP US NIMBLE BY MINIMIZING COMPLEXITY AND FINDING TIME TO SIMPLIFY

COURAGE

· YOU SAY WHAT YOU THINK EVEN IF IT IS CONTROVERSIAL
· YOU MAKE TOUGH DECISIONS WITHOUT AGONIZING
· YOU TAKE SMART RISKS
· YOU QUESTION ACTIONS INCONSISTENT WITH OUR VALUES

PASSION

· YOU INSPIRE OTHERS WITH YOUR THIRST FOR EXCELLENCE
· YOU CARE INTENSELY ABOUT NETFLIX'S SUCCESS
· YOU CELEBRATE WINS
· YOU ARE TENACIOUS

HONESTY

· YOU ARE KNOWN FOR CANDOR AND DIRECTNESS
· YOU ARE NON-POLITICAL WHEN YOU DISAGREE WITH OTHERS
· YOU ONLY SAY THINGS ABOUT FELLOW EMPLOYEES YOU WILL SAY TO THEIR FACE
· YOU ARE QUICK TO ADMIT MISTAKES

SELFLESSNESS

· YOU SEEK WHAT IS BEST FOR NETFLIX, RATHER THAN BEST FOR YOURSELF OR YOUR GROUP
· YOU ARE EGO-LESS WHEN SEARCHING FOR THE BEST IDEAS

Table 23: The nine Netflix values

Netflix exemplifies three broad HR trends that can inspire other organizations: an increased focus on skills, more use of vision and values as a coordination mechanism and increasing objectivity in human resource processes. This sounds nice, but the mechanisms are also harsh. If your capability is no longer valued by the market, your salary will drop or you may have to leave.

INCREASED FOCUS ON SKILLS

Many new organizational forms tend to focus more on skills than on function levels for their HR policies. The capabilities of employees are increasingly relevant in a dynamic and challenging world. Whereas in an industrial society much labor required relatively low skills and hence people were exchangeable, in the information society highly skilled work becomes more important to gain a competitive advantage. In addition, new knowledge emerges on a daily basis making existing knowledge obsolete. Continuous attention for the skills of employees is a prerequisite for firm survival. For that reason, team members in the Spotify model report to the chapter lead, who is responsible for skill development and knowledge exchange.

One popular approach to operationalize the focus on skills in IT organizations is the Dreyfus model of skill development[2]. This model describes how IT staff can develop from a novice to an expert, somewhat along the lines of the development from apprentice to master in the guilds of the middle ages. The Holacracy movement also proposes a skill based approach to HR and remuneration[3]. They propose a system of badges that represent different skills and skill levels. Somebody can receive a badge when two people already holding the badge award it. A badge will have different levels of experience reflecting that in certain skills some may be beginners while others may be highly accomplished. Badges expire after two years, unless renewed. An individual holds several badges and the set of badges is tied to a certain compensation level.

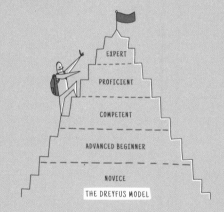

In true holacracy fashion, the entire system is based on rules and meetings and that may seem cumbersome. Yet it has some advantages as well. One of them is that the badge mechanism is transparent. It is clear to everybody who has which badges and therefore which salary. It also is a non-hierarchical system. There is no manager who negotiates a salary or a pay rise with employees. Instead the salary is earned by displaying skills. The strongest point however may be that it allows each individual to build up their own specific profile with badges. Employees do not have to fit into the often narrow boxes that are defined in traditional function schemes. The focus on skills is another strength. The system focuses on the development of the individual and because of the possibility of losing a badge, there also is an incentive for continuous development. Moreover, it may not only fit with individual development but also the organization's development, because there is a possibility to propose new badges when new skills become more important for the organization.

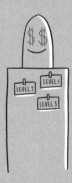

VISION- AND VALUE-DRIVEN

Despite the vast differences between the new organizational forms, there is agreement around the increased importance of vision and values. From a traditional perspective, new organizational forms face a clear control gap. The multidimensional organization

closes this gap through improved information sharing. The Spotify model closes the control gap by using product owners and agile/scrum methods. In holacracy, the double bind provides a form of control. And so on. The control gap however is never closed in the way it was closed in traditional hierarchies. And neither is it desirable to do so, because more than in the traditional hierarchy, new organizational forms deliver flexibility and innovation. The control gap therefore needs to be bridged in a different way.

New organizational forms point towards two relevant elements that are instrumental in this: vision and values. A clearly articulated vision, that is also continuously emphasized and discussed, can replace traditional mechanisms by which strategy is implemented. The traditional, waterfall method of setting the vision, translating it to strategy, incorporating it in business unit scorecards and finally in individual scorecards (and next reporting all that back up again) is slow and not well-suited for fast paced business environments. The current method in many new organizational forms is to articulate and share a vision and then work towards its realization iteratively. It pays to invest in creating a clear and shared vision, as it will guide employees' day-to-day actions.

The second element is to create a culture around values that matter to the company to realize its vision. In general that means there is more emphasis on teamwork, collaboration and sharing rather than keeping to yourself, learning, improvement instead of efficiency. This is also one of the reasons why traditional hierarchies may have so much difficulty in transferring to a new organizational form. Their cultures and hence their employees are often at odds with these values. Start-ups can begin hiring people who fit with the new cultural demands from day one.

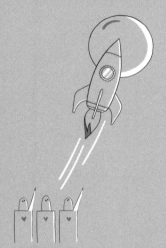

INCREASED OBJECTIVITY

A third trend is the search for increased objectivity in HR. This search is rooted in the need to be more objective about the capabilities of the individual as mentioned above. Also, in dynamic organizations a happy and healthy workforce is a significant plus, so research into how employees can be made happy and healthy should be more thorough. Finally, objectivity is also enabled by the fact that so much more is measurable nowadays. This has led to a whole new field of inquiry: HR analytics. There are a number of ways to find out what works best:

- *Surveys.* This is the most traditional approach. If no other data are at hand, a survey may provide input about employee behavior.
- *Experiments.* A well-known example is that Google lowered the caloric intake of its employees by using smaller plates in the cafeteria. Firms can measure how much their staff eat and what they eat. By experimenting with how food is presented and where in the cafeteria it is presented, staff may be nudged into healthier eating.
- *Measure online engagement.* For example, it is possible to measure how long employees take to fill in their expense account. If it takes too long or there is a wide discrepancy between employees, this may indicate that the tool for claiming expenses needs to be simplified.
- *Search through HR records.* It may be possible to predict when people may think of leaving the company. Perhaps there is a point after four years when certain people think about a taking a next step. Or maybe after a pregnancy many women do not return to work. Finding such patterns may help companies to retain their staff.

The champion of this drive for objectivity is Google. It has even dedicated a whole site to the various ways in which it tries to objectify its HR practices[4]. One interesting practice is the installation of hiring committees. Managers cannot decide to hire people on their own. Instead hiring committees need to agree with hiring a certain person. This limits the influence of biases that individual managers may have when they do job interviews.

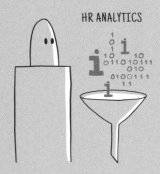

DIFFERENT CHOICES

Together with the new organizational forms, new options for HR policies are emerging. For salaries, the market based top salaries of Netflix may not be a good choice for every organization. Functional based salaries may be a better, albeit more traditional option. In an age where skills are more important, a focus on skill-based compensation may fit more with the times. The bonus culture has led to some public debate since the financial crisis, especially because of the size of bonuses in the financial sector. Bonuses however may still play a role in supporting an organization structure in some cases. Alternatives to bonuses are the Netflix approach of paying

top salaries, team-based rather than individual bonuses and rewarding the development of skills.

IT'S NOT ALL THAT NICE

All this sounds nice, but is it? The attention on skills, values and objectivity does not necessarily mean that companies are friendlier to their employees than they used to be. The attention on skills also means employees may continuously have to prove they have the skills to do their job and plenty of people will not be able to live with that pressure. In addition, the continuous change in organizations also puts a burden on people. Some platform organizations have been criticized for how they deal with the people who are not on their payroll but still depend on them, Uber is a case in point. Again, not every individual fits in these new HR systems and these systems do not work for all organizations. But that was also true of the HR systems of traditional organizations.

"Intellectual complacency is not our friend and learning – not just new things but new ways of thinking – is a life-long endeavour"

> Blair Sheppard, PwC

1 The most recent (2017) version of Netflix's policies can be found at https://jobs.netflix.com/culture. However it is worth reading the original 2009 version, because this version also explains why Netflix has these policies. This version is found at: https://www.slideshare.net/reed2001/culture-1798664. Also see: McCord, P. (2014). How netflix reinvented HR. Harvard Business Review, 92(1), 70-76.
2 Dreyfus, S. E., & Dreyfus, H. L. (1980). A five-stage model of the mental activities involved in directed skill acquisition (No. ORC-80-2). California University Berkeley Operations Research Center.
3 For more information see holacracy.org: https://www.holacracy.org/wp-content/uploads/2015/08/Badge-basedCompensationApp-v1.0.pdf.
4 rework.withgoogle.com. This site also provided most of the examples mentioned here.

NEW ORGANIZATIONAL FORMS: A ROUGH GUIDE

The organizational models that form the core of this book are the multidimensional organization, the Spotify model, Holacracy, open source, the platform organization and the value proposition based ecosystem. We present a rough guideline on when each of the organizational forms is applicable. However, the cases in the book showed that in real life companies adapt these models and take inspiration from across the business landscape, to tailor them to their specific needs and circumstances. Therefore we highlight the risks of using a copy-paste approach to organization design. Because of the risk of copy-pasting and the necessity to adapt models to the specific organization, hybrid models may emerge. We describe some of those.

WHEN TO USE WHICH FORM

The organizational forms discussed in this book have many characteristics in common that distinguish them from more hierarchical organizational forms, as we showed in Chapter 1. Despite these commonalities, there is still substantial diversity. Table 24 highlights the unique characteristics of each organizational form to help clarify the distinctions between them. The table gathers insights from the earlier chapters with the aim of helping managers get a picture of when they may apply each form. Keep in mind that this is a rough guide. In practice there are many gray areas and the applicability of the forms may be broader than the table suggests.

The multidimensional form's unique characteristics are that the client acts as the profit center and that a manager is accountable for each relevant dimension. Such a set up works

The idea in brief
- **None of the models discussed in this book should be used in a copy-paste manner**
- **Instead, they are sources of inspiration and present ideas that managers need to adapt to their specific circumstances**
- **We present some guidelines as to when which form is suitable and how they can be combined into hybrid forms**

well when clients require integrated solutions rather than individual products and when an organization can gain substantial advantage by coordinating multiple rather than single dimensions. This form therefore presupposes the presence of a multi-product, multi-unit, multi-geography firm. To deliver the solution to the client, departments in the organization depend on each other. This model is less applicable when departments are able to be successful in the market on their own.

The unique characteristics of the Spotify model are multifunctional teams with prescribed roles for team members and the presence of the product owner/client in the team. They are grouped in tribes and chapters. The Spotify model is suitable in a project environment with non-routine operations, such as when information products need to be developed. The multifunctional teams have great value when solutions are unclear, because the combination of insights from people with different backgrounds may lead to more creative solutions. The short cycle time and the presence of a client in the team also make it possible to adapt to changes in requirements during the development process. If no such changes are expected or close collaboration with an end user is not possible, this model is less applicable[1].

Unlike the Spotify model, holacracy does not prescribe roles. Roles can be defined by the people in the organization, who work in consent based circles. Double links ensure vertical coordination. In holacracy everybody is involved in the governance of the organization and everyone is involved in changing, adapting or transferring roles. This contrasts with the Spotify model where the structure of chapters and tribes is fixed. This difference is rooted in the fact that holacracy focuses on improving the management of the flow of work. This is best done by involving those who know most about the work: the people doing the work. In keeping with this focus on the flow of work, holacracy tends to be used more in routine operations, where similar tasks need to be performed on a daily basis. Because of the more routine tasks, the client is not present in holacracy. Co-creation with clients is less relevant in holacracy than in Spotify. The bol.com case shows holacracy can be useful in sales and marketing as well. Holacracy improves entrepreneurship by giving people a sense of ownership of the business and enabling them to make decisions about which new products to sell or which products discontinue.

On the right hand side of the of the table, we find the organizational forms that cross organizational boundaries. The platform organization may still be within a single organization, but its surrounding ecosystem permeates the organizational boundaries. Unique for the platform organization is that it tends to support several value propositions. For example, complementors like app developers offer a wide variety of information services, entertainment and tools that support work. A further unique attribute is the use of standardized contracts that platform owners use to orchestrate their ecosystem. Building a platform organization is particularly attractive when high economies of scale can be reaped by using the platform for a variety of purposes. Alternatively, network effects need to exist that create economic value. Platforms also require the definition of standardized interfaces for all partners. Without them, platforms cannot flourish. Finally, platforms assume clients are able to integrate complementing services themselves. When those services are too complex or demand high skills from clients to integrate them, the platform may be less successful.

This last point differentiates platform organizations from value proposition based ecosystems. These ecosystems are a suitable organizational form when clients demand integrated solutions, that no individual firm is able to deliver on its own. Multiple partners integrate their offering and next jointly deliver a single value proposition to clients. As the value proposition requires the combination of specialized competences of these partners, contracts between the partners are customized. Partners coordinate their activities jointly. Value proposition based

ecosystems fit in environments where there are high economies of skill: results are better when each partner focuses on its own competences[2]. This form also assumes a high level of collaborative behavior between partners.

Finally, the unique characteristics of open source organizations compared to the other forms we discussed lie in the fact that it consists of volunteers, executing work under enlightened dictatorship. Coordination is mainly online and physical, face-to-face meetings are absent. Because of the voluntary nature of open source organizations, speed is sacrificed for quality, so this model is less suitable when speed is important. It also demands high intrinsic motivation from the volunteers, often this is achieved by the fact that they are also users of the products they produce. Open source also demands that tasks can be broken down into discrete activities that can be performed in a standardized way. This is a marked difference from value proposition based ecosystems that tend to work well when unique outcomes need to be delivered based on unique processes. Though not unique to online environments, most open source organizations develop software online.

Table 24: New organizational forms compared

	UNIQUE CHARACTERISTIC	APPLICABILITY
MULTIDIMENSIONAL ORGANIZATION	· CLIENT AS PROFIT CENTER · MANAGER FOR EACH DIMENSION	· MULTI-PRODUCT, MULTI-UNIT, MULTI-GEOGRAPHY FIRMS · CLIENTS REQUIRE INTEGRATED SOLUTIONS · DEPARTMENTS ARE INTERDEPENDENT
SPOTIFY MODEL	· PRESCRIBED ROLES PER PERSON IN MULTIFUNCTIONAL TEAMS · TRIBES AND CHAPTERS · SHORT CYCLE TIME WITH CLIENT / PRODUCT OWNER; CLIENT IS PART OF THE SYSTEM	· PROJECT ENVIRONMENT, NON-ROUTINE OPERATIONS · DEVELOPMENT OF INFORMATION PRODUCTS · UNCLEAR SOLUTIONS AND HIGH LIKELIHOOD OF CHANGE IN REQUIREMENTS · CLOSE COLLABORATION WITH END USER IS POSSIBLE
HOLACRACY	· CONSENT BASED CIRCLES WITH NON-PRESCRIBED ROLES · DOUBLE LINKS · EVERYBODY INVOLVED IN GOVERNANCE (BUT NOT A CLIENT)	· ROUTINE OPERATIONS · FLOWS OF SIMILAR TASKS ARE OPTIMIZED · LIMITED NEED TO CO-CREATE WITH CLIENTS · INCREASE ENTREPRENEURSHIP IN SALES AND MARKETING
PLATFORM ORGANIZATION	· SINGLE PLATFORM SUPPORTS MULTIPLE VALUE PROPOSITIONS · COMPLEMENTORS WORK ACCORDING TO STANDARDIZED CONTRACT · PLATFORM OWNER HAS ORCHESTRATING ROLE IN COORDINATION	· HIGH ECONOMIES OF SCALE OR NETWORK EFFECTS EXIST · STANDARDIZED INTERFACES FOR ALL PARTNERS CAN BE DEFINED · CLIENTS ARE ABLE TO INTEGRATE COMPLEMENTING SERVICES THEMSELVES
VALUE PROPOSITION BASED ECOSYSTEMS	· ONE ECOSYSTEM DELIVERS ONE VALUE PROPOSITION · ECOSYSTEM PARTNERS WORK ACCORDING TO CUSTOMIZED CONTRACT · JOINT COORDINATION	· CLIENTS DEMAND INTEGRATED SOLUTIONS NO FIRM CAN DELIVER ON ITS OWN · HIGH ECONOMIES OF SKILL · PARTNERS HAVE A HIGH LEVEL OF COLLABORATIVE BEHAVIOR
OPEN SOURCE	· VOLUNTEERS · ENLIGHTENED DICTATORSHIP · ABSENCE OF FACE-TO-FACE MEETINGS	· GOOD SOFTWARE/PRODUCT MORE IMPORTANT THAN SPEED · HIGH INTRINSIC MOTIVATION · TASKS CAN BE BROKEN DOWN IN DISCRETE ACTIVITIES · BUILDERS ARE USERS

THE RISKS OF A COPY-PASTE APPROACH

The model that works best for any organization depends on many different variables. Any organization implementing a new organizational model must also make that model its own. When forms become a hype however, organizations may start to copy-paste them without a thorough analysis of which form is most suitable. Organizations that have taken a copy-paste approach towards any of the organizational models discussed in this book, have often failed to reach their objectives. Among the many reasons why the copy-paste approach does not work, some important ones are:

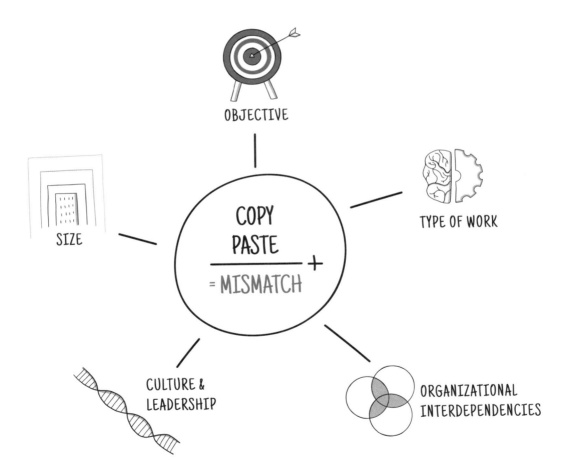

OBJECTIVE

TYPE OF WORK

COPY
PASTE
———————— +
= MISMATCH

SIZE

CULTURE &
LEADERSHIP

ORGANIZATIONAL
INTERDEPENDENCIES

- *Mismatch with overall objectives.* Depending on the organization's objectives, some forms are more suitable than others. The Spotify model allows organizations to deal with uncertainties and enables them to respond fast to changes in their business environment. In a small municipality this form may therefore not be the best option.
- *Mismatch with type of work.* Some forms presuppose routine work (holacracy), others non-routine work (Spotify). Some forms require high task standardization (open source), others are suitable for unique tasks (value proposition based ecosystems). Without a thorough understanding of the nature of work, no choice between organization models can be made.
- *Mismatch with organizational interdependencies.* The expected level of interdependencies between departments within the organization is an important area of consideration when selecting the right organizational form. The multidimensional organization recognizes such interdependencies; value proposition based ecosystems recognize interorganizational interdependencies and propose a method of dealing with them. The Spotify and platform models, on the other hand, assume more simplified organizational environments, with fewer interdependencies.
- *Mismatch to organizational culture and leadership.* Organization culture and leadership are key elements to consider when selecting a new organizational framework. Some models are based upon a high level of autonomy and trust. Organizations and their leaders need to be able to demonstrate behavior that fits this. If culture and leadership do not fit the chosen model, either the model has to change or the culture and leadership.
- *Mismatch with size of the organization.* Some of these organizational forms contain assumptions on the minimum and maximum number of people in teams and how teams should be structured in an organization. Complex structures for smaller organizations or smaller department will not be effective.

TAILORING ORGANIZATIONAL FORMS TO YOUR CONTEXT AND NEEDS

A thoughtful adaptation of an organizational idea to the needs of the organization is necessary for it to succeed. The examples of bol.com and ING show they were very much aware that they needed to adapt holacracy and Spotify to their specific situation. They consciously chose not to follow some elements and added others. As a further illustration we present some examples of how organizations have successfully tailored underlying principles from the Spotify model to their specific context.

- All tribes should be maximum of 150 people. Spotify has approximately 3,000 people working in its tribe and squad organization. Many large organizations struggle to group related squads into tribes that are smaller than 150 people. Some organizations have adjusted this *tribe size* principle to allow for scaling the model within their company. Tribes may be larger than 150 people when all squads have a strongly related purpose and their backlog requires them to collaborate. Large tribes may assign Product Area Leads as a layer across multiple squads to reduce the span of control.
- All people in squads need to be *co-located*. Many multinationals have teams with people that work from different locations or time zones. Some organizations have adjusted the co-location principle to be able to work in a geographically dispersed team. Principles we have seen are:
  » Teams are distributed across maximum two locations.
  » Team size is equally divided across two locations (with a minimum of three people at each location).
  » There should be a minimum of two hours overlap in daily working time between the two locations taking time zone differences into account.
  » Team leads need to be present at both locations for an equal length of time to work with the team and to manage stakeholders.

» Teams share a single backlog and follow the same cadence and meetings.
» Teams split functions e.g. one part of the team defines the customer journey, another team in another location builds it.
- Tribes should consist out of features-, client app- and/or infrastructure squads. Many existing organizations carry an IT legacy and simply cannot transition to a Spotify model with just three types of *self-service* teams. The concept of self-service means that any squad can start developing and iterating on a service in the live environment without having to interact with the rest of the organization. So organizations adjust this principle, for example by assigning additional temporary roles at tribe level that help to orchestrate and align activities between squads.

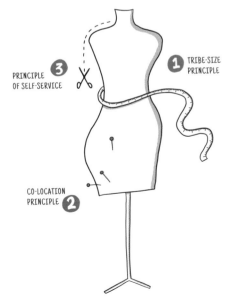

PRINCIPLE OF SELF-SERVICE ❸

TRIBE-SIZE PRINCIPLE ❶

CO-LOCATION PRINCIPLE ❷

HYBRID STRUCTURES

A step further than tailoring one specific organizational form to specific needs is hybridization, in which several forms are combined. Hybridization can come in two forms: one is mixing elements of different forms, another one is using multiple forms within one organization but in different parts of the firm. The bol.com case shows how bol.com renamed holacracy into spark and combines it with a traditional functional structure. Next to such mixes, organizations may also choose to use one form for department A and another form for department B.

A good example of an organization that has analyzed its needs in different environments and has cherry picked inspiration from different organizational forms is ING. They have recently implemented different models and mechanisms, inspired by Spotify, Zappos, Google and Netflix, for different purposes across their organization. Below we present an overview of how and where they have used these organizational forms to replace traditional ways of working within the bank.

- *Spotify Model.* ING reorganized its traditional business and IT organization into tribes, chapters and squads. In this organizational form, small autonomous multi-disciplinary teams work together to build a digital banking platform and improve the customer experience around its existing products and services.
- *Holacracy.* ING has reorganized its traditional sales and service organization (including branches, client contact centers and back office operations) into (super) circles and self-organized loyalty teams. In this organizational form, small teams are responsible for delivering a superior omni-channel customer experience towards a specific client segment or a group of related customer service requests.
- *Centers of expertise model.* ING has reorganized its traditional supporting functions like HR, Finance and Risk in Centers of Expertise. In this organizational form, scarce and deep know-how is centralized and offered to all parts of the organization on demand.
- *Lean start-up model[3].* ING has reorganized its development efforts and platform based innovations into a centralized innovation factory. In this organizational form corporate accelerators use a combination of agile, lean start-up and design thinking practices called PACE to develop prototypes and minimal viable products with Fintechs and third parties.
- *QBR & OKR Model.* ING has adopted the Quarterly Business Review (QBR) and Objectives Key Result (OKR) methodology to replace traditional performance and portfolio management mechanisms. In this QBR and OKR model, all parts of the organization reflect on their performance and align on priorities and business goals.

In summary, there are many new organizational forms. They often share similar underlying principles, but they have different assumptions on the right scale, scope and context in which they can be implemented. Organizations looking to adopt these types of organizational forms should not simply copy-paste the model but tailor it to their needs and the context in which they operate. This could very well include mixing concepts from multiple organizational forms for different purposes.

"Firms don't have to be "born Agile," like Spotify. Even big, old firms can undertake an Agile transformation if they set their minds and hearts to it—and stick with it."

> Stephen Denning

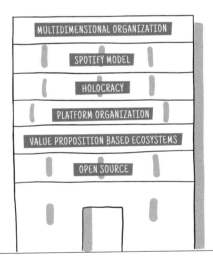

[1] Rigby, D. K., Sutherland, J., & Noble, A. (2018). Agile at Scale. Harvard Business Review. 96(3), 88-96.
[2] De Man, A.P., & Luvison, D. (2019). Collaborative business models: Aligning and operationalizing alliances, Business Horizons. 62(4), 473-482.
[3] Ries, E. (2011). The lean startup: How today's entrepreneurs use continuous innovation to create radically successful businesses. Crown Books.

CASE STUDY:
IMPLEMENTING TELSTRA'S NEW WAYS OF WORKING

An interview with Natalie Peters, Ways of Working Lead at Telstra

Telstra is Australia's leading telecommunications and technology company offering a full range of communications services and competing in all telecommunications markets. In Australia Telstra provides 17.7 million retail mobile services, 4.9 million retail fixed voice services and 3.6 million retail fixed broadband services. Telstra has an international presence spanning over 20 countries. Currently Telstra has 360 retail stores across Australia and employs more than 30,000 people.

Natalie Peters is Telstra's inaugural Ways of Working Executive. In this new role established in early 2018, Natalie is accountable for defining, designing and embedding the transformation of how Telstra works. Simplifying and accelerating how Telstra works is essential to Telstra's new corporate strategy, T22, which was announced half way through 2018. With T22, the company aims to simplify product offerings and create all digital experiences for customers with new platforms as well as simplifying the structure and ways of working.

How do new ways of working and organizing tie into your strategy?

Telstra has had many teams applying different agile ways of working methods for some time. The application of these methods provided a blueprint for how the single suite of new ways of working needed to be applied successfully across all parts of the organization. It also highlighted a number of impediments that were blocking our ability to accelerate the adoption of the method and mindset elements of our ways of working transformation. We were also able to identify areas of our operating model that were getting in the way of our ability to deliver outcomes at speed. We were clearly seeing the benefits of adopting the ways of working however we knew that we would be unable to structurally embed and integrate agile successfully across our organization into everyday work and behavior of our people. Under the T22 strategy, the strategic pillar on simplifying and embedding the new ways of working will affect all of our 30,000 employees – from across all functions within the company including all customer and non-customer facing employees and corporate functions.

Telstra's T22 announcement to the market in June 2018 included the following key remarks from our CEO Andy Penn that highlight the importance of new ways of working and the fact that it requires a paradigm shift for the organization as a whole. It has put new ways of working in the public spotlight.

"The rate and pace of change in the telecom and media industry is increasingly driven by technological innovation and competition. In this environment, traditional companies that do not respond fast are most at risk. We are now at a tipping point where we must act more boldly if we are to continue to be the nation's leading telecommunications company. Telstra will implement a new organizational structure, breaking down silos and enabling the sizeable transformation to which Telstra is committing today. In the future, our workforce will be a smaller, knowledge-based one with a structure and way of working that is agile enough to deal with rapid change. This means that some roles will no longer be required, some will change and there will be new ones created. This also includes the reduction of two to four organizational layers and removal of one in four executive and middle management roles to flatten the structure".

Breaking down silos

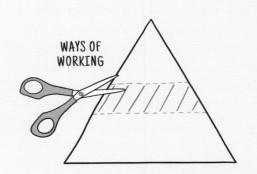

Reduction of 2-4 organization layers

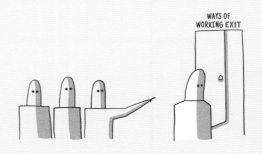

Removing 1 out of 4 managers

What are the key principles behind the design of your new organization and ways of working?

We have looked at how other large companies, both inside and outside telecommunications, have transformed their operating model. We have seen that there are multiple organizational models to scale new ways of working across a company.

The biggest key take away for us is that you cannot simply copy and paste any model into your organization and expect that it will work perfectly from day one. Designing a new target end state for your organizational structure and ways of working starts with understanding your company DNA and the context in which it operates.

At Telstra, we have a strong history built on an engineering mindset and culture. Whenever we design and build something for our customers we want it to be 100% right. As a result, we tend to strive for perfection in everything that we do and our organization typically does not accept mistakes. This has led to increased governance and heavy documentation requirements when we want to implement change. Whilst there are some positives in having this as part of a culture, when you want to create an organization with agility, it can limit your ability to respond fast to changes in your environment.

Our company plays an important role in Australia to provide essential services, particularly in times of crisis or natural disaster. This is when our organization can come together out of our functional silos, collaborate and think about pragmatic solutions and act fast to implement them. With this foundation and mindset, much of the design of our new operating model builds upon the principle of cross-functional and empowered teams that demonstrate that kind of working practices and behavior every day.

Who is driving the transformation to change the way of working within Telstra?

At Telstra, Human Resources (HR) is the driving force behind the organizational transformation and implementation of new ways of working. The reason why HR is driving the organizational transformation is that it also closely relates to the culture we are creating as we deliver on our T22 strategy. However, HR is not designing the new organization and ways of working in isolation or in a dark room. Everything that the ways of working team does to transform our organization, is in collaboration and co-designed with our functional teams across the company. We practice the concept of co-design, co-creation and facilitation to allow parts of our organization to lead the organizational and way of working change by themselves. Together we set out what ways of working means for Telstra and develop a common set of language and practices based on design thinking, lean (start-up), agile and DevOps. Our philosophy is also very much to learn by doing and therefore every person engaged as part of the transformation learns the method through the design process.

Where did the new ways of working transformation start within Telstra?

The first major intervention to set up the new ways of working strategy started with a focus on our organizational impediments. In March 2018 our top 300 Telstra leaders came together to focus on our top 20 impediments and designed real solutions using agile tools and methods. Looking back at that event, I believe it was as a catalyst and sparked our leadership to commit to enable more agile ways of working in the company. The mindset shift that started on this day was a leap forward to building deeper understanding from our leaders as to what needed to change and how they as individuals were going to invest in their development and understanding to enable their teams to successfully transition to the new way.

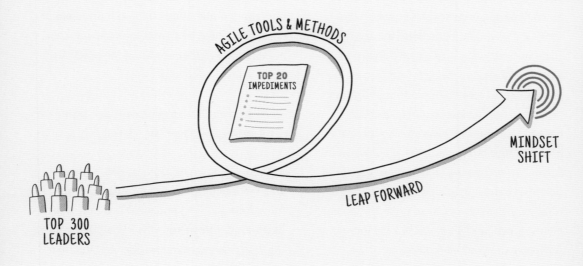

At Telstra it was particularly important to bring people together regularly to understand the strategy and progress. This was an integral part of the strategy as we were designing our transformation. We created a physical space where people could come to see the way of working program in action and see the work come to life. It also functions as a collaboration space for anybody or any team that is looking to accelerate on a specific outcome or resolve an issue. At first, we started transforming the organization from inside out with a bottom-up approach. However, we soon realized that in order to transform our organization, we needed critical mass to move faster, top down and bottom up, and to continue to push harder.

What was causing you to realize that you had to move faster on the transformation?

Transformations needs to take place rapidly otherwise you are just adjusting incrementally on a current state and may not reach your target end-state. Transformation also takes a lot of energy and focus for an organization to sustain over a long term and means you can be too internally focused for too long. Therefore, when you are transforming an organization, everything is about momentum. Even if it is imperfect, momentum and moving forward is critical over standing still and debating the perfect outcome. Once people reach the point of frustration and realize

that you cannot keep doing things the same way and expect a different outcome there is an opportunity to be bold. Being bold also means providing extreme alternatives and then adjusting to a new normal. Moving too slow and cautious on a transformation allows the organization to put up roadblocks, sabotage, shift priorities and raise concerns. When you break through functional silos, you have to realize that you are also effectively challenging a comfortable status quo. This can be challenging to navigate. However having success stories, good data to substantiate the case for change, and critical mass in the company supporting the transformation, can ensure momentum is maintained and makes this easier.

How do you pick up the pace for such a massive transformation?

Instead of going through a huge long-term operating model design phase and big bang implementation, we wanted to test a beta version of our new operating model and ways of working. We wanted to experience various constraints and challenges that we would face and have to overcome before we scaled the operating model and new ways of working across the entire company. That is where the concept of "frontrunners" came from within Telstra. Using the vehicle of frontrunners, we moved parts of the business early to our new organizational model with the ways of working, learn from this implementation within a manageable sample size, and then incorporate the necessary changes into the organizational design iteratively.

How did you setup this concept of frontrunners?

Our way of working team selected four front-runner groups across our organization to build the new cross-functional organizational design, ensuring agile capability and way of working uplift across participants. Our first wave of frontrunners started in our digital, consumer segment and product and technology groups. We took an end-to-end holistic perspective in the organizational setup of frontrunners. This meant that all required competences to create value for our customers were involved, including marketing, product development, user experience (UX) design and system engineering. Concurrent to this we ran campaigns to identify ambassadors to create a coalition of the willing for the company. We also sourced strong internal talent who could make the transition into agile coaches. The way we were applying coaches to the frontrunners provided us with a deeper understanding of the quality and skills of the coaches we needed as we scaled the model in the company.

How do the frontrunners start adopting new ways of working?

Together with the participants of the frontrunners we identified the best possible way to deliver value to our customers and how to get work done using new ways of working. The roll out of these new ways of working practices follow a learning by doing approach. For this purpose, we created an intense three-day simulation design experience for frontrunners. Part of this accelerator event was practicing and learning the Telstra new ways of working, but much more, it is about new cross-functional teams spending time together getting to know each other. During the three-day accelerator event, we helped the new teams to define their purpose, why they exist and what their commitment is to one another. During the three-day accelerators, we spend time with teams on the intersection of the being and doing side regarding our new ways of working. Our experience is that teams were comfortable talking about the doing side of new ways of working like methods, practices, structure. However much of where our coaches facilitate and challenge the frontrunner groups lean into the 'being' side of ways of working. It addresses the way we feel, think and what we value as individuals, teams and groups of teams. We have been able to bring together successfully how people feel in the moment and how their experience in the past can fit into practicing our new ways of working.

Can you give an example on how you address the being side of new ways of working?

The coaches from our ways of working team enable the leaders of the frontrunners on transitioning towards the new organizational model and the adoption of ways of working. We fully acknowledge this is a learning journey for everyone. In the beginning, the new organizational setup and new ways of working within the frontrunner teams often feels imperfect and awkward. This is normal and to be expected. It was also common for us to hear feedback from people either loving the new way or wanting to revert back to traditional ways of working. The agile coaches from our ways of working team help our leaders to drive the change and help the individuals and the teams to build resilience.

What positive impact have you seen from the new ways of working?

In our frontrunners groups we have seen the development of features and solutions to problems speed up immensely. In some

cases things that could take four weeks are now done in four hours. Our leadership team and board members also visit our frontrunners. During these visits, the participants of the frontrunners explain how new ways of working have helped them to deliver more value for our customers. That has been very powerful.

You are halfway in your transformation. Are you looking to change your approach?

We are moving full steam ahead on our frontrunner approach in 2019 to transform the entire company and scale agile ways of working. We continue to demonstrate the positive impact of new ways of working to our

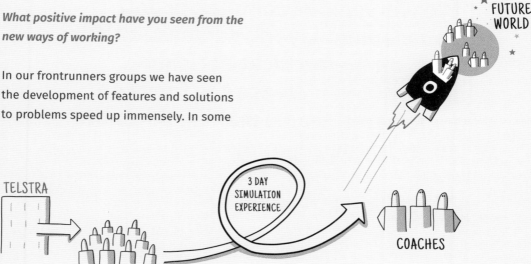

executive leadership team and board members. It clearly shows how we successfully tackle organizational impediments that get in the way of delivering value for our customers. In our next waves of frontrunners that we will be launching we are planning to strengthen the communication activities internally to ensure all parts of the company understand the changes. The ways of working changes are a very positive part of our company's strategy. Ensuring people understand it and are connected to it is very important. We want people to feel positive and passionate about their role as we move towards being a more agile organization.

"We will remove complexity and management layers, decrease the focus on hierarchical decision-making, and increase the focus on empowered teams making decisions closer to the customer"

> Andy Penn, Telstra